What reviewers have to say about

Writers of the Future

Volume 1

". . . There's an explosion of talent in these pages."

Larry Brown
Rocky Mountain News
Denver

"L. Ron Hubbard Presents Writers of the Future . . . it is an exceedingly solid collection, including SF, fantasy and horror . . ."

Chicago Sun-Times

"All the stories are provocative, imaginative, and entertaining . . ."

Richard Langford
Deland News
Florida

". . . this volume is worthy of praise."

Booklist
American Library Association

L. RON HUBBARD
PRESENTS
WRITERS OF THE FUTURE
VOLUME II

L. RON HUBBARD
PRESENTS
WRITERS OF THE FUTURE

VOLUME II

Commentaries by
FRANK HERBERT
ANNE McCAFFREY
LARRY NIVEN
GENE WOLFE

Edited by
ALGIS BUDRYS

Bridge Publications, Inc.

ISBN 0-88404-254-5
Library of Congress Catalog Card Number: 84-73270

First Edition Paperback
10 9 8 7 6 5 4 3 2 1

Printed in the United States of America

Contents

L. Ron Hubbard

March 13, 1911 - January 24, 1986

Author
Philosopher
Humanitarian
Photographer
Composer
Researcher
Explorer

After the stories for this volume of Writers of the Future had been collected and just prior to publication of this work, L. Ron Hubbard departed his body. He is greatly missed by his many friends and colleagues who worked with him over the years and by the many many readers who have enjoyed his fascinating works of fiction and non fiction.

The legendary L. Ron Hubbard, born in 1911, lived his early years in Montana which was yet part of the great American frontier. Learning to ride before he could walk, he became well acquainted with a rugged outdoor life before going to sea. The cowboys, Indians and mountains of Montana were balanced with an open sea, and the temples and urban throngs of the Orient while Hubbard journeyed through the Far East as a teenager. By the time he was nineteen, he had traveled over a quarter of a million sea miles and thousands on land, recording his experiences in a series of diaries mixed with story ideas.

On a return to the U.S., Hubbard's insatiable

curiosity and demand for excitement sent him into the sky as a barnstorming aviator, where he quickly earned a reputation in skill and daring. He again turned his attention to the sea. This time it was four-masted schooners and voyages into the Caribbean, where he found the adventure and experience that was to serve him later at the typewriter.

Drawing from his travels, he produced an amazing number of stories ranging from adventure and westerns through to sea and detective fiction.

By 1938, Hubbard was already established and recognized as one of the top-selling authors, when Street & Smith, publishers of Astounding Science Fiction *magazine called for new blood. Hubbard was urged to try his hand at science fiction. He protested that he did not write about "machines and machinery" but that he wrote about people. "That's just what we want," he was told.*

The result was a barrage of stories from Hubbard that expanded the scope and changed the face of the literary genre gaining Hubbard the repute of one of the founding fathers of the great "Golden Age" of science fiction. At the same time, he was greatly responsible for the success and popularity of Astounding's newly created sister publication, the now legendary Unknown Worlds *fantasy magazine.*

Hubbard soon had a reputation of not only being one of the best authors of the Golden Age but also the fastest. His great classic Fear, *for example, was written in a single weekend. His prodigious output, now with more than twenty-two million copies of his fiction works in a dozen languages sold throughout the world, is a true publishing phenomenon.*

Hubbard is fondly remembered in the field for his

early classics—Final Blackout, Death's Deputy, Slaves of Sleep, Typewriter In The Sky, To The Stars *and many others. He interrupted his fiction writings in 1950 to pursue his research into the subject of Dianetics and it was not until 1980 that he returned to the SF genre celebrating his 50th aniversary as a writer with the blockbuster adventure,* Battlefield Earth. *The epic became a national bestseller, remaining on the country's major lists for an incredible 32 weeks.*

But his Magnum Opus was yet to come. After completing Battlefield Earth, *Hubbard accomplished what few writers have even dared contemplate. He wrote the 10 volume space adventure satire,* Mission Earth. *So unprecedented in size a new term—"Dekalogy" (meaning a story in ten volumes) had to be coined just to describe the magnitude of the work.*

The entire dekalogy is now being released, with a new volume coming out every two to three months throughout 1986 and 1987.

Throughout his career as a master author, L. Ron Hubbard never forgot his own roots and a tradition, inherent particularly in the SF genre, of older hands helping the new. Hubbard is undoubtedly the most stellar example of this tradition. His help to new authors dates back to the early 1930's when he was a young author himself and authoring columns for 'how-to-do-it' magazines on the writing craft. At one point he even established a writing contest over the radio from Alaska.

In 1983 he launched the Writers of the Future Contest to give recognition to hitherto undiscovered talented authors. L. Ron Hubbard created the concept of the contest, sponsored it, and established the procedures it would follow in order to be successful. Indeed it was successful and one result was this series of anthologies publishing the winners each year.

L. Ron Hubbard left behind a timeless legacy of unparalleled storytelling richness for readers the world over to enjoy. And he left behind the spirit of his actions to assist and guide new writers, which shall always be remembered, and which is carried forward through these pages.

Theodore Sturgeon

1918 - 1985

and

Frank Herbert

1920 - 1986

To the last days of their remarkable lives, they continued their work in the contest, and maintained their lifelong concern for newcomers to their art. For this as well as their many other accomplishments, the world of speculative fiction is in their debt.

Acknowledgements

The success of Writers of the Future is a direct reflection of the dedication of the noted authors who give their special expertise as judges in selecting the contest's winners.

The contest judges for the 1985 year are—

Gregory Benford
Algis Budrys
Stephen Goldin
Frank Herbert
Anne McCaffrey
Larry Niven
Frederik Pohl
Robert Silverberg
Theodore Sturgeon
Jack Williamson
Gene Wolfe
Roger Zelazny

It is through their contributions to the Writers of the Future contest that this volume has been made possible.

On This Book
by
Algis Budrys

About the Editor

Algis Budrys edits the Writers of the Future *books and acts as a judge in the contest from which the book springs.*

His career in science fiction began in 1952 with his first SF story sales and his simultaneous employment as an SF book editor. Since then his work has been published many times, and he has pursued an effective editorial career within and outside of the speculative-fiction media.

He is a well-known teacher and critic in the field, having served as an instructor at numerous writing workshops, and having written regular columns and several books of SF reviews.

This book contains fifteen good stories; brand-new tales of science fiction and fantasy. Some are short, some are longer; some are funny, some bend the mind in a different way. They're all here because world-famous SF writers judged them to be among the top stories of the year by new writers.

That alone might well be worth the modest price of admission. *Writers of the Future Volume I,* the anthology preceding this one is still being bought and enjoyed by more people than most "best-sellers." The stories this time are just as good.

In addition, this volume, like the last, contains valuable essays of advice and insight by some of our judges. If you're a writer at any level, the advice on writing is wisdom from winners. If you're "just" a reader, you might appreciate this chance to look at some of the hard thought that top professionals devote to pleasing you.

The judging and judges are part of the Writers of the Future contest sponsored by L. Ron Hubbard and conducted according to the guidelines he laid down when the contest was initiated in late 1983. As far as we know, this is the biggest and best of all writing competitions in any field of literature.

For one thing, it regularly gives substantial cash prizes purely on merit. The contest requires little but amateur standing and an original story. There's no entry fee, and there's no obligation on an entrant to give us any rights in the story. (When we put these anthologies together, we do so by going back to the writers and making them a separate offer; it's an excellent one.)

Another factor is our judges' panel, which is always comprised of people whose status clearly puts them above pettiness or pressure. They have the final say. And these judges in turn, as we mention again elsewhere, don't see authors' names on the manuscript copies distributed to them. So they judge only what's in the manuscript. What we're interested in is finding good new people; if we already knew who they were, we wouldn't need a contest.

The critical commentary on the stories has been overwhelmingly positive. That's deserved. A fair number of winners and finalists have gone on to what are already quite substantial careers. For that matter, one of the writers appearing in *this* book has already signed a major publisher's contract for his first novel, and others are being approached by noteworthy literary talent scouts.

The prize money awarded each quarter is, as we said, substantial. Elsewhere in this book you'll find a set of the contest rules in which that's spelled out. It adds up to far more than most beginning writers ever see. In addition, this year L. Ron Hubbard instituted a $4,000 Master Prize award, for the top story among the four First Prize winners. That's major recognition—it means the Master Prize winner has gained a total of $5,000 even before he or she begins licensing any rights in the story, and that is, believe me, extraordinary.

Who among the people included here is the Master Prize winner? Ah . . . we don't know yet. That judging is going on as this is written and set in type. Our judges' selection will be announced at our annual awards dinner. It's between Howard V. Hendrix, Camilla Decarnin,

Bridget McKenna and Robert Touzalin. Read their stories here and make your own pick . . . and bear in mind that the eleven other stories came very close to qualifying; you might well like one of them better. You're the reader, and the only vote that counts for you is your own.

This volume contains stories received in the contest during the last three months of 1984 and the first nine months of 1985. That sort of fiscal year enables us to complete the quarterly judging, edit the book, and get it out early in the calendar year. We have brought you the twelve winners from those four quarters, and three of the finalists. There were five finalists in each quarter this past year; each writer received a certificate and the story had a chance at inclusion here.

We arrange the stories to make the book a varied and, we hope, entertaining reading experience for you. We do the things editors do—we follow long stories with short ones, or vice-versa, and we try to balance mood and tone. We commission essays from our judges, and we write introductions to each piece, in the hope that we can say something interesting and useful. Somewhere in that process, the final content of the book takes form.

The editorial process of handling the entered stories you see here began with a talented, conscientious man named Stephen Goldin, who is an excellent SF writer and a long-time student of the field. Then it passed on through me as an intermediate judge in the contest, and thence to the finalist judges, before it doubled back into this book. As I think you can see from the results, none of us look for any preferred kind of science fiction or fantasy. We don't work to some criterion that is either nonliterary or tries to separate acceptable literature from unacceptable literature. We just want good speculative fiction stories. That's a tough-enough standard, as some of our essayists explain.

The beginning writer has a hard time of it at best. Mind you, there's more short-story publishing in SF than in any other field, and there's just enough recompense and just enough editorial feedback so that it *is* possible for a novice to start and continue a viable writing career if one is very energetic, very well organized, and rather lucky. But that's well below ideal conditions. As a practical matter, beginning writers today almost inevitably launch their careers under needless pressures—financial pressures, and pressures to produce work they might not want to produce. In particular, the money paid for short stories is hardly enough to sustain an apprenticeship, and yet it's writing short stories that teaches you the basics.

The "good old days" of pulp writing were hardly like Paradise; rates were terrible, and every writer constantly raced deadlines. But there was very much a sense of the process of apprenticeship, and a writer of promise quickly found support from colleagues and editors. It was often the established writers who found ways to provide food, clothing and shelter to the talented apprentice.

The Writers of the Future contest was originally set up to institute a contemporary form of that support; to provide encouragement, recognition, and something more than an honorarium—a realistic reward that would give its recipients a chance to draw breath, assess their future opportunities, and pursue them clearheadedly. Not too much of a chance . . . enough of a chance. The objective is not to subsidize the future, but to discover it.

When it became evident we could do a book, we did a book to embody those same precepts. And, again, we were not sure we would ever do another book. But that decision was made for us by the number of people who praised that book—as critics, and, more important, as readers who paid out money to purchase copies, and thus spoke with the clearest voice of all. *Writers of the Future Volume II* is part of what is now a set of books that continue to be available to the reading public, that offer good reading to those who like speculative fiction, and that clearly meet a continuing demand.

For their parts in this, we thank the judges whose choices are included here. Their names are listed on our covers. The finalist judges give the most; the world's demands on their time, and the consequent value of that time, are very great. What they do for us is their gift.

The contest administration and the staff of Bridge Publications set an example of industriousness, efficiency, and integrity. All of us on this project do a little better than we have to, I think because we believe in this project harder than we have to. And nobody believed in it harder than L. Ron Hubbard.

Finally, we would like to list for you here the people who have given us our reward:

Camilla Decarnin	1st Place, 1st Quarter
Laura E. Campbell	2nd Place, 1st Quarter
Jerry Meredith and Dennis E. Smirl	3rd Place, 1st Quarter
Robert Touzalin	1st Place, 2nd Quarter
Kenneth Schulze	2nd Place, 2nd Quarter
Sansoucy Kathenor	3rd Place, 2nd Quarter
Howard V. Hendrix	1st Place, 3rd Quarter
Don Baumgart	2nd Place, 3rd Quarter
Marina Fitch	3rd Place, 3rd Quarter
Bridget McKenna	1st Place, 4th Quarter
Parris ja Young	2nd Place, 4th Quarter
Ray Aldridge	3rd Place, 4th Quarter

as well as Jon Gustafson, Marianne O. Nielsen and Jay

Sullivan and the other finalists. These are the sort of people who will be bringing you reading pleasure for a generation to come.

See you in the future.

—Algis Budrys

Introducing L. Ron Hubbard On Art

In putting this book together, we had asked four of our judges to contribute essays of advice to beginning writers. Specifically, we *asked them to concentrate on the single most important piece of advice they'd give to apprentices.*

This seemed like a sensible idea that would yield a broad spectrum of useful information. The one common denominator among Frank Herbert, Anne McCaffrey, Larry Niven and Gene Wolfe as SF writers was that they are enormously respected popular authors. Otherwise, they wrote very differently from each other—as master artists tend to do, while nevertheless being indubitable masters. While most professional writers in our experience agree on the same set of broad-stroke imperatives, it seemed reasonable to expect they'd arrange them in various orders of priority.

Two things happened. One, it turned out that all four of our experts had the same single most important piece of advice to give. Some spoke of "story" and some of "idea," but in either case they were reacting profoundly to the discovery all we "experts" make—that the biggest difference between the gifted amateur and the solid professional is that the amateur thinks about parts and the pro thinks about the whole.

The second thing that happened was that we were struck by how closely this matched with something L. Ron Hubbard had said in a 1965 statement on the fundamentals of art:

> *"The order of importance in art is:*
> *(1) The resultant communication.*
> *(2) The technical rendition.*
> *(2) is always subordinate to (1). (2) may be as high as possible but never so high as to injure (1).*
> *The communication is the primary target. The technical quality is the secondary consideration. A person pushes (2) as high as possible within the reality of (1)."*

In working on a story, the amateur stops at each detail and asks "How does this look?" whereas the professional asks "Does it work?" and pauses only an eyeblink before going on. It's not that the pro disregards matters such as characterization, dialogue technique, narrative style, and all the other aspects of prose composition and artistic aesthetics. Hardly. It's that one becomes a professional on the day when one realizes that all the school details exist only to serve the art; get a story going, and the rest follows. Get the car started and see if it will bring home the groceries. Then *polish the fenders.*

No matter what kind of story they tell—that is, no matter what audience they pick—professional writers get their satisfaction from the plaudits of the audience. And what the audience wants is not style or syntax or characterizations done in the first, second or third person in the past or present tense. What it wants is a satisfactory story. Professional writers think about engineering details, and they work toward clean solutions to storytelling problems, but they concentrate on making the delivery.

Professional artists, whatever their art form, are people who are bound to their audiences by the tie of mutual satisfaction in the art. "Self-expression" is for amateurs, and the audiences are properly impatient with it. Doing the art, and appreciating the art, are what matters over the long haul, and the best of the art is what then outlives today.

But what is art? What is good art?

Between 1929 and 1941, L. Ron Hubbard counted some 15 million words of fiction sold to audiences who clamored for more. Along the way to that total, he participated heavily in a still fondly remembered "Golden Age" of science fiction and fantasy. He was the author of milestones along the path of contemporary SF's development from a clumsy pseudoliterature into a form that pays serious attention to classic human problems. Characteristically, he presented such topics to his audiences in tales that were notable for their pace and their occasional lightheartedness as well as for his commentary on the nature of things. But for those who feel art can only be couched in serious tones, this aspect can also be found in his work—not that he'd agree with such a narrow-minded criterion for art.

Returning from World War II, Hubbard resumed his SF career with the same velocity and in the same manner. Had he stayed in the pages of Astounding Science Fiction *and the specialist SF book publishers, he would have continued as a giant in the regard of the popular audience for SF. And even after he temporarily stopped writing fiction, he continued thinking on it.*

As a major insight into how a major creative talent regarded the role of artist, art and audience, we're pleased to bring you here a 1973 essay that has never before been published to the general audience:

Art, More About
by
L. Ron Hubbard

How good does a professional work of art have to be? This would include painting, music, photography, poetry: any of the arts whether fine or otherwise. It would also include presenting oneself as an art form as well as one's products.

Yes, how GOOD does such a work of art have to be?

Ah, you say, but that is an imponderable, a thing that can't be answered. Verily, you say, you have just asked a question for which there are no answers except the sneers and applause of critics. Indeed, this is why we have art critics! For who can tell how good good is. Who knows?

I have a surprise for you. There IS an answer.

As you know, I searched for many years, as a sort of minor counterpoint to what I was hardwork doing, to dredge up some of the materials which might constitute the basis of art. Art was the most uncodified and most opinionated subject on the planet—after men's ideas about women and women's ideas about men and Man's ideas of Man. Art was anyone's guess. Masterpieces have gone unapplauded, positive freaks have gained raves.

So how good does a work of art have to be, to be good?

The painter will point out all the tiny technical details known only to painters; the musician will put a score through the Alto horn and explain about valve clicks and lip; the poet will talk about meter types; the actor will explain how the position and wave of one hand per the instructions of one school can transform a clod into an actor. And so it goes, art by art, bit by bit.

But all these people will be discussing the special intricacies and holy mysteries of technique, the tiny things only the initiate of that art would recognize. They are talking about technique. They are not really answering how *good* a work of art has to be.

Works of art are viewed by people. They are heard by people. They are felt by people. They are not just the fodder of a close-knit group of initiates. They are the soul food of all people.

One is at liberty of course to challenge that wide purpose of art. Some professors who don't want rivals tell their students, "Art is for self-satisfaction," "It is a hobby." In other words, don't display or exhibit, kid, or you'll be competition! The world today is full of that figure-figure. But as none of this self-satisfaction art meets a definition of art wider than self for the sake of self, the professional is not interested in it.

In any artistic production, what does one have as an audience? People. Not, heaven forbid, critics. But people. Not experts in that line of art. But people.

That old Chinese poet who, after he wrote a poem, went down out of his traditional garret and read it to the flower-selling old lady on the corner had the right idea. If she understood it and thought it was great, he published. If she didn't he put it to the bamboo trash can. Not remarkably, his poems have come down the centuries awesomely praised.

Well, one could answer this now by just saying that art should communicate to people high and low. But that really doesn't get the sweating professional anywhere as a guide in actually putting together a piece of work and it doesn't give him a yardstick whereby he can say, "That is that!" "I've done it," and go out with confidence that he has.

What is technique? What is its value? Where does it fit? What is perfectionism? Where does one stop scraping off the paint and erasing notes and say, "That is that"?

For there is a point. Some artists don't ever find it. The Impressionists practically spun in as a group trying to develop a new way of viewing and communicating it. They made it—or some of them did, like Monet. But many of them never knew where to stop and they didn't make it. They couldn't answer the question "How good does a piece of art work have to be to be good?"

In this time of century, there are many communication lines for works of art. Because a few works of art can be shown so easily to so many there may even be fewer artists. The competition is very keen and even dagger sharp. To be good one has to be very good. But in what way and how?

Well, when I used to buy breakfasts for Greenwich Village artists (which they ate hungrily, only stopping between bites to deplore my commercialism and bastardizing my talents for the gold that bought their breakfasts), I used to ask this question and needless to say I received an appalling variety of responses. They avalanched me with technique or lack of it; they vaguely dwelt on inherent talent; they rushed me around to galleries to show me Picasso or to a board fence covered with abstracts. But none of them told me how good a song had to be, to be a song.

So I wondered about this. And a clue came when the late Hubert Mathieu, a dear friend, stamped with youth on the Left Bank of the Seine and, painting dowagers at the Beaux Arts in middle age, said to me, "To do any of these modern, abstract, cubist things, you have to to first be able to paint!" And he enlarged the theme while I plied him in the midnight hush of Manhattan with iced sherry and he finished up the First Lady of Nantucket's somewhat swollen ball gown. Matty could PAINT. Finally, he dashed me off an abstract to show me how somebody who couldn't paint would do it and how it *could* be done.

I got his point. To really make one of these too too modern things come off, you first had to be able to paint. So I said well, hell, there's Gertrude Stein and Thomas Mann and ink splatterers like those. Let's see if it really is an art form. So I sharpened up my electric typewriter and dashed off the last chapters of a novel in way far out acid prose and put THE END at the bottom and shipped it off to an editor who promptly pushed several large loaves down the telephone wire and had me to lunch and, unlike his normal blasé self said, "I really got a big bang (this was decades ago—other years, other slang) out of the way that story wound up! You really put it over the plate." And it sent his circulation rating up. And this was very odd because, you see, the first chapters were straight, since they'd been written before Matty got thirsty for sherry and called me to come over, and the last chapters were an impressionistic stream of consciousness that Mann himself would have called "an advanced, rather adventurous over-Finneganized departure from the ultra school."

So just to see how far this sort of thing could go, for a short while I shifted around amongst various prose periods just to see what was going on. That they sold didn't prove too much because I never had any trouble with that. But that they were understood at all was surprising to me for their prose types (ranging from Shakespeare to Beowulf) were at wild variance with anything currently being published.

So I showed them to Matty the next time he had a ball gown to do or three chins to paint out and was thirsty. And he looked them over and he said, "Well, you proved my point. There's no mystery to it. Basically, you're a trained writer! It shows through."

And now we are getting somewhere, not just with me and my adventures and long dead yesterdays.

As time rolled on, this is what I began to see: The fellow technician in an art hears and sees the small technical points. The artist himself is engrossed in the exact application of certain exact actions which produce, when done, his canvas, his score, his novel, his performance.

The successful artist does these small things so well that he also then has attention and skill left to get out his message, he is not still fiddling about with the cerulean blue and the semiquaver. He has these zeroed in. He can repeat them and repeat them as technical actions. No ulcers. Strictly routine.

And here we have three surrealist paintings. And they each have their own message. And the public wanders by and they only look with awe on one. And why is this one different than the other two? Is it a different message? No. Is it more popular? That's too vague.

If you look at or listen to any work of art, there is only one thing the casual audience responds to en masse, and if this has it, then you, too, will see it as a work of art. If it doesn't have it, you won't.

So what is *it?*

TECHNICAL EXPERTISE ITSELF ADEQUATE TO PRODUCE AN EMOTIONAL IMPACT.

And that is how good a work of art has to be to be good.

If you look this over from various sides, you will see that the general spectator is generally unaware of technique. That is the zone of art's creators.

Were you to watch a crowd watching a magician, you would find one common denominator eliciting uniform response. If he is a good magician, he is a smooth showman. He isn't showing them how he does his tricks. He is showing them a flawless flowing performance. This alone is providing the carrier wave that takes the substance of his actions to his audience. Though a far cry from fine art, perhaps, yet there is art in the way he does things. If he is good, the audience is seeing first of all, before anything else, the TECHNICAL EXPERTISE of his performance. They are also watching him do things they know they can't do. And they are watching the outcome of his presentations. He is a good magician if he gives a technically flawless performance just in terms of scenes and motions which provide the channel for what he is presenting.

Not to compare Bach with a magician (though you could), all great pieces of art have this one factor in common. First of all, before one looks at the faces on the canvas or hears the meaning of the song, there is the TECHNICAL EXPERTISE there adequate to produce an emotional impact. Before one adds message or meaning, there is this TECHNICAL EXPERTISE.

TECHNICAL EXPERTISE is composed of all the little and large bits of technique known to the skilled painter, musician, actor, any artist. He adds these things together in his basic presentation. He knows what he is doing. And how to do it. And then to this he adds his message.

All old masters were in there nailing canvas on frames as apprentices or grinding up the lapis lazuli or cleaning paintbrushes before they arrived at the Metropolitan.

But how many paintbrushes do you have to clean? Enough to know that clean paintbrushes make clean color. How many clarinet reeds do you have to replace? Enough to know which types will hit high C.

Back of every artist there is technique. You see them groping, finding, discarding, fooling about. What are they hunting for? A new blue? No, just a constant of blue that is an adequate quality.

And you see somebody who can really paint still stumbling about looking for technique—a total overrun.

Someplace one says, "That's the TECHNICAL EXPERTISE adequate to produce an emotional impact." And that's it. Now he CAN. So he devotes himself to messages.

If you get this tangled up or backwards, the art does not have a good chance of being good. If one bats out messages without a TECHNICALLY EXPERT carrier wave of art, the first standard of the many spectators seems to be violated.

The nice trick is to be a technician and retain one's fire. Then one can whip out the masterpieces like chain lightning. And all the great artists seem to have managed that. And when they forked off onto a new trail they mastered the technique and *then* erupted with great works.

It is a remarkable thing about expertise. Do you know that some artists get by on "Technical expertise adequate to produce an emotional impact" alone with no messages? They might not suspect that. But it is true.

So the "expertise adequate" is important enough to be, itself, art. It is never great art. But it produces an emotional impact just from quality alone.

And how masterly an expertise? Not very masterly. Merely adequate. How adequate is adequate? Well, people have been known to criticize a story because there were typographical errors in the typing. And stories by the non-adept often go pages before anyone appears or anything happens. And scores have been known to be considered dull simply because they were inexpertly chorded or clashed. And a handsome actor has been known not to have made it because he never knew what to do with his arms, for all his fiery thunderings of the Bard's words.

Any art demands a certain expertise. When this is basically sound, magic! Almost anyone will look at it and say Ah! For quality alone has an emotional impact. That it is cubist or dissonant or blank verse has very little bearing on it; the type of the art form is no limitation to audience attention generally when it has, underlying it and expressed in it, the expertise adequate to produce an emotional impact.

The message is what the audience thinks it sees or hears. The significance of the play, the towering clouds of sound in the symphony, the scatter-batter of the current pop group, are what the audience thinks it is perceiving and what they will describe, usually, or which they think they admire. If it comes to them with a basic expertise itself able to produce an emotional impact they will think it is great. And it will be great.

The artist is thought of as enthroned in some special heaven where all is clean and there is no sweat, eyes half-closed in the thrall of inspiration. Well, maybe he is sometimes. But every one I've seen had ink in his hair or a towel handy to mop his brow or a throat spray in his hand to ease the voice strain of having said his lines twenty-two times to the wall or the cat. I mean the great ones. The others were loafing and hoping and talking about the producer or the unfair art gallery proprietor.

The great ones always worked to achieve the technical quality necessary. When they had it, they knew they had it. How did they know? Because it was technically correct.

Living itself is an art form. One puts up a mock-up. It doesn't happen by accident. One has to know how to wash his nylon shirts and girls have to know what mascara runs and that too many candy bars spoil the silhouette, quite in addition to the pancreas.

Some people are themselves a work of art because they have mastered the small practical techniques of living that give them a quality adequate to produce an emotional impact even before anyone knows their name or what they do.

Even a beard and baggy pants require a certain art if they are to be the expertise adequate to produce an emotional impact.

And some products produce a bad *mis*emotional impact without fully being viewed. And by this reverse logic, of which you can think of many examples such as a dirty room, you can then see that there might be an opposite expertise, all by itself, adequate to produce a strong but *desirable* emotional impact.

That is how good a work of art has to be. Once one is capable of executing that technical expertise for that art form he can pour on the message. Unless the professional form is there first, the message will not transmit.

A lot of artists are overstraining to obtain a quality far above that necessary to produce an emotional impact. And many more are trying to machine gun messages at the world without any expertise at all to form the vital carrier wave.

So how good does a piece of art have to be?

Beast
by
Jon Gustafson

About the Author

Jon Gustafson is a massive, jovial, bright man with nearly innumerable ties to the speculative-fiction community. "Beast" first saw the light of day at a 1984 writing workshop. This was conducted as part of MosCon, an Idaho SF convention that Jon and his wife, Victoria Mitchell, serve as organizers. Jon is a graphic artist and illustrator, as well as being a semiprofessional pool player, and owns what he describes as the country's only science fiction and fantasy art-appraisal business.

A contest finalist, "Beast" is set in one of the most breathtaking parts of North America—the rolling-hill wheatfield country of eastern Washington State and the Idaho panhandle. Known as the Palouse Empire, named for a long-vanished Indian tribe, this part of the world has given rise to, among other major talents, Elmer E. ("Doc") Smith, Ph.D., author of the "superscience-fiction" Skylark *stories in the 1920's and '30's, and of the "Lensman" series that appeared in the Golden Age. These days, the central community of Moscow, Idaho, houses PESFA—The Palouse Empire Science Fiction Association, which Jon helped found. PESFA in turn gave rise to a group called Writer's Bloc, sometimes known as the Moscow Moffia (sic) for its ability to produce winning stories and writers. Last year,* Writers of The Future Volume I *published work by Moffia members Nina Kiriki Hoffman and Dean Wesley Smith. This year, talent and dedication have struck again.*

"Beast" is Jon's first published story. He describes it as his first real attempt at fiction. He has, however, sold eighteen articles on SF topics, and his book on classic SF illustrator Alex Schomburg is appearing at the same time as this volume. He can honestly say that he has sold everything he has ever written for publication, an exceedingly rare accomplishment.

"Beast" is a simple vignette . . . an incident, really, in the life of a traveler . . . or two travelers, one as bewildered as the other.

The tractor lay on its side, the farmer's left hand and part of his arm still clinging to the steering wheel. The bright green paint of the machine was splotched with drying blood and the metal was twisted and bent.

Nicholas Bishop took all this in as he was slamming his foot down on the brake pedal of his car. The shriek of rubber sliding on asphalt echoed through the rolling hills, through the fields of wheat and barley waving gold in the hot August sun. He had noticed the tractor lying on its side several seconds earlier and started to slow; seeing the rest made him react.

Bishop staggered out of the Impala and threw up into the ditch beside the road. The gravel dug into his knees as he gasped and choked, his eyes watering, his throat and nose burning. He spat into the ditch and rubbed his lips on his shirt sleeve, then lurched to his feet and walked unsteadily back to his car. The powerful engine still burbled as he slid in and shifted into reverse. He backed the car until he was beside the overturned tractor. He shut off the engine, took a deep breath, and got out.

Good God, what a mess, he thought, as he walked around the car to look at the carnage. The farmer's hand and arm were dark and muscular, the fingers clutched tightly around the steering wheel. Bishop looked away for a moment, fighting the surging in his stomach, breathing heavily, cold sweat on his forehead in spite of the hot sun. He looked back. The tractor looked as if two insane giants, one armed with a sledgehammer and one with a pickax, had taken out their anger on it.

Bishop jumped the ditch and climbed over the fallen fence. His feet sank into the soft soil. This area had just been plowed and raked, and the dark brown made a sharp contrast with the ripe grains on the nearby hills. He made a wide circle around the tractor, expecting to see the rest of the farmer's body. There was none. He stumbled in a large, trident-shaped depression in the ground, recovered his balance, then went back to the car.

Sitting behind the wheel, Bishop tried to remember what was in this desolate area. He had passed through it many times when he was going to college; the two-lane asphalt road was a short cut that he usually took because there were never any cops patrolling it and he could drive seventy-five or eighty miles per hour, saving him over half an hour on the trip. He shut his eyes.

"Just passed Kahlotus," he muttered, "and the big wheat rancher's spread not too long ago. Yeah, there should be a house in the next mile or so." A sudden thought struck him. *Oh, Jeez, I hope the guy wasn't from that house!* He shuddered.

With a last glance at the grisly scene, he started his car and threw it into gear. The powerful engine accelerated the large vehicle effortlessly, the rear wheels spinning and squealing. His mind was racing, too.

What if the guy's wandering the hills, bleeding to death? What the hell happened, anyway? What if he's dead? He slewed the large Chevy around a curve, tires protesting. *What if he's—ah, there's the house and—what the Hell's THAT?* He slammed on his brakes and slid to a stop.

THAT was pulling a hind leg off a very dead steer and gulping it down in one piece. At the sound of the squealing tires, it turned and Nicholas Bishop found himself looking into the impossible golden eyes of a *Tyrannosaurus Rex.*

As a child, Bishop had gone with his parents to a museum and stood in awe at the immense skeleton of the dinosaur. Later, he had looked at the diorama, showing a *Rex* feeding on some smaller, unnamed dinosaur. But the atmosphere there had been calm, almost serene; this was hot and confused.

"Holy sonuvabitch," Bishop muttered under his breath, knuckles white on the wheel. "I think I'm losing my mind!" The two-story-tall reptile opened its huge mouth and, for an instant, Bishop thought he was still sliding to a stop. The sound that came out of the monster sounded like the screeching of tires. Frozen, all he could do was watch as the immense reptile returned to its meal, satisfied that its warning had cowed the stranger. Six-inch-long teeth, yellowish-white and streaked with red, tore another huge chunk of meat out the steer's carcass. The blocky head swung up and the bloody meat disappeared. *Just like the guy on the tractor!* Bishop's mind slipped back to the tractor and to the indentation he'd stumbled in. *Footprints!*

The beast was in a large, flat area near the farmhouse Bishop had remembered. The road crested a small rise and he had been heading down it when he'd seen the dinosaur and stopped. The road curved to the right slightly, then ran straight for almost a mile between a series of cutbanks before it began to rise again. Bishop looked at the house.

Nestled in a small group of poplars, the farmhouse appeared unharmed by the giant carnivore. The same could not be said for the family car, which lay on its roof, mauled in much the same way as the tractor. Bishop saw what looked like a shirt sleeve hanging out of one window. He looked at the house and saw with despair that the power and phone lines were down, resting in the brown grass like black snakes.

Bishop looked back at the *Tyrannosaurus,* sweat pouring from his brow, his hair plastered to his skin. The reptile had finished its meal and was looking around the farmyard, his back to the road. Bishop knew that he had a chance to get by and make it to Pasco, the next large town, where he could get help.

He laughed bitterly. "Get help," he muttered. "Sure you'll get help . . . help right into a straitjacket." He struck the steering wheel with the palm of his hand.

He slammed the shift lever into drive and gunned the engine. The car leaped forward, down the slight incline, and past the yard. At the first sound of the tires, the dinosaur turned its massive head toward the moving car, then turned and lunged at it as Bishop careened past. The huge mouth bit at the roof on the passenger's side, breaking the windows and gouging the metal of the roof. Bishop caught a whiff of the beast's rank breath and almost vomited again. The car jerked and broke loose.

As he sped down the road, Bishop looked into his mirror and was astonished to see the *Tyrannosaurus* sprawling on the pavement, its tiny forearms trapped under the massive body. Its tail was thrashing about as it struggled to regain its feet. Unconsciously, Bishop slowed the car and watched as the rust and green body slowly heaved itself upright. One of its tiny forearms was broken, dangling uselessly. It opened its mouth, screamed, and began lumbering after the car.

Oh, hell! thought Bishop. *If I keep going, it'll follow me and there's a farm every mile or so all the way to*

Pasco. And if I don't go, it's going to make a goddamn snack out of me! Oh damn oh damn oh. . . . He tromped on the gas again, thinking furiously. When he reached the end of the cutbanks, he had put half a mile between himself and the enraged reptile. He stopped and carefully turned the car around. The dinosaur continued to come on, striding at a surprisingly rapid pace. Bishop fastened his seat belt and patted the dashboard of the car.

"Sorry, old girl, it's me or him and you're the only weapon I've got." He sighed, and stomped on the gas once more. The tires broke loose, screaming, and were answered by the shriek of the *Tyrannosaurus Rex* a half mile away.

By the time he was halfway to the beast, Bishop's car had passed seventy miles per hour and was continuing to accelerate. Its powerful engine roared out a challenge to an ancient adversary. Just before contact, the car was traveling almost ninety, and had become two-and-a-half tons of lethal metal. Shaking and yelling at the top of his lungs, Nicholas Bishop twitched the car to the left and aimed for the massive right leg.

The impact was tremendous. The dinosaur had stopped and bent down to bite at the small, strange creature charging at it, and its lower jaw caught the roof right at the windshield. The safety glass exploded into thousands of harmless pieces, but the roof kept going, its metal shearing through the jaw as the roof peeled back off the car. The bumper struck the leg squarely and collapsed, as did the front sheet metal and the radiator. The engine, however, was over a quarter-ton of nearly solid iron moving at ninety miles per hour. It did not collapse.

The leg all but exploded. The bones shattered, the flesh pulverized; the huge animal crashed to the ground, shrieking in pain. Bishop's car spun out of control and ground to a halt in the ditch a hundred yards farther on.

The engine, which had been shoved through the firewall, coughed, sputtered and died. Bishop, bruised and bleeding from a dozen small cuts, tried to unfasten his seat belt with his right hand first, but the pain from his broken thumb stopped him. His right leg throbbed where the transmission bellhousing had struck it. He unfastened the seat belt, shouldered the door open and staggered from the car. He looked back at the shrieking, dying beast, the most ferocious carnivore that had ever lived, and cried.

Illustrated by Greg Petan

In the Smoke
by
Howard V. Hendrix

About the Author

Howard V. Hendrix served for a time in the administration of Palm Springs, California, just west of the setting for "In The Smoke." He is, however, a career academic, currently on the faculty of The University of California, Riverside, having passed his Ph.D. exams in June, 1985. Most of his teaching career has involved writing and composition, or teaching English, but he also holds a degree in biology and was briefly the manager of a fish hatchery.

He began his acquaintance with SF as a fan, reading Alan E. Nourse's Raiders From the Rings *at the age of nine, in 1968. While in college, he was a member of the Cincinnati Fantasy Group, a club long noted for its activities within the SF community. But his interests have included being a disc jockey and an energetic participant in various drama groups, as director, actor, and playwright.*

He has won or placed high in various competitions over the years . . . among others, a nonfiction writing contest with a piece on genetic engineering, the English Award for his graduating class at Covington (KY) Latin School, and a 1980 award for a poem entered in the Jacques Barzun Writing Contest. He has published several scholarly articles, presented papers on SF topics at the Eaton

Conference in California and at its counterpart in England, and published some fiction in small-press magazines.

So while winning First Place in the third quarter of this year's W.O.T.F. contest is the high point of his creative career to date, he can expect to be seen on innumerable daises of various sorts over the years to come. Meanwhile, turn the page and see what he *has done with dinosaurs . . . of various sorts, some of them flesh and blood, none of them innocent.*

There is only the highway ahead, only the sunrise behind. The sun is a burning clock, the highway the arrow of time. The driver sails along the arrow under the clock in his big rig with the brights always on. He has nowhere to go, nowhere to come from. Only the highway goes on, broken where there used to be cities, burned where there used to be towns.

Beyond his windshield, Interstate 10 is a concrete river through the desert. His rear-view mirror monitor traces the tenuous strand of still-passable highway along which he has come. It is a thread dropped from the tapestry of another world, a lost world. Its real name is the Christopher Columbus Transcontinental Highway, a name maybe the driver alone in all the world remembers. This is the highway that fulfills Columbus's ancient quest for a route to the east by sailing west. I-10 is the passage across that continent that got in Columbus's way.

The road's true name is forgotten. It was never very well known, displayed as it was only on the large, white-lettered, green signs at the ends of the road. Those ends were in cities, the signs of which are fast disappearing, quickly becoming unreadable. On one of his monitors he punches up an old map tape. Sign and city—ghosts made of light—appear on the monitor. He stares at them and then punches them as out of existence as they really are.

His rig is an eighteen-wheel, info-assisted cold storer

that stores only emptiness at present. Its license plate reads LEVITHN, a title more appropriate perhaps to the driver's former handle—"Ishmael"— and the rig's former color—plain, Moby Dick white—than to its present incarnation. The driver, wanting to make it new, painted everything over with a gaudy rendition of a sailing ship and changed his handle to "Dutchman." No doubt this incarnation, too, will also lose its novelty and will change again. Only the license plate will remain the same; nobody's making them anymore.

Levithn plows through the headwind blowing down the Pass. Truck and driver climb the grade toward where the Whitewater flows beneath the highway—a confluence of rivers in the desert, one of stone and one of water, coming together at the highest point between here and Cabazon. They are passing through the valley of the windfarms now. Beneath the setting moon, the trembling fingers of date palms reach to caress the wind that moves them, always reaching and never catching, shackled to the earth forever by their roots. Out the windows and on the monitors, the driver sees the cyclone fences that surround the windfarms where windmills spin beneath searchlights dawn has not yet turned off. Prisoners in a prison yard plodding round and round, trapped in a nightmare of flight that once powered whole cities, the windmills now power nothing through a grid leading nowhere.

Seeing acre after acre of them, the driver thinks of scarecrows and the Bird Man of Alcatraz. He thinks of Icarus and wings melting in the sun. He thinks of skyfeathers and cloudwings of a ruined god stooping to earth, soaring motionless in incalculable gyres, then diving arpeggio down the steadfast song of the sky, bearing a burning gift and a passion not even the vultures perched on his chains can tear from him. He remembers a dream of a

LEVIT

Illustrated by Brian Patrick Murray

billion children dancing in a circle around a mushroom cloud. He thinks of what his eyes have seen and unseen, and wonders if he has ever been honest with himself. His thoughts, such rare desert birds, always fly away from him—never toward.

He remembers owning an automotive albatross that died and left him stranded in this very place he's now passing. The junkyard for Don Wells Towing is still there, deserted, its owner most likely killed in the fallout from the nuke strike that took out Twenty-nine Palms—the same bystander calamity that transformed Palm Springs and all the other desert cities into ghost towns overnight. Dutchman was a language mechanic back then, before the fire, someone who could tell you Alcatraz and Albatross were from the same root, someone who could tell you about *The Rime of the Ancient Mariner,* someone who had yet to learn that in all the motion of history there is no final freedom, only mad windmills whirling in darkness and children born insane who would catch the wind in their hands and never let it go.

He listens now, trying to catch the meaning in the wind as it moans over the desert. In it he hears no meaning, only sound, the screams of mobs out for blood and the screams of their bloodfeast victims, indistinguishable, no nobility at all in the sound, only twisted pain.

He thumbs on the entertainment scan. Music: *La Damnation de Faust* by Berlioz, switching to *Big Science* by Laurie Anderson, switching to something by the Grateful Dead. Selections from the microvideo library: "But why a poodle?" says a sitcomedian, "Poodles aren't even real dogs—they're hairdressers working off bad karma from past lives"; switching to a Famous Talk Show Author saying, "Godel's Theorem means that every Eden must necessarily have its Forbidden Tree, every Imaginary Garden its requisite Real Toad. Fantasy is the sword and sorcery used to kill it yesterday, science fiction the laser and logic used to kill it tomorrow, and horror the realization that the Toad never dies, that the Tree must always remain Forbidden"; switching to a selection from his personal Video Record, a scene at The Wheel Inn in Cabazon. He hits the SCAN STOP button, then the one labeled PLAY.

The Wheel possesses all the glory one can reasonably expect of a pre-Apocalypse truckstop, a survivor from the old time. As the camera pans over the surrounding area, the numerous tents and lean-tos huddled about make it clear that the old truckstop is the center of a settlement of sorts, a pariah settlement, Dutchman knows, one housing Blacks, Hispanics, a few Indians and—most unlikely of all—a considerable number of Laotians brought to this country to resettle after the debacle of a brush-fire war in a far-away land. Even before the War, the white populations of Banning, Beaumont, and Cherry Valley had resented the presence of such minorities in the Pass area. With the massive rad death and collapse of order brought on by the War, this resentment flared into a full scale pogrom in which those ethnics the White Cowboys had failed to kill at the outset were driven into the desert to die.

But the tenacity of human life prevailed. The ethnics had, instead of dying, settled at Cabazon: in abandoned shacks, in the long-since condemned Desert Sands Casino, in The Wheel Inn itself and the trucks that had stopped permanently around it, in hastily constructed lean-tos and tents, even in the great hollow bellies of the monumental concrete brontosaurus and tyrannosaurus on the premises there, the outcasts had housed themselves. They became a community huddled in the great empty belly of the beast.

It was the dinosaurs that had intrigued Dutchman, caused him to record this. The massive, olive-drab sculptures were the brain children of one Clarence Bell, one-time amusement park caricaturist, who held simply that "people will stop to look at something big." That, perhaps, was the reason these replicas were built to two-and-a-half-times life size, why they survived the War, why they so clearly dwarfed their abandoned metal children, the dinosaur semis come to eternal rust there.

The video ends and the scan starts again. On the monitors appear the image of an astronaut using a manned maneuvering unit—black arch of heaven, blue bow of Earth, wingless faceless white-spacesuited Technological Angel adrift against the horizon of black and blue. He joins a group of faceless Angels at work on a space station—plump white Doughboys of Space, Astronaut Service Guards, the scientists, engineers, technologists and space soldiers who worked for Orbital Defense and Intelligence Network (ODIN). Over their suit radios comes the announcement of the commencement of hostilities. The Angel in the manned maneuvering unit refuses to go to battle stations. The blue-white Earth is reflected in his face-plate as he looks upon it. Explosions, the acne of apocalypse, bloom and shroom across the Earth, his face.

Dutchman punches the video off. He has never been able to figure out whether that particular video is a dramatization of the End or a document of the End itself. He obtained it off a trader who said he got it from government files stored underground not far from Edwards. The same trader had told him that many of the surviving ASGuards had returned to the broken Earth they could not infallibly defend, that they had shuttled down into the Mojave, the salt flats, the dry lake beds, anywhere they could put their craft down. He claimed that they walked the same Earth as other men, Angels fallen from the sky, failed guardians. Dutchman doubts it, but he does not place it outside the realm of the possible. He has seen strange things aplenty since the Fire.

"Old news, old news," he says to the tomcat sprawled asleep on the truck's broad dashboard. "Doesn't mean a thing, anymore."

In his rear-view monitor the sun is rising. The burning clock. He recalls his stop in Flagstaff. He had parked and camouflaged his truck outside town and hiked down the rails to scare up provisions. In the streets of that dying town, he'd heard the ragged wild-eyed crowd crying, "Simplify him! Simplify him!" as they dragged an old man, a heretic, to the pyre of their justice.

He had, of course, seen Simplifications before. "Smash the Machines, smash their slavish masters!" It was the voice of long reptilian reflex, the voice of hitting back, the voice of the future and the voice of the past. It meant revenge on technology, revenge on technologists, revenge on the sinful Thought that created a world of evil, selfish destruction, a world that valued Technology more than people.

So the Simplifiers claimed. Whatever the case, their notions could mean the destruction of both Dutchman and his rig, so he was constantly wary of them, as he had been on his approach to Flagstaff.

The Simplification he saw there, though—that *had* been different from the ones he'd seen before. Apparently, the elderly heretic there had been a collector of timepieces. The mob immolated him atop a pile of his burning clocks. Dutchman could do nothing to stop the suffering that time had brought upon the old man, but seeing it made him realize that that was what Simplification was all about: burning clocks to kill the old time.

He had gotten some food, then spent the night sharing an abandoned rail car with a stray tomcat. In the boxcar, he'd eaten, sharing his food with the battered old tom, reflecting for the thousandth time on the luck that left him still alive in a land where nearly four-fifths of the population had died within three months of the Fire—despite the attack-ameliorating powers of ODIN. He had been between targets and driving a truckload of foodstuffs when the War came. A miracle, maybe—the simultaneous action of chance and necessity. Or maybe just dumb luck. And who could ultimately say whether the luck that left him alive to endure such times as these was good luck, or bad?

Thinking on it, he fell asleep. In the light of the following morning, before hiking back to his truck, he had noticed a poem scrawled on one wall of the car by some previous (and surprisingly literate) drifter. It read:

in the bowels of America
in the bowels of Russia
I can tell the future
the way the ancients could tell the future
in the bowels of animals destined for holocaust

they could see the pattern of time veined in a goat's gut
they could read it inscribed in the entrails of the
sacrificial beast
I can watch it on TV
I can read it in the papers two women from Chicago
two women from Leningrad
talking about 'defending our way if life,'
'freedom of self-determination,' and
'bargaining from strength'

I can hear it
I can diagnose it in the ulcerous silos
perforating the national bowels,
in the gut rumblings of war machines,
in the full-stomached talk of bravado leaders

I can tell the future
but what am I going to tell the future?

"Dated a full six years before the war," Dutchman had said to the tomcat. "Guess we all really knew Doomsday was coming—every day. All our lives."

The cat hadn't replied, though it did follow him back to his truck and had stayed with him since. The sound the old cat made reminded Dutchman of something a woman he'd known had said. She told him that in foreign countries the animals didn't speak English. In France or Germany pigs didn't say Oink, Oink; they said Cronk, Cronk or Nuff, Nuff. French cats didn't say Meow, they said Miaou, which in French sounds like the word for 'better.' To him, what the old cat said sounded more like Miauo than Meow, and it seemed to mean something very much like 'better' all the time, so he'd named the old rat-killer Pierre.

Pierre at the moment is sprawled across the dashboard, no longer asleep but with—at most—only half an eye on the desert scenery rushing past. They are crossing over the Whitewater. To starboard, Whitewater Canyon cuts back and back, starkly scenic in the zoom monitors and only slightly less so out the window, as it gouges its way from mountains to desert. To port, the river flows its rocky way before disappearing into the desert. Abaft, the sun is rising fast; forward, the shadows are racing back across Cabazon, across Banning, across Beaumont. The ocean of the desert is calm, this dawning; nothing, save the truck, is moving in any direction for as far as the eye or the zoom cameras can see.

There was a time, in the first few months after the Fire, when the big rigs still haunted the interstates like the ghosts of a dinosaur culture. One by one, though, the fuelholes had dried up. The dinosaurs had ceased their haunted roaming, scattering their corroding metal bones beside a thousand highways at a million truckstops and roadside rests. At the bottom of the downhill grade from Whitewater, Dutchman passes one such behemoths' burial ground, the roadside rest oasis not far from the off-ramps for Highway 111 and Verbenia. Over fifty truck carcasses line the lots and ramps hereabouts, all picked clean by the parts-locusts and vehicle vultures.

"Yeah, we must be right lucky, Pierre," Dutchman says to the cat, "or smarter than these guys were. We're still on the road. I can sniff out the fuelholes like a Bushman tracking water in the Kalahari. Find where nobody suspects. Sure, these other guys, they could Geiger out the hotspots and avoid them, figure ways around dead road ends, scrabble up parts or cobble together versions of their own, like I can. But they couldn't scam up the fuel, no sir. . . ."

He roughs up the scruff of the old cat's neck then smooths it down again.

"All these dead trucks we're passing, cat. Look at 'em. And to think they all died within fumes' reach of one of the largest secret fuel caches left *anywhere!* My depot! They just didn't know it was there, that's all."

The cat gives him a disinterested look.

"You bet—right behind The Wheel Inn at Cabazon, just up the road a little bit. One-thousand-gallon fuel tank, buried underground. Used to service it regular before the War. I got ten others just like it set up all along the length of the whole damn Christopher Columbus Transcontinental Highway. Safe harbors, Pierre, and I'm the one that's got 'em."

The thought occurs to Dutchman that other truckers have been growing fewer and fewer all the time. In fact, he hasn't seen any other over-the-roaders at all on this trip. Could he maybe be the last of the breed? But, no, he puts that thought out, out of his mind, out like an unwanted fire.

The roadside billboards that used to line this stretch of highway from 111 to Cabazon are limp and broken, their messages long since reduced to tatters, all victims of the high winds that venturi through the pass here.

On the horizon a cloud of smoke, increasingly distinguishable from morning haze, rides like a ghost ship.

"Holy Nike, Mother of Missiles," Dutchman mutters, tugging absently at his neckerchief and punching up ZOOM on his monitors, "what the hell's going on here?"

For a moment he fears Simplifiers may have discovered his fuel depot and exploded it—but no, this doesn't look like a fuel fire. . . .

As he approaches, Dutchman clearly sees that the smoke is coming from Cabazon, even if not from his fuel cache. In his monitors, he sees The Wheel Inn a burning ruin. Smoke and fire rise from the mouths of the olive-drab concrete reptiles. The dinosaurs have a fire in their bowels. Around them, the abandoned trucks, lean-tos and tents are burning too. Dragons stride the Earth again, and all is flame and carnage.

Soon he doesn't need ZOOM or even his monitors, he can see the devastation with his own two naked eyes. He takes the off-ramp a bit too fast. The parking area is bodies and blood and fire, a spillage of mud and blood and bones.

Blood on the crumbling gray asphalt. Red and gray-white skull-smear on the olive-drab flanks of the concrete dinosaurs where children, babies, have been headbashed and flung again and again against that unyielding flesh, that too too solid flesh that would not melt to spare their lives. Men and women spitted upon sharpened stakes. . . .

His eyes and his cameras pass over all of them, and soon enough he sees that every one has been marked. All of them have had the Civil Defense glyph seared into the flesh of their foreheads by branding irons.

All around, the stench of burning flesh, the smoke rising from the hollow bowels of the concrete beasts, from the bowels where the outcasts of many nations made their homes. All around a shambles of bodies, some naked as well as bloody, all chill in the early morning wind, blood-soaked clothing rags fluttering like the flags of the nations of despair.

Dutchman looks over the scene of blood and smoke. The lesson of history—his eyes have seen it all before—the lesson of history is that no one—yet still he must wait for the shock to die out of him—the lesson of history is that no one learns —before he can think right again—the lesson of history is that no one learns from the lesson of history—and it never dies out of him completely.

"What good was surviving the War," he mutters in his mind, though God or the cat might be listening, "if this is what it still all comes to? Surviving to kill, killing to survive—what's the point? Why not better to have died, if we've lived through the Fire only to perish in the smoke?"

The only answer is the wind which, like the cat, seems to be crying 'better' in another language. Also on the wind he hears hoofbeats and cries, sees a cloud of dust blowing behind a column of horsemen as he rounds a corner of the burning Inn. The horsemen are white men, dressed in white, on white horses. Above them, leading them onward is a White Angel—a spacesuited somebody atop a flying platform.

White Cowboys, then, but led by a Death Angel, a fallen angel, apparently one of the ASGuards who had returned to Earth and whom he'd thought were mythical. But this myth is brandishing a very real revolver and hovering at the head of this posse, which is armed with branding irons, blades, torches, a few guns. They are in pursuit of a fleeing young couple—very young; a boy and girl, really.

The Faceless Angel that fell from the sky takes aim at the couple.

"Off the dash, Pierre," Dutchman shouts to the cat as he jams the truck into gear, tromps the accelerator, hurtles into the fray.

The fleeing young couple are almost to where his fuel cache is hidden—they've just crossed the dirt road that runs beside it, the dirt road he is hurtling down. The Angel fires, the boy goes down, hit, unable to run. The girl goes to her knees, cradling the boy's head in her arms, as if to protect him from the madness bearing down upon them.

Dutchman sounds his airhorn. The cat, already off the dash, dives under the seat. In the portside monitor, an ancient white humpback diesel Cadillac wheeled-whale comes surging out of the horseguard's dust cloud, comes roaring across the desert, aiming to reach the fuel depot before LEVITHN.

"Cut me off at the pass, huh?" Dutchman smiles peacefully, even if the presence of the ancient fuel-guzzler here must mean they've discovered his fuel cache. Is that also part of the reason for this raid on the settlement? Had the pariahs discovered his fuel depot? They must have seen him here often enough. . . . Is this the Cowboys taking control of that precious resource? Is he, Dutchman, somehow responsible for the death and carnage of this raid?

The smile vanishes from his face, to be replaced by set determination. The airhorn is sounding. The Cadillac's license plate reads BUCUBUX. The horsemen are just behind it, the Angel on his flying platform almost directly overhead. The downed young couple watch as the lines of force converge.

To the drone of the airhorn the hollow noise of crumpling metal and shattering glass is added. The Cadillac is disabled, stranded. The horses bolt in a dozen confused directions, their riders unable to restrain them. Dust everywhere. Even the deadly Angel pulls back, momentarily disoriented.

Dutchman brakes the truck to an abrupt halt beside the couple. A cloud of dust swirls around him as he leaps from the truck and runs toward them. The girl, a young woman of Asian ancestry, is dumbstruck with fear. As Dutchman approaches she cradles her companion still more tightly, as if to ward off whatever evil this newcomer might represent.

"I'll help you," Dutchman says. The girl does not move. Dutchman squats beside the boy, a young Mexindian who stares with the wide, wide eyes of shock. He is hit badly, high in the right leg. From the ugliness of the wound, it is clear the Angel is using hollow-point bullets. The boy is losing a great deal of blood.

Dutchman lifts the boy in a fireman's carry and heads toward the truck. The girl, snapping free of her catatonia, runs ahead and opens the passenger side door. Dutchman lays the boy out on the seat. Glass shatters as a gunshot punches through the windshield. The cat burrows more deeply beneath the seat.

Dutchman turns.

"You can't save them, nigger trucker," says the

Angel, floating out of the swirling dust, gun drawn. Somewhere he can hear horsemen shouting as they regroup and prepare to head toward them. "You can't save them and you can't save yourself."

The young girl, her hair blown back, is walking toward the faceless Angel that floats winglessly toward them. Neither seems to touch the ground. Dutchman watches incredulously as the girl goes to her knees before her tormentor. She lifts her empty, defenseless hands toward her attacker.

"Man of future, man of past," she says brokenly, "please leave us! Please you, leave us alone!"

Dutchman sidles slowly out in the girl's direction, slowly fingering loose the clawhammer in his workbelt. In his head, this tableau before him is the children dancing their ring around the mushroom cloud. It is President Kennedy waving from his motorcade. Missiles rising on pillars of fire by night, columns of cloud by day. White lab coats locking a baboon by its head into a vise. Out-of-control-CIA operatives sighting down the barrel from the railroad bridge. Final stage rocket shutoff punching out of atmosphere in tragic trajectories, arcs of covenants with gravity. The lab technician cocking back his hammer arm like Vulcan at the forge, preparing to test the effects on baboon behavior of repeated concussive blows. Shots ringing out above the grassy knoll, the hammer plunging toward the baboon's skull, the nuclear fireworks delivering portable hell. The President's head jerking back, the baboon skull's audible crack, the burning blasts erasing history's tracks——

Dutchman hears the dry click of the Angel's suit amplifier.

"Shit," hisses the Angel as he aims the gun at the young girl's face, as he clicks back the gunlock's hammer.

"These subhumans can't even talk right."

Dutchman yanks the clawhammer from his workbelt. The aim shifts from the girl to him as he releases the tool in a strong end-over-end arc toward the flying platform. The Angel releases the hammer on the gun. Dutchman is diving, wondering if the billion children dance around the death cloud to conjure it into being or to abjure it out of existence. Genies and bottles. Corks, stoppers, hammers rising, falling.

A gunshot. The claw end of the work hammer slamming into stabilizer board. Sound of metal puncturing at both ends of this exchange of ballistic information, this reptilian communication, this highway moment. Bullet puncturing trailer, pinging round inside. A shower of sparks and smoke from the disabled flying platform as it veers to the right, as the Angel struggles to keep it aloft, gyring farther and farther afield in the process. The horsemen behind are daunted at the sight.

Dutchman grabs up the girl, drops her in the cab beside her wounded companion. Seeing the convection rising from the makeshift pump and nozzle the Cowboys have mounted on his fuel cache, Dutchman snatches off his neckerchief and begins soaking it in the #2 oil, nearly as light as gasoline, that dribbles from the aperture as he threads a corner of the rag into the throat of it. As he lights the rag a bullet whizzes past—fired by the Cadillac driver, who, unhurt, has extricated himself from his vehicle.

The rag is afire. Dutchman reverses the pump. Air and flame are sucked down toward the volatile vapors adrift above the fuel in the partially empty tanks. Dutchman sprints away. He dashes round to the driver's side and puts the rig into gear like a ghost ship hoisting sail. The Cadillac driver chases after on foot and is able to shoot out two of LEVITHN's many tires before he too must take

cover as the fuel tank behind him explodes in fine imitation of a mushroom cloud, engulfing the white whale of his car. The cloud hangs in the air, unbroken for a quite a while, as the wind has stopped blowing.

Well, Dutchman thinks, at least I only destroyed things and not *people.* The destruction saddens him, nonetheless. And still, in the back of his mind, he wonders how responsible he might be for all that has happened in this day's dawning.

When they reach the highway again, the girl looks at him from out of eyes much used to seeing darkness.

"God send you," she says.

Dutchman doesn't know quite what to make of that. The look of dark wonder in the girl's eyes and the strange tone of her voice make her statement a question—Did God send you?—an affirmation—God sent you!—and a benediction—God send you!—all rolled into one.

He shrugs.

"What you've got to believe in," he says, gripping the wheel a bit more tightly, "is what you've got to believe."

Somewhere ahead there will be more fuel. There will be a doctor or at least medicine for the boy. There will be the ocean Columbus never saw, a place where mountains wade into the water. There will be a place where he will drop these children off and they will go their way.

This is what Dutchman has got to believe in. For now, and perhaps forever, his way lies down the arrow of time, beneath the burning clock.

The Book of Time
by
Camilla Decarnin

About the Author

Camilla Decarnin has been writing since the Third Grade. She now has a Masters degree in the subject, received from a school she declines to name "since they nearly destroyed all desire to write."

This can happen. Different academic programs have different effects on different people. So do different informal programs. In the end, the writer's best teacher is the writer herself, and the writer's best precept is to persist in writing.

Case in point: the charming, deft, and markedly professional story that follows. Selected for First Prize in the first quarter of the year by a distinguished judges' panel of heavily experienced SF writers, "The Book of Time" had previously been submitted fruitlessly to all the professional SF magazines, including one that felt there was something wrong with the syntax.

There certainly is; it is not dull; it is not always what you would expect, and it is wholly ingenious. That's true of the story as a whole . . . in which you will find a host of memorable characters figuratively pulling rabbits out of their hats at every turn, centering on a character we hope we shall often see again as her author's career expands and flourishes. Sometimes it just works that way . . .

many a now-famous writer, with a now highly-praised story, had to begin despite a series of rejections that seem inexplicable now.

Meanwhile, Camilla Decarnin is a radical feminist who works at the San Francisco AIDS Foundation and weighs her options, while listening to Mozart . . . who also had trouble getting people to see what he was driving at. Whether her career will display other parallels to his remains to be seen . . . but in SF, it begins on the next page.

For JR, SRD, and all who see themselves in The Book of Time

Making the dreams of time, gray mother of this night weave me your mirror light into a journey.

The streets were cobbled with black stone, the walls were gray rock; she would have led him to the high gate, to see the beams of ebony bound in bronze. Instead, she went into the city alone. She understood everything at a glance, and saw how the locks would fall amorously open for someone like her.

It was no use inviting him. He did not understand the hearts of true thieves, born thieves. He built a house of which he had stolen not a nail. It looked exactly like every other house she had ever seen. When he played chess he always knew what his next four moves would be, no matter that she had the set made for him out of amber that washed up in the sand away north (you were supposed to turn it in to the government) and of smuggled unmatched jades. But a thief in a new city must be drawn among the wakes of time, not hurled before it like a surf-rider. This is the only way to see an act the split second before it happens, and to know what is going on in the mind of a lock.

So she left him at home. The city was just as she imagined it, with canals of flat green water on the lagoon side, arched footbridges, kiosks selling spun glass.

A young boy looked up at her from under his black lashes. Apronned, he was kneeling, unpacking shiny fish in the door of a market. The look of stunned love told her she was his first thief, so she must not speak or smile, but commended him to the mother of dreams—she swaggered a bit, after that.

A scarlet-uniformed man steering his official conveyance in through one of the other gates also took cognizance of her—she faded into a crowd.

The streets seemed endless.

Even a city this size, she said to herself sardonically, must have something worth stealing.

"The Book of Time," a passing mother announced to her daughter, "will be on display in the Rotunda the first of the month." She was reading from a newspaper with the ink still wet. The daughter, who was thirteen, hunched her shoulders and sighed loudly. They turned the corner.

A good thief knows when it is time to find an inn.

Nearby, a façade was crusted with light—purple, blue, red, orange, pink, flashing messages: BED AND BOARD, DANCING NITELY, ROULETTE, WIN, VACANCY. Sounds of laughter and merriment floated out mixed with a kind of music she particularly enjoyed. On a sign over the door, a neon person demonstrated an exotic dance.

No born thief is that kind of fool.

She crossed the square and engaged a room in that shuttered and shabby place where the lighting is distinctly poor. Anyone who has ever visited such a city knows the one. The atmosphere is homey though the shadows cast into the corners by the oil lamps are a little odd.

The sound that awakened her that night was like a tent-flap in the wind. It came from the shadowy corner by the wardrobe. But she knew at once by the texture of the air that she was alone in the room.

From next door, however, issued muffled rumplings, tinkles, hisses, muted sounds of crisis, an opening door; a rapid progress of the hall ended in the *clossh* of a flushing sanitary device.

She slipped out of bed and cracked the door an inch.

Down the long perspective of the hall, a man in voluminous black robes emerged from the lavatory, clutching an empty alembic. He regarded some curls of indigo vapor that heliced insinuatingly along the floorboards, and avoided them in his return passage. His robes of black taffeta, so new that the folds whined against each other, were embroidered with silver keys, coins, flamesticks, and arcane symbols in general; across the left breast was neatly stitched the name of a well-known alchemical supply firm. His headgear, black sequined, was of a complicated nature, his expression uncordial. When he entered his chamber the door slammed; in a whisper, the light that spilled into the hall sliced off.

Quick as a thought she was out there, crouched to one of the commodious keyholes with which these inns abound.

Within: suspended from a chain, a lantern dropped a teepee of gold light over two cross-legged, sullen, naked albino teenagers, in an effect of overexposed daguerreotype.

The skinniest one wound long, near-luminous hair round his finger. The other one hunched theatrically, features squeezed and orange-rimmed eyes crossed, to stick her tongue out at the shadows. Presently from that direction a slant of black cut the thief's field of vision, with a *zeet zeet* of taffeta.

"If you're sure," it hissed, "quite sure you have no further aesthetic reservations." The albino mouths got sulkier. "No lingering doubts? No qualms about meter as an authentic expression of the technological zeitgeist?" The robes whisked out of sight.

The boy muttered something with "alliteration" and "archaic" in it. The girl muttered back about "accipiters" and "accuracy."

Zeet zeet zeet. The wizard planked down a tray of beakers, phials, caskets, Petri dishes, eyedroppers and measuring spoons; in the center rose the uncapped alembic, over a lighted candle. "Begin again. And this time, if you don't mind," the hiss rose to a whispered shriek like a strangling teakettle, "*no editorial changes in the spell!*"

Together the two poured black liquids into the alembic.

"Near for strange,"

they chanted in bored unison,

"We call the change;"

The boy went on alone, adding blue powders.

"Aleph, izzard;
Gut to gizzard;
Wing from finger;
Talon springing—"

In the alembic, indigo vapor tumbled. The girl eye-droppered blood-colored viscosities, droning,

"Marrow, hollow;
Feathers fallow
Force to fledge;
the Word our pledge—"

The boy's voice joined hers while they tossed triangular silver pills down the neck of the alembic and capped it:

"The hour our range—
We call the change!"

The heaving vapor went silver and started pushing out at the nozzle of the alembic. It rose curling to the suspended lantern and cloaked it in a cone of silver vapor. As the mystic steam spouted, the hovering cone spread downward. It covered the albino heads, blotting them from sight; covered the shoulders; the girl scratched the white fuzz at her crotch; the cone came on down. It snuffed the candle under the alembic; it reached the floor.

It shone. It looked like a pyramid of live mercury.

*

*   *

*   *

The silver shivered and broke, to a fine precipitate, and amid the falling silver dust two huge white falcons blinked. The skinnier one sneezed. The bigger one spread its wings a little for balance.

The thief's passionate attention was just then broken by a vaporous indigo sensation insinuating itself across her instep. She looked down but the hall was too dark for her to see anything. The sensation began to tendril around her ankle.

Hastily she arose and slid into her room, where by the light of a pocket flash she determined that her move ment must have dislodged the thing. Thoughtfully, she jammed small items of clothing into the crack under her door and into the keyhole. Then she retired to her bed and her interrupted sojourn among logics the other side of sleep.

Illustrated by Brian Patrick Murray

In the morning, from her upper-story window, the roofs of the town lay like a mist, green-gray, blue-gray, pink-gray, shot with black and green veins of the streets and canals. East, the lagoon showed as a bit of blue skirting, while young hills rose green, narrow, almost perfectly conical, to the north.

The thief ran jauntily down the multiple stairs. The world was hers for the taking.

Breakfast was served by a thirteen-year-old in overalls and a white jumper-apron who kept giving her short intense looks when she wasn't watching (but that is just when true thieves see the most). The wizard and the albino teenagers were not there.

After breakfast she ambled across the square. By daylight the neon of the grand hostelry was wan and embarrassed. The drab inn where she had stayed looked solidly wholesome. This is the way it works, as the thief well knew, and as she made her way up a narrow street she thought complacently, "It was just a matter of——"

"Hisst!" said someone from a deep doorway.

The thief, who had not been watching, said, "Come out of there; you are making yourself conspicuous."

A thirteen-year-old in overalls, tubby, with freckles and rusty frizzed electrical hair materialized, matching step with her, saying, "My name is Tetikte. Tik to my friends, Tetik to my enemies. That's a pun in another language."

The thief grinned. "I know that language. Best we be friends, then. Some call me Skylla." And some did.

"After the Great Bitch?"

"On the contrary. She was named after me."

"I believe you. Thousands wouldn't. Bet you didn't know I was a girl."

"I did indeed." She looked into the girl's squinted

yellow eyes. "Even the *first* time I saw you."

"My aunt owns the inn," Tik explained. "So I wait table there."

"Ah, but I saw you once before that."

"I'm pretty ubiquitous—— That's the Rotunda," she said quickly.

They had come out onto a gray-flagged plaza. One green canal cut a third of the way across, interrupted once into a rectangular pool full of fountains and statuary, to become a moat around the Rotunda, which rose there as a perfect shimmering hemisphere. Several drawbridges spanned the moat. People were crossing them, in and out.

A portico fringing the plaza sheltered the kiosks that sold food, wine, coffee, drugs, flowers, blown glass, jewelry, stamped leather, baskets, rugs, pottery and other items familiar to travelers. Dancers and acrobats wiggled and rebounded on spread carpets, vendors wove the throng, leafletters nabbed passersby.

"This square is the exact center of the city," remarked the girl Tetikte while they strolled. The thief called by some Skylla, paying no particular attention to their surroundings, said, "Yesterday I traversed this city from end to end three times and never saw this place."

"It's a big city," said Tik. At that moment a carpet flung itself out and a troupe of jugglers sprang up before them—dizened in bright silk rags, clicking their bootheels, doffing their clever hats—and cried: "Ho!"

Woman and girl stopped perforce.

"You never know what you'll run into here," Tik continued. "You go down a different street and——"

"That Rotunda," Skylla mused, "does look familiar, but I'm certain I have never been here before."

"*Dejà vu,*" Tik suggested. The jugglers' clubs slapped into their hands and flashed out again. "You can only see half of it, actually. The other half is underground. It's a . . . sort of museum."

"Art treasures?" Skylla inquired with unfeigned interest.

"They've got all kinds of things. It's pretty big, once you get inside. There are thirteen floors devoted to different periods."

"Precious relics of the past?"

Tik's eyes slid away to watch the jugglers bowing with clutches of clubs in their hands. "Something like that."

"I would like to see the inside of that place."

" 'No time like the present,' " Tik quoted agreeably.

Away from the arcade the crowd thinned. They walked almost alone in the great square, on slabs of the purest slate-gray stone. One lone block they passed framed neatly incised lettering: WHAT HAPPENS WHEN YOU FIND OUT—the thief's head turned as they walked and she read the rest upside-down over her shoulder —YOU WANT SOMETHING THAT DOESN'T EXIST? with a name and date below she couldn't make out.

It was a problem she personally had never encountered. She thought it must be an interesting one to solve.

The drawbridge rang hollow under their feet.

"These can be drawn up in time of siege," Tik said slapping the rail. "Only there never has been a siege." Her voice held the regrets of the young at all untenanted possibility. Skylla smiled and rubbed her palms lightly together.

"My treat," Tik stipulated with upraised forefinger. She bought their tickets and they passed into the foyer. A stand held a sign:

THE BOOK OF TIME
will be on display in
the Rotunda
the first
of the month.

Skylla paused. Down the long hall to their right the skeleton of an animal had been arrayed: hung on wires, clawed toes dangling, fanged jaws open, tail curved serpentinely. The wingspread was approximately forty feet.

The thief cleared her throat. "Remarkably well preserved," she said, and coughed into her fist.

"This way." They went down the other hall, between cases of ornaments. There were a lot of armbands of beaten gold, crowns of pearls designed for massy dark hair, odd rings and harnesses of jewels displayed on velvet mannequins, together with diamond-, emerald-, ruby-, sapphire- and turquoise-encrusted hilts and scabbards of swords, daggers, bodkins, cutlasses, dirks and swordsticks, and similarly encrusted battle-axe hafts. Many of the gems, she noticed, were vulgarly large.

"Along here." Abruptly the blades were replaced by an elegant and unintelligible weaponry of silver tubes and flanges, wire-spoked tori, sinister needley projectiles; interspersed with unabated empearled headgear and halters of jewels. "Come on, I want to start at the beginning," Tik cried, and the thief hastened to catch up with her at the entrance of a broad coiled stair, walled with lucite. Below their feet the steps spiraled glitteringly in flattened perspective, like a sparkling snake.

"Come on!" Tik was already a flight down.

Skylla started circling the descent.

Visions printed themselves on her retinas, between glances down the stairwell, of beasts, vehicles, consoles, and costumery, statuary, muraled vistas, bulks for which she had no names. She descended, following Tik off the last spiral. Above, the stair seemed a wheeling galaxy. She steadied. Under her feet now fish warped green water, weed undulated. She straightened. Tik had run on. The thief took a step and the Rotunda shook.

Ahead, Tik stopped with arms out stiffly. Below, Skylla was sure that something that looked like an immense barnacled cable had rippled, just slightly, on the floor of the sea.

"Krake-quake!" Tik skidded back, lit with excitement. The thief pointed.

"What is that," she stated.

Tik looked down. "A kraken."

"*A* kraken."

"Sure. A giant squid. Let's see what the Richter is."

"Is that the sea? We are in the middle of the city. . . ."

"A lot of this place is built over a system of caves, hollowed out ages ago under the sea level, before the city was ever thought of." She pushed into a cluster of people by a glass-covered graphed scroll, onto which a pen point was tracing a crotchety line. Someone whistled.

"Not bad," Tik breathed. "Five-five." They backed out of the crowd. "Of course, the krakograph at the university is supposed to be a lot more accurate.

"What's the matter?" she added.

The thief paced beside her a moment in silence. "Nothing, my young friend. But I would see this museum of yours."

Tik nestled her hands into the pockets of her overalls. "Well, that's what we came here for, isn't it? Now, over this way . . ."

They ascended floor by floor.

"What *is* all this?" said the thief on the seventh. She cast another glance at the door of startling design and contrivance by which they had entered the room.

"Plasmoids." Tik picked up a big, translucent orangish loaf and stroked and patted it. "This is the children's room. I used to love this place. Watch." The thing elongated submissively to a fat rope under her modeling. Holding it by one end, she put her face close to it and shouted, "BOO!" Then she rapped it smartly against the floor. "When you scare it, it goes rigid for thirty-one seconds. In fact, it's one of the most rigid organics known. That's all they've ever been able to figure out that it does. Now, that one over there——"

"Tik." The girl turned from the much, much bigger green loaf being scaled by means of rope ladders by several children in overalls. "Not this room. The museum. Where does it come from?"

"You mean where do they get all their exhibits?" She looked down. The orange rod limpened, hung like a dead anaconda out either end of her fist. "See? And if you let it alone a while it goes back to the shape you saw first.

"The Rotunda . . ." She watched the little girls climb. "It's been here a long time." Her soft rust-brown lashes fluttered as she looked at Skylla. "They say," she continued in the mode associated throughout the civilized world with the imparting of significant information, "the whole thing was laid out by a foreigner; the major and minor themes of the floors were set up then."

"But she could not have brought all this with her."

"No," Tik agreed. "Most of the actual exhibits have been . . . acquired since her time."

Obscurely but immensely relieved, the thief yet raised a black eyebrow.

"People bring them," Tik replied to it. "Visitors . . .

wizards, a few warriors . . . and . . ." She shrugged.

Two children grabbed the plasmoid rope she had dropped and ran for opposite ends of the room, with it stretching to glistening filament between them. The thief studied somberly red, purple, gold, blue, tea-brown depths in gels more or less bean-shaped all around them.

They went up.

On the thirteenth floor they stood under a bowl of black sky through which stars approached and passed them. The girl was tired and the thief preternaturally silent.

"I guess that's about it," Tik said finally.

As the thief watched, suddenly from the deeps of space in the ceiling floated a dot that became a triangle that bloomed to a galleon in full sail, hoist on three stripèd gasbags. From the hull, twin combs of oars swept the ether; from the topmast, thin colored banners streamed; and as it passed near, people on deck, including two of oddly marsupial aspect, waved their handkerchiefs.

Tik looked slightly embarrassed. "The projectionists get bored. You know."

The stars flowed down the sky.

Skylla rubbed her palms together gently, and spoke. "Much food for thought and an empty stomach were ever a bad combination. What do you say to lunch?"

But when they left the Rotunda the sun had already dipped behind the western rooftops and the air in the gray plaza was cool. The thief was mildly perturbed that time had got so far ahead of her.

"I know a place near here," Tik volunteered.

"Good food?"

"It has atmosphere."

"The inn——"

"If we went back there my aunt would put me to work."

"Work enriches the soul, they say."

"Sort of like horse manure?" Tik asked dryly. "*You* don't work, I bet." She glanced at the flat pouch—it contained small tools—the thief wore on her belt and at the plain brown dagger at her hip.

"My occupation," Skylla replied "is very demanding." Her teeth grinned privately behind her serious face and she felt through her boot an irregularity in the gray flags. When she glanced back all she could read in the settling dusk, looking worn rather than carved into the stone, was, ". . . YOU CAN HAVE ANYTHING YOU WANT . . ." and the next moment she could not be sure there were any words there at all. "Well," she said, tilting her forester's hat, with the long pheasant feather, over one eye, "if the place is nearby, then."

"In fact, it's kind of a dive," Tik confessed, her face like an amber moon with a russet aureole in the gloom of the alley they turned into; adding, "Not that it's dangerous or anything."

"Thank goodness for that," replied the thief chastely, and followed the girl down damp stone steps.

The door was wood, deeply carved with graffiti; the room—big, noisy, full of tables, lit by lamps in sconces, warmed by bodies and kitchen-heat—enveloped them in a smell of food like a lover's rapturous and importunate embrace. Skylla snapped her fingers at a serving-boy even as they wended to their table.

The boy had heated cheeks and black hair, and lowered his eyelashes before the thief's bold and hungry stare. "Give us your best, and plenty of it," she instructed simply. Someone at the next table said something in another language that warmed the lad's cheeks a degree, to scarlet. He hurried off.

"A pretty callant," the thief nodded, lounging on her bench against the wall, "and one I've seen before."

"Oh, him? His name's Min. He's a sort of very distant cousin of mine."

"Do tell."

"Well, we're all more or less related here. One way or another."

"When I saw him, he had a different job."

Tik pointed. "Looks like we even get some entertainment."

A curly-haired youth on a high stool strummed for quiet and sang, heavy on authentic gutturals:

"I am a lonesome farmboy,
with boots up to my hips . . ."

—wrenched into another octave—

". . . Yes, I'm just a lonesome farmboy,
My boots up to my hips.
I walk the red dust deserts . . ."

—and let his voice drop into haunted regions (as the door opened on two night-framed figures with luminously pale hair)—

". . . Among the bouncer chips."

Tik leaned conspiratorially. "What you want to bet he's never even been on—— Hey, those two are staying at the inn, too." The door swung closed, ushering cold air; the albinos found a table in the shadows.

Min brought them beer in mugs, and bread—"Saltless," Tik warned—cut from a long, thin loaf. "That's just the way they make it here. The butter, too." She spread butter on a piece and sprinkled it with salt from a minute bowl. Her teeth wrenched at the crust while the thief sipped beer. "I never can wait for the real food when I'm hungry." The curly-haired singer stopped, amid a flourish of guitar chords.

"Where do you suppose they came here from?"

Tik followed the thief's indicative glance across the room. "Caves?" she suggested. Skylla looked at her obliquely. "Well, how did they get so white, then?"

"They were born that way." On the thief's face was an expression compounded of several recollections. "This city looks as though it were designed for tourists, but the dining room at the inn was empty this morning. None of the people I've seen dressed like travelers."

"We . . . um . . . don't get many visitors." Min came and set down for them plates of a salad that had artichoke hearts and anchovies in it, glanced quickly from Tik's face to the thief's and ducked away among the tables. Tik scrutinized her salad. "Just a few wizards and warriors and . . . well . . ."

"Thieves?"

"Um."

"Why is that?" The thief's travels had taught her when to be blunt, which is harder to learn than other subtleties.

"The city," Tik said through spinach leaves, "lies under a tilsim, a spell of obscurity. Because," she scanned the room and lowered her voice, "it contains the greatest treasure in the universe."

"Your museum."

Tik's brows peaked. "The Rotunda? No. I mean The Book of Time."

Something, perhaps at the advent of food, unknotted in the thief's interior.

"A book is more valuable than . . . all that?"

"Well, first of all, it isn't really a book."

"It isn't."

"It just looks like a book. It's really a mirror. Except it doesn't reflect anything." Out in the kitchen, a glass smashed.

"This is a riddle?"

"No, no. I'm telling you exactly what it is, just literally."

"And what good is a mirror that doesn't reflect anything?"

"They say it will reflect the face of one person." Shadows from the lamps wavered solemnly over the girl's cheeks. "The person who will steal it."

Skylla felt chills tampering with her vertebrae.

"Why would anyone want to do that?"

Lamplights gleamed in Tik's shadowed-amber eyes.

"Because: the wayfarer who reaves away The Book of Time past the city gate can have anything . . . anything at all." She swallowed beer. "Or so they say." The thief began to eat again, tidily.

"Who owns it now?"

"No one—that is, it belongs to the city."

"And it will be on display tomorrow in the Rotunda."

"Yes." Tik spread a napkin and drew on it with a tine of her fork.

"It's kept in a room in the exact center of the building. The room is spherical with a mezzanine running around the inside. The book is suspended in the middle of the room."

"How far out from the mezzanine?"

Tik hesitated. "Maybe five feet from the rail."

"On wires?"

"No, it just sort of hangs there."

"Magic?"

"Could be. Although here, you never know."

Just then Min offered them a boned pike rolled in

galantine, which Skylla sliced neatly into small oval steaks with her dagger.

The noise around them was jolly, with other singers succeeding to the high stool. They ate the pike. Then they ate tortellini and were waiting with considerable indifference to see if anything else emerged from the kitchen on Min's tray when the street door was flung open by a black-draped arm.

The wizard poised on the sill, scanning. Robes of taffeta moved in the draft, in one slow piece, like a black bell.

Skylla's ankles were crossed and her fingers laced around her empty beer mug as she regarded with tolerance the banjo-hung singer now mounting the stool—this one wore a tall pointed cap in which, if precedence were any guide, he would collect coins after a song or two—and spared not a glance for the cold doorway . . .

"My girl knows my mind,"

(sang the pointed-hatted boy)

"She always comforts me.
She is a real woman,
Yes, she is my lay-dee——"

. . . as the wizard crossed the room in a commotion of drapery, seized the albino boy, dragged him from his bench and shook him, thrust him staggering toward the door and reached toward where the girl had scooted back in the shadows. Then he stopped. He continued to stand, arm outstretched, 'til a small, squarish hand stilled the brown hilt of a dagger that nailed several folds of his sleeve to the wall, and a voice said courteously,

"Excuse me. I believe I dropped this."

The wizard then backed up, to the sound of ripping taffeta.

The thief examined her blade.

When she looked up, the wizard was gone.

Pleased, for it is not every day you can pull off something like that in a dim light, Skylla, inclining her upper body punctiliously, expressed a hope that the pair—the boy had walked back brushing his white sleeves—might join her and her companion at their table.

Their progress among the diners was preceded by marked silence. Conversation reanimating behind them took up at a higher pitch.

Min's gaze as they came up was wholly worshipful. He proffered a clean stein of sleety beer.

Tik accepted the newcomers with a small glance of reserve. In the exchange of names they hesitated before the white girl said, "I'm Tasneem. He's Adaja. We use other names professionally, of course."

"Where are you from?" asked Tik.

The boy shrugged and sipped the coffee Min brought. "We travel around."

"What do you do?"

"Birds."

Tik blinked. "What?"

The boy took his lips from his cup again. "We do birds. Mostly."

"We're freelance *enchantées,*" enlarged Tasneem gruffly.

Adaja glanced with eyes the color of ball bearings at the enthralled waiter and turned back to Skylla. "That means we whore around for the alchemical corporations."

Tik looked from one to the other, revolving her empty glass on its wet ring. "How come he was so mad?"

Tasneem shrugged. "He thinks we should be where he can watch us all the time. They get like that."

"Possessive," Adaja put in.

"You do them one raven and they think you're their

familiar or something."

Adaja rubbed his shoulder. "Amateurs," he muttered all on one pitch as though it were a comment on moral habits. Tasneem snorted tolerantly. Adaja turned on her. "It isn't a joke," he insisted. "Like last night."

Tasneem's eyelids flickered, but the white boy brushed at the air. He leaned intently across the table at the thief; she noticed that his eyes, between lashes ghost-blond in lamplight, jiggetted uncontrollably. "Last night this nit interrupts a spell at the worst possible moment, just because we'd introduced a few improvements——"

"He thought we'd *forgotten* the right lines, 'til we told him."

"And these were standard variants. He didn't even recognize them." He leaned back, bounced his palms once on the table top.

"I had thought," said the thief carefully, "that exact wording was considered critical in these matters."

"Sure," Tasneem granted, "if you know what you're doing it's the difference between a simple cantrip and a major glamour."

"But this guy gets everything out of a book we in the trade refer to as 'Gracious Grammarye'."

Skylla frowned. "*The Spellbinder's Fireside Companion?* You're not serious."

Adaja crossed his wrists ceremonially over his heart. "So you see. Of course, you can paint by numbers and still end up with a picture. But . . ." Mollified, he picked up his coffee.

His hands were slender, with strong, precise fingers —Tasneem's more square. Her eyelids were puffy, her lips full. While both of them handled the language familiarly, his vowels dragged, hers curled like combers. Looking between them the thief decided they were probably from two different continents just as Tik asked, "Are you twins?"

Tasneem sighed almost inaudibly.

"Sometimes we do admit to it," the boy said with a sweetened smile the thief winced at slightly, "for the jaded. You'd be surprised the touch of the *troublant* it adds to the coital spells, even in this day and——"

The jerk of his torso showed that Tasneem kicked him under the table. "Actually he's two years younger than I am and we aren't even related."

A clash of chording interrupted. On the tall stool the young man in the pointed hat announced, "I've just written a completely new song," and cast a roguish look toward their table. He strummed at length, and sang,

"My girl is a tigress,
Don't no one mess with me,
She is a real woman,
Yes, she is my . . ."

Tasneem had wrinkled her nose, gone back to her coffee. But Tik watched an increasingly suppressed, explosive sort of look gathering on the thief's dark countenance. She jumped up, slapping a handful of coins on the table.

"We have to go," she announced, and actually tugged Skylla's sleeve. The albinos rose politely. "It's late." The thief let herself be dragged.

Adaja looked back.

"You coming?"

Min in his white apron still held the coffee. After a moment in which his body seemed to lock, he shoved the tray onto the table, and hurried.

Tik bundled them all out the oak door into the black stairwell and there Skylla exploded. She collapsed on the stairs and laughed with her head between her knees, slapping the wall, slapping her insteps and shrieking appallingly. The children watched open-mouthed. She lay back on the stairs, tears barring her cheeks with spectral warpaint.

"Oh," she gasped, "yes. Yes. This place does need more visitors. Tetikte," she said, "help me up."

But she kept reeling against the wall of the alley. The four smiled uncertainly. None of them felt privy to the joke, and none of them had had as much beer, either.

Where the alley debouched between porticos onto the square was a wire newsstand plump with fresh four-star editions. The thief took a paper.

On the moonlight way back to the inn, Tasneem and Adaja patiently explained their profession.

"Ontogeny," Tasneem said, as though it were obvious. "Every human body knows how to be a bird. Given the right spell——"

"You mean I could do that?" Tik's demand fell somewhere between derision and plea. Her hair and lashes looked powdered with platinum, her face gone to darker grays. Beside her the two albinos had become lunar royalty, crowned with cold fire. Min, behind, bobbed, white-tabarded. The thief felt that she walked in some incorporeal company, and wondered what the moon made her.

"Of course she could," Adaja was arguing. "It's just the spells"—he leaned across Tasneem, who interjected "The older spells"—"call for a lot of white."

"How come?"

Adaja shrugged. "Superstition."

"And you can fly, and everything?"

"Of course. We *are* birds. Only bigger, of course."

"Though not as big as you might think," Tasneem

emended. "Quite a bit of the mass aligns itself in the energic mode, for the binding. Naturally."

"Well, of course," Tik said. Skylla shot her a glance. There was an uncoordinated silence in which their footsteps took on echoes and echoes of echoes. They cornered by a dark shop window; reflected among the glimmering children Skylla saw herself, a black shadow, pass. They walked into music and neon.

"There's the inn." Something in the white boy's tone revived basic allegiances.

"Look." Tik halted. "My aunt will give you a room of your own, for the night. In the morning you can sneak out the back."

Adaja looked down and toed a sandal at the cobbles.

"My mother——" Min stuck as everyone turned to look at him. "She'll give you food to take with you. If you want." It ended as an apology, for Tasneem was shaking her head. Where they stood, blinking signs cast temporal rainbows over the white girl's face, the boy's waist-length hair.

"We have a job to do." Tasneem put her hands in the pockets of her white jacket, tailored exactly like Adaja's, looked at them, looked at the inn.

"Thank you, though," Adaja added politely.

They all stood, gazing in various directions, until Tasneem said, at last, with the gentleness of terrific embarrassment, "You don't break this kind of contract." She moved, and they were walking again.

"It will be all right." Adaja smiled.

"But what do you have to *do* for him?"

Tasneem looked at Tik and smiled, too. "That's confidential, I'm afraid." To the thief, they suddenly appeared strictly capable. It was a look she recognized and respected, in artists, workers, other thieves. They entered the inn.

In the doorway Min stopped. The thief's raised eyebrow struck him mute at mouth, hand, and eye.

"I guess you have to be going," Tik said helpfully.

The lamplight seemed to be seeping color from the waiter's cheeks. With a dare-all breath, he raised his black eyes: a head-on stare that bespoke her in untranslatable oratory.

The thief, adept at languages, but still slightly drunk, returned a slightly more rakish grin than she intended.

"Good night!" said Min valiantly, and then fled.

"Kind of a weird kid," Tasneem commented. She missed the oblique look Tik gave her. "Is there anything we could get to eat at this hour?"

"Leftovers, if you want them."

As Tik steered them through the darkened dining room they could hear splashes and clatter.

The kitchen was bright and hot and filled solid with the smell of bread baking. The cook stood with his back to them, washing up. Pastries crowded a table. By one wall were racks and racks of floury noodles.

"Don't touch those tarts," the cook remarked at the dishwater. Tik drew back her hand, then beckoned the albinos into the pantry. Skylla drifted toward the sink. On the drainboard were bowls, rolling pin, silverware, beakers and measuring spoons. The cook washed something made of aligned curved blades that glimmered menacingly through the suds. Rinsed, it proved a pastry-cutter.

"Passing through?" The cook nodded his crew-cut head in self-confirmation. "You look like you might be from the north. We get a lot of interesting folks through here.

"There was a fellow last month. Philosophical. Had

this theory: everything is really just a reflection of this other world, see. All we are is like shadows of the things on that higher level. 'Well,' I said, 'how do you know *they* aren't the shadows and *we're* the real thing?' " He chuckled and filled the sink with pots. "I had him there all right. But we get all kinds. Makes you stop and think. New ideas and what-all."

He slid his eyes at the albinos as they perched on a bench, biting into biscuits and cold ham. He lowered his voice. "I don't hold with magic though. Sex and drugs and carrying on? You can't change things overnight, I say. I grew up here and it's good enough for me. Not but what I don't think about it. What's it like out there—up north and all? Different, huh? I hear you go up there far enough, even time changes. Fellow read an article where a day lasts half a year up there. I said, 'Son, I've had days like that myself.' 'I don't need to travel for that,' I said." The cook raised his head suddenly and sniffed. "That bread's done," he decided. "I'm going to chase you all out of here."

They departed without demur. "Uncle Jube," Tik allowed, doesn't get that many people to talk to, stuck in the kitchen all day. I hope you weren't too bored."

"Not at all," said Skylla. Early in her career someone had told her you could learn a lot by listening to the garrulous. She had found it the usual leavened sort of truth. Nevertheless, she had not been bored.

They bunched together up the flights of wooden stairs, trying not to make noise. But as they shuffled along the dark hallway a door flew open and with a *WHEEET!* of taffeta the wizard was before them. He inhaled and then gasped on top of it. His mouth stayed open. In the lantern light his blond goatee quivered.

Tasneem and Adaja filed past him through the doorway, the light transmuting them to white gold before they disappeared.

Looking inscrutable, Skylla melted backward into the shadows toward her own room. The wizard edged back through his door, closing it rapidly and throwing the bolts.

Woman and girl withdrew to the thief's chamber. Over the lamp Skylla lit, they listened. There were no sounds of immediate hostilities from the next room.

Outside, the wind was rising. Skylla turned up the lamp. On the table where she had laid it, the fat rolled newspaper showed an arc of bold print:

POLLUTION HAZARD SCARE
"No Danger," Says Official

Tik was looking around. "You didn't bring much luggage."

"I travel light. At least, when I'm just visiting."

Tik gave her a wise look. "You travel a lot—'just visiting'—don't you?"

"Some." The thief removed her hat and belt, and stretched.

"Where have you been?" She had knelt on the bed and now leaned intently across its high brass footrail.

"The north and the east." Skylla yawned, unlacing her jerkin.

"What's it like?"

The thief smiled. "Which one? The north . . . is green and white: green forests, green grass high as your waist in summer; snow higher than that in winter, with the sky white, too. Even farther is the sea. In the sand on the milder shores you can find young boulders of amber. The farther you go, the more water there is. The ocean freezes. At last everything is white, or if the sky is clear it fills with portents. The mountains there are made of ice. Even the animals have turned white from cold. You must change your life entirely to live there." She paused. "The east is even less variable. Its primary export is languages. The farther east you go the less room there is to maneuver in. The men are not fond of loose women—by which they mean women who wander around loose. I only go there to . . . 'just visit'."

"You don't make it sound like much fun. I'd think it'd be wonderful—traveling. You must like it or you wouldn't do it so much."

"Try it and see."

"Well, I meant for you, of course. Because here, we already have everything we could want." She gestured artlessly. "They don't have half the stuff we do anywhere else. So why would we want to leave?"

The thief contemplated her. "You can't get out."

"Well," Tik said, "no."

"Because of the tilsim."

"Not 'til . . . that is to say . . ." Red crept up her neck to her ears. "We aren't supposed to talk about it."

From the corner there came an odd sound, as of wind opening the canvas sail of a ship on some distant sea. However, when they both glanced there was nothing among the shadows but more shadows.

"The woman you were with the first time I saw you: her voice had a remarkable carrying quality."

The girl's face took on the most complicated expression Skylla had yet seen there. In tones that contained pride and acute mortification, like those of a martyr twitted about the one true deity, Tik explained, "That was Mother." After a pause, "She's not always too subtle. But you can count on her."

"I thought there might have been a family resemblance, at the time."

"Pretty safe bet in this place. We really are all over.

When you—that is, if you get back to the Rotunda you might even run into another cousin of mine. She works as a guard there now." Her plump fingers hooked on the bedrail as she leaned back; her nails blanched, the bedsprings squeaked. "There are six of them to a shift, she told me. Besides a couple of guides and the curators."

"That is rather few to patrol thirteen floors."

"Well, it's not as if any of our citizens would try to steal anything. They wouldn't get far, would they?"

Skylla conceded her point.

The conversation hovered. Tik's brow wrinkled.

The thief looked down. Out one end of the rolled newspaper protruded a wooden cylinder, carved like a handle. The startlement did not leave Tik's face even when she averted her eyes. She turned them to the shadows, which obliged with a *flap* as of a large, leathery wing. Then she slid her leg over the edge of the bed and stood up. "You'll be wanting to get to bed early." She resisted glancing as she passed the table. "So I guess I'll turn in. See you"—her eyes darted X-rays at the newspaper—"at breakfast." As she looked back from the doorway, it seemed to the thief that for an instant her whole being, from lightning-struck hair to the very snaps on her overalls, blazed and glittered with a passion of anticipation. Then she was gone.

It had probably been a trick of the light.

Yawning, the thief unwrapped the newspaper. The print again caught her eye. POLLUTION HAZARD. Sitting on the edge of the bed, she toed her tall, supple boots off as she read:

> *Officials assured residents of the Old Town canal district that the blue vapor sighted over two neighboring canals earlier today is harmless.*

> *"Tests show no abnormal levels of concentrates in the water," said a Health Department spokesperson. He added that the early dawn phenomenon might have been an effect of unusual light conditions reflected from ordinary mist.*
>
> *"Whatever the case may be," he added, "there is absolutely no cause for alarm."*
>
> *Several residents this morning claimed to have seen the "fast-moving blue fog" as one described it. "It kind of spiraled," said another. "I saw it when I stepped out to get the milk from the landing. It came down the canal in separate wisps."*
>
> *Complaints prompted a statement from alchemical industry representatives. It expressed continuing concern with the safe disposal of alchemical waste and denied reports of uncontrolled dumping. "We observe the most rigid standards in all areas of production and storage," the statement maintained. "Health officials are perfectly satisfied that our present procedures safeguard the best interests both of our customers and the general public."*
>
> *A company worker who asked to remain anonymous added that "whatever the stuff was, it must be harmless since it hasn't done anything yet. A powerful agent doesn't just hang around, it's got to react with* something."

The thief tossed the paper back on the table, stripped off her trousers and blew out the lamp.

Weather may be creative without heralding revolution; that is what makes it a safe topic at formal entertainments. At dawn the atmosphere was making itself felt. Thunder rolled like tumbling organ chords across the sky, while lightning danced—*plié, plié, entrechat*—above it. None of this need disturb the dreams of any proper thief.

What she woke to at length was a different noise, like the rattling of wind in a canvas backdrop, or a throttled alarm clock.

It stopped abruptly when she sat up. The room was unnaturally darkened on account of the clouds.

She pushed open the casement windows and the storm air rushed in, bouncy with negative ions, and ruffled the raw silk of her tunic. There was no rain, despite histrionics aloft.

More thunder fumbled to a crescendo. She dressed and descended to breakfast with a cloak prudently bundled under one arm.

Tetikte was nowhere to be seen. The thief even dawdled a bit over her cocoa, then shrugged, then looked thoughtful. She hummed as she strode into the day, over cobbles and flags, a captious wind tussling with the pheasant feather in her peaked hat, flashing the kitten-gray underdown of the pigeons policing the square, roostering the fountains' gleaming tresses.

The drawbridge rang under her heels. This time she would have to pay her own way. She fingered forth a piece of that city's unwonted money.

The change was more than she expected. The freckled curly-headed youngster in the ticket booth nodded in explanation toward the interior: "Today, you know . . ." Skylla touched a forefinger to her cap and passed in.

Above her glided pointed teeth . . . awkward neck bones . . . innumerable ribs . . . vertebrae in an endlessly sinuous diminishing contrail; then she entered the next vast hall. Lingering at the foot of a large stuffed saurian, she allowed a field trip of shrill eight-year-olds to be shepherded past. At her leisure, she followed them.

The door dilated.

Three were already traversing the lucent green mound. Two were inflating something red. One played in a hillock of giant purple beans.

In the middle of the room stood a guard.

The uniform was a stand-out kilted affair in five colors, the angle of the shako on her red curls alert. But as the thief inspected the next plaque but one to Tik's orange plasmoid, the guard, with the timeless good breeding of a professional wrestling referee, turned her back. When she turned again, Skylla made inquiry and received directions. She set out briskly for the heart of the Rotunda.

Was there a flutter of black disappearing behind a door as she rounded the last corner? Perhaps.

Stuck top and bottom into ceiling and floor, cheeks brushing at the walls either side, the sphere of light filled half her vision. It was only on approaching nearer that she saw the transparent stairs, only on mounting them that the door in the globe became visible; the interior's same cool-white illumination united within and without. She admired the effect.

She had actually to step through the door to see the book.

She stood on the mezzanine, a circular balcony, as Tik had described. Below, abyssal featureless light; above, the radiant vault. She advanced to the rail. Before her, The Book of Time seemed almost within reach in the perspectiveless arena. The big front and back covers of ornately worked, studded and darkened leather were winged wide, facing her. On the front cover an untooled oval was wreathed by demoniacally arabesqued recomplicated lettering that she had to crack character by character to extract the legend.

J'ai suel la clef

She was alone. No one had entered the hall below. The crowds, she supposed, would turn up later. Quickly she pulled from her rolled cloak the heavy orange loaf of plasmoid and a rolling pin. The plasmoid's surface was cool, slightly tacky without sticking to her fingers. She squeezed it into a snake as Tik had done, only longer and thinner, and laid it out carefully straight on the floor. She grasped the rolling pin.

She rolled the creature out flat. It did not protest. As it spread into a strip five inches wide and over seven feet long, its translucent orange paled to gold.

The hall was empty still. With cloak and rolling pin under one arm, the thief gently lifted the plasmoid.

To give herself time should anyone now intrude, she ran lightly round the mezzanine to the point opposite the door, sparing only a glance for the mirror in the book. Time was now of the essence.

Flipping six feet of the plasmoid over the railing to hang plumb, reckoning distances and angles carefully, she wrapped the obliging tail of the thing three-fourths round the rolling pin, held it out right-angled to the rail and—feeling as nigh kin to a fool as she ever would—yelled *"Boo!"*

It was then a simple matter to pull out the rolling pin, lift the paralyzed plasmoid, hook the curl under the second rail, snap the ninety-degree bend into place over the top rail, and leap up to crouch, one foot on the rail, one on the rigid beast. Five seconds. She stood up, balancing nonchalant as a cat on a fence.

She walked the golden plank.

At the end the book awaited her, larger than she had thought and further away, but within reach. The thief crouched, grasped the covers, looked full into the inset mirror: an oval silver emptiness. Her pale shadow, cast from behind by the luminous shell of the sphere, moved there, but no reflected face appeared. It looked as a mirror might look if you could catch it dreaming.

Fifteen seconds. Bracing, she gripped the top and bottom of the spine and pulled. There was a moment when the book weighed nothing in her hands, but had terrible inertia. It sucked forward. Then the weight hit, uneven. The covers of the book swung. Her crouch staggered. Recovering, she closed the heavy, wrought volume over the mirror and rose erect. Twenty seconds. Two enormous white falcons, spread wings tipped near-vertical, baffed through the door and dove at her.

She twisted and threw herself flat, the book under her chest, legs and arms seized round the plasmoid. She hunched ahead under a tumult of wings, 'til white sheared off on either side of her, falling into tight-banked turns. Twenty-five seconds. She sat up, shoved the book forward, pulling herself after it. The falcons' wings battered around her. Sheltering the book, she fended them with one arm, glimpsing small-feathered mail of breast, a fist of furled talons, remiges spread like white fingers at the tip of a wing. They fell away again. The thief gathered the book to her, sprang up and leaped for the rail as the plasmoid wilted beneath her. It slithered off the rail into the bowl,

rumpling, 'til it lay humped like a piece of gold ribbon candy among the light. Skylla, meanwhile, hung by one arm, with clenched teeth.

The falcons were having trouble with their cramped turns. One came at her as she heaved The Book of Time, getting a corner over the mezzanine edge. She boosted it with her knee and slid it flat onto the floor. The falcon put its wings straight up, talons stretched wide, but it could not get close enough to the railing for the snatch. It wobbled away and flapped madly for altitude. Skylla swarmed over the rail.

She had meant to wrap her prize in the cloak but now there was no time. The book clamped to her body, dodging the second falcon, she dashed for the door. She made it down the stairs before the falcons, wings folded, bombed into the hall. She ran.

They fell at her, snapping their eight-foot wings open before her very face, flapping about her like insane moths however she ducked or darted. She made headway as against a raging blizzard.

The corridor. The white storm cleared suddenly—here their wingspan again hampered them. Still, they harried her as she ran.

She burst out amid displays. In a landscape of paper maché boulders, a metal being with a glass head flashed its lights and milled its arms, emitting cries of alarm that blended with the scream of a falcon. Skylla plunged among smooth-clad automatons seated before screens or panels of switches; a dark woman wearing minute earphones appeared to look at her in surprise where she crouched behind the thronelike central chair, brandishing her hat to drive off a white-winged fury. She bolted and the falcon, off balance, flopped to the floor. It hopped, raging, after her, wings umbrellaed, unable to get loft among the crowding tableaux. She ran the aisle, the other bird bearing swiftly down upon her. It followed her experimental swerves at speed. Curling the heavy book tight in her arms the thief dived and rolled between the fat pointy fins of an upright rocketship. Behind her there was a desperate thrashing of wings, succeeded by a thud. She rolled to her feet, unpursued.

Breaking into the next gallery, she slowed to an inconspicuous walk and doubled over, giggling. To her right, a frowning man stuck his head through a doorway. She saw his expression change, his mouth open. He pointed. He yelled. She was already out the door speeding down a corridor. There were more yells and running feet.

She turned into another gallery where she immediately hid in the hollow behind a desk-like console. As she caught her breath, waiting, she placed The Book of Time on her crossed legs and lifted its nubbled, whorled cover. In the dim light shapes seemed to move within the sleeping silver. It was as if, just below the surface, there were texture and depth from another universe. Something seemed to writhe, there, in the sliding toils of an immense silver serpent.

Hullooing, the pursuit thundered through the gallery.

Nowhere in the mirror's shifting deeps could she find a reflection of her own face.

Frowning, she crawled out of her hole and resumed her course down the corridor. Her brisk gait attracted no special notice.

She glanced toward a creaking sound: from the roof of a niche was suspended by chains an oil lamp, bronze bodies lolling or romping its branches. Over the groins of fauns, behind the tongues of winged reptiles, colored flames jittered.

Nearby, the rather elaborate fetters of a bound captive rattled.

She checked her steps; the floor was wiggling under the soles of her boots.

Ahead and behind alarms clanged. The thief sprinted.

No alarm, she reasoned, had sounded during the last quake. Therefore——

Shouts and pursuits.

Through an arch strode the kilted guard from the children's room.

From the rear came a cry that sounded like "Ginger!" And then, "Stop her!"

The guard did a classic take, and with the best will in the world ran out waving her arms into the thief's path. Skylla aimed herself straight at the redhead's crossed bandeaux. At the last instant she feinted right and broke left, hips swiveling. The only hand laid on her felt like a slap on the back. With clattering boots and blowing on a whistle, the guard joined the chase.

The weight of the book was beginning to tell.

Passing through a narrow portal formed of a snaky golden dragon in the Eastern style, she risked a glance back. Just under the scaly loop, skirts flying and whistle shrilling, galloped "Ginger," and tripped spectacularly. Seven people fell over her.

With a skip of sheer exuberance, the thief charged down the Hall of Weapons. Dead ahead lay the lobby. She saw the freckle-faced ticket taker glance over her shoulder and then go back to fumbling energetically at something set into the wall. The thief felt a pang of apprehension. As she dashed into the lobby, a gibbering man pushed the ticket taker aside and gave a wrench, a heave, a lot of rapid twirlings to the thing in the wall. There was a whine of machinery.

They all fell down.

The building shook again, once, hard. Heart pounding, Skylla rose up and loped, somewhat rickety, for the door; she could not help noticing that everyone else clutched the floor, faces leaching of color. With a grind, the mechanical sound started again.

The doors stood wide. But as she set foot on the bridge, the thief became simultaneously aware of four things. First, the wind that had played with her had grown up into an ambitious young gale that plastered her clothes against her right side, trying to throw and pin her with its first rush. She clapped her hand to her hat. Second, there was something wrong with the water. The canal surface surged, heaved, whirled and foamed, and a small boat down there staggered like a drunk. Third, converging across the plaza at a run were some forty or fifty uniformed persons. And fourth, the drawbridge was rising.

The drawbridge was rising: at every step her foot bent more sharply up from the ankle, her stride shortened on the increasing grade. The wind veered toward the railing. She stuffed her hat into her belt and grabbed the fretwork between the rails. She looked up. The bridge blocked most of the sky. She looked out. She thought she would not be able to swim with the book and, moreover, the water sucked and vortexed in a singularly uninviting manner. She looked back. Her pursuers clustered below with upturned faces. By now she was climbing the bridge rather than running it, bracing her feet in the iron lattices of the rail. The angle neared seventy-five degrees. Even if she reached the summit—and it was too far now—she would not be able to jump to the plaza. She swore in her native tongue, always a sign, with her, of the most active concern.

The walls of the Rotunda had slid back to form a niche for the drawbridge. The thief looked down at the particolor guard, the ticket taker, the men in suits. They would pluck her from that niche like an escargot from its shell. Suddenly the faces below lost all expression. The next instant a deluge of rain struck Skylla, slacked abruptly.

Something . . . *hit* the bridge.

The rail yanked almost out of her fist and rebounded. Her cheek pressing an iron curlicue, eyelids crimped against the water, the thief looked up.

Across the bridge, crushing segments of the rail each side, tautened a dripping cable twice the thickness of her body. The lower surface was a writhing flap covered with giant suckers.

The huge muscle convulsed. Somewhere below, gears screamed and stripped. Skylla hugged the bars as the bridge began to fall.

As from a great distance she heard panicked screams. Then the drawbridge struck the plaza, and bent. Then it stopped.

The thief disentangled her bruised arms, picked up the book, and staggered, downhill now. Athwart her path lay the quiescent tentacle, slanted severely to the water either side of the buckled bridge.

Picking their way through cracked stone onto the bridge-head were a goodly number of the uniformed persons from the plaza.

"Here!"

The shout came neither from behind nor before.

"This way!"

On the water below, the small boat still tossed like a cockleshell. A figure in the bow waved its arms, then cupped hands to mouth.

"Hur-ry!"

The boat nosed lollopping to starboard, bunted the tentacle.

The thief leaped onto the kraken's arm. She would have run down its sharp slope even against the buffeting wind but, having the book, she turned herself about, straddled the monstrous limb, and slid. The grab of her trouser material on the marbled-gray wet skin kept her speed sedate. Roiling water grew louder. The small outboard turned broadside to the tentacle. Skylla dug in with knees, heels, and the fingers of one hand to stop herself. Vast muscle rippled, shuddered beneath her, causing an unexpected variety of sensations to course her viscera. She jumped.

The bottom of the boat was shaped like cupped hands. She landed in a half crouch there, between the stowed oars. Tik's arms caught round her. A swerve of the craft plumped them onto facing seats. Tik, a new orange-striped t-shirt under her overalls, clutching the gunwales with her back to the bow, yelled something. The thief twisted. From the stern, both hands on the tiller, Min, in jeans and a long-sleeved jersey, looked ahead out of a face that was chalky white. The bow rose and spanked down onto a wave, the sound almost lost among the motor's roar and the splashing and wind all around them.

Skylla shouted to Tik, "Watch our course!" She crouched aft, keeping her weight as far down and forward as she could, and reached to put her hand on the boy's arm. "Go and lie down in the bow!" she yelled. A gulf opened under the screw, letting the boat slew searchingly atop a wave that turned them sideways and tried strenuously to climb into the boat. Min slammed the tiller over; they scaled water at perilous angles; green glass poured around them, broke to white sleets that drenched them. They wallowed through into a whirlpool that expired under the keel.

Min's lips were blue.

"Go!" she shouted, and tugged his arm. He let her take the tiller before he ducked by her. Shoving The Book of Time beneath it, she slid onto the stern seat and took her bearings. The Rotunda loomed starboard; the bridge veed astern. To port, waves dashed themselves insensible against the seawall of the canal; ahead writhed insane water out of which just then rose, sea-monsterlike, three croquet-hoops of thick gray tentacle undulating toward them. A premonitory feeling came over her. The motor was of that type whose speed is increased by twisting the end of the tiller. She twisted it.

The boat leaped into the mad water.

Min was looking back at her, black hair whipped across his mouth. She gestured, palm down. He dropped into the bilges, gripping a cleat. Leaning on the bow cover, her rusty hair bunched behind her by the wind, Tik scanned the canal. Her right arm bent up, swept slowly straight out; the thief steered starboard before she had repeated the signal. Gurgling horribly, something of the vortex nature broke surface to port and reeled away. A part of her mind that was not glaring slit-eyed into the wind and spray had already surmised that this canal went far, far deeper, in some of its reaches, than anyone would imagine. They navigated the disaster. Suddenly Tik semaphored frantically to port.

Skylla heeled over but the signal only became more frenzied. Hard port ahead were the rolling loops of tentacle; between them and the seawall waves crashed and bounded. Tik's arm threshed. The thief cut hard aport.

Then she saw it. An enormous shape, swimming the murk with jerky motions between them and the right wall of the canal, was expanding, changing color—rising. They sped across the bows, as it were, of the kraken. The water tried to bounce them off the wall. The thief heeled around and made a dash back—the shadow of the moving tentacle, with the drops cascading from it, fell on Tik, who stared up at the vast suckers; on Min, who threw up his hand to shield himself; on the thief, who heeled over again to port. They slalomed the sinuous arches, shooting by the last into clear water. Then the shape on the canal stood up.

It was a Dead Man.

The thief had viewed one before, from a grateful distance. She had never before smelled one.

The water swashed as in an extensive bathtub.

Tiny in the roaring came miniature screams again from the plaza.

Dead Man: conjured of the sedimental refuse of ages. Flotsam of a horrid nature cleaved to him. Bits hurrying even now through the water joined themselves to his thighs in ecstatic affinity. Gummy indigo clung the whole, thin as a scum on seething jelly; indigo vapors flared and collapsed and heliced about him. When he turned, corruption exhaled from him in billows.

He turned toward them. They quailed down in the boat. He lurched a step.

There might have seemed a disarming inexpertise to his organization. Where he ought to have had features there were but squirmings and extrusions; when he moved, the draff and scurfs avalanched under the blue pleura; there was about his accumulated lumber the slack of eternal incompetence.

Yet when he lurched, he lurched yards at one step, and if he swatted you, you died. A Dead Man is impelled to swat, since his true food is entropy.

These are things that a real thief knows by instinct, and besides, she had seen one before. Quick waves slapped their stern as the Dead Man lurched again, and again. Skylla glanced back; sucking water burled by his thighs, he loomed on the lightning-shot iron sky. She evaded perilously. Where they had been, water exploded under the rude paddle-hand. She tried for speed. Forward, Min had covered his mouth and nose against the sorcerous stench. Tik clung to the bow ropes. She pointed and shouted, words lost in the wind. Far ahead something narrow wavered in the air. Then half the canal lifted.

Out of the water rose the kraken's arm. It curled hugely, with muscular speed. It encountered the Dead Man and whipped about him in a trice.

Skylla, at once deducing the source of all the kraken's agitation, considered that their odds had materially improved. She bucketed the little boat over the lashing water into the rectangle of fountainworks.

Openmouthed, the children in the bow stared over her head. When she could, she looked. Towering, staggering, the Dead Man chopped at the tentacle, heaved at it; it wrapped his torso like an induction coil. He curled flaps of hand round the groping tip and yanked. This did him no good. Even as she watched, lightning crashed down behind the struggling titans; the storm broke.

They drove on down the canal, through tall sheets of rain illumed by lightning and beaten by wind into wavering silver auroras. She looked back again: obscured by the bright curtains, the Dead Man plunged in the kraken's toils, 'til a final, transcendent thunderbolt tied him to heaven an instant, cracked like doom, fingered his pecs, and withdrew. A moment he stood, covered in white ash. Then washed by rain, he sagged, the colors of mud and gristle. No wisp of indigo survived. Slowly the gravitic haul of the kraken overbore him—they waltzed together—he toppled.

"Hold on!" Skylla shouted. The concussion wave lifted them over the canal wall. Skylla instantly put about and raced down its back slope, yet still it raised them. Then it dropped them, hard. She felt the strop of the screw on stone, flung herself into the bow. The boat's hind end flounced up and they cleared the wall. Scrambling back, she gunned the little engine. It vroomed gamely. They shipped water over bows and gunwales, but the boat squatted and duckwalked after the receding wavefront. The torrential cloudburst was easing. They left the plaza and glided between tall pastel façades. Tethered dories bobbled in the wave's wake.

The Book of Time had skidded forward, was half awash, and one of her own footprints stamped its saucy legend. It was a wonder, she thought, it hadn't gone overboard.

Chrysoprase bow-waves cataracted from their keel, the boat seat trunketed pleasantly on the seat of the thief's trousers, the wind was only blowing enough to be pulling away the cloud pack, and as Tik struggled from where she had wedged herself in the bow, sun lit droplets in the ruddy-gold nap of her hair. To laugh so merrily at those it's drenched, a day must needs be prepubescent. A check of the sun showed it not yet nine o'clock.

Holding his right biceps, a familiar bootprint diagonal on the shoulder of his jersey, Min rolled himself to a cross-legged sitting position. Flipping wet hair out of his eyes, he found a can clamped under a seat and, left-handed, bailed. Tik clambered past him.

The prow angled steeper, sniffing out their course.

Tik, after one glance of scandalized recognition, tucked her hands, which shook, between her overalled knees and looked out over the widening canal filled with black and green and white wavelets, at a little sailboat that passed like a butterfly, at the pale pink, pale blue, pale gold houses wavering under the still ones, at Skylla planted, legs apart, in the roar of the motor—anywhere but at The Book of Time. Scenery, it soon appeared, was to supply their sole means of amusement, as conversation in the neighborhood of an outboard motor must be acknowledged to be impossible. The scenery, therefore, was examined, not without some share of private relief.

In this manner the beautiful city was got through with expedition. They ran out under a last chryselephantine bridge into the broad mooring pool by the Western Gate, its circumference toothed with piers, its deep waters lapping calm around the pilings. Passenger craft for hire bumped their tall carved prows in idle clusters over by the cafés.

Skylla reversed, cut the engine, Tetikte gripped the dock as the boat wallowed up to it, Min lassoed a bollard. Skylla scooped up the book. As Min, then Tik, then she herself trod heavily on the gunwale, the boat curvetted in farewell.

A plaza—here, too, flagged in gray—not much traversed, lay before the gates, higher above the water than the other, reached from the docks by wooden stairs. Climbing, time pushed past her. She was not surprised, therefore, when she stepped onto the plaza, to discern a fluster of black robes pacing angrily before the gates and scanning the heavens. A tinny sound came at intervals from the striped guardhouse.

Skylla rounded on her two companions crisply.

"I thank you for the ride," she said. "Now I must be

going and I'm sure you have your own pressing affairs."

Tik smiled kindly. Skylla eyed her.

She sighed. "Very well," she acknowledged, "but wait here 'til I am beyond the gates." She put her free hand on the girl's shoulder, looking into her yellow irises, as one does with comrades in these lands, then drew her near in the embrace of her own native country. She repeated the ceremony with black-eyed Min and—this woman had lamentable morals—kissed him on the mouth besides. With a wave of her hand she set off across the plaza, hoping to have rooted them in their tracks for the necessary few moments.

The wizard still presented a mime of outraged impatience. He stalked hither and thither. He gesticulated. It was the most realistic thing imaginable. He noticed the figure of the thief approaching, turned and craned at the sky. He glanced her way again—froze—pressed his splayed hand to his collarbones and backed away at a trot. Then he braked. He peered. He raised his fists above his head and called down imprecations which by now Skylla was quite close enough to hear. He took a quick step toward her but then instead fumbled among his whickering robes.

The regular noise from the guardhouse proved to be a jangling telephone. It hung on the wall, black, rectangular, sprouting a black flange on its front, with a similar cone-shaped hook at one side, a little crank at the other. Before it, seated on a tall stool in his bright uniform, the guard beamed over the counter at her. The telephone branged. Clearly a spell of selective perception obtained within the booth. Skylla nodded pleasantly to the guard.

The wizard stood feverishly thumbing the pages of a paperback book.

Suddenly he reached forth with his fingers pointed toward her like the prongs of a heavy-duty electrical plug and, with rapid peeks at his book, incanted. She dodged. A slat fell off the guardhouse. She dodged again but the edge of the ballooning witchment caught her: her next pace spanned the plaza, the city, the hills, distant forests. Time, like the poltroon it is, ran out on her.

She strode between planets, across stars, the galaxies shrank to her stepping stones and still she had not passed the striped booth. The universe wandered through her, serene, black, jeweled.

With every step she took the weight of the book doubled. The wizard gabbled, flipped more pages. Before her rose a massive barrier of stone, clearly modeled on Semiramis's walls, unscalable, stretching miles in either direction. As Skylla walked on, it sifted away into a view of interminable dunes, rippled desert like an ocean seen from a great height; it was perfectly obvious she would never cross it with that heavy book weighing her down. She walked. The distant dunes rolled toward her like tiny sausage curls, the ocean came up to her chin, the book would drag her under. She sank, and walked the water. Forests of redware weed undulated, swayed in wind as wheat she waded. Snow-leopards rosetted with purple and lilac wreathed about her, tendrils pressed up the guardhouse chased by a rustle of leaves unfurling; grape clusters framed the beaming guard. He held out a crystal jug of sparkling vintage. Smoke went up from rosy-gold lamps of scented oil, clouded the roof of the pavilion. Among the cushions pricked the bare feet of the dancing-boys. The woman shaking the tambour put her fingers before her mouth and ululated a shrill incitement. The thief's boot brushed a pillow.

The dark-turbaned boy who neared her gazed frankly into her eyes, wrists gyrating, tassels and bangle-belts at his hips switching and flashing, fringed ends of his sashes swaying between his ankles. His liquid eyes were impudent, a smile lurked his brief moustache, as he delicately touched his fingertips together at the back of his neck. Lamplight ran gold on the brocade of his vest, shadow hollowed his belly. Something in her relented. A moment's dalliance with illusion . . . The boy turned gracefully. Back over his shoulder he flaunted her a look under his long eyelids. He perched the backs of his hands low on his hips and, stepping away to the double-time of the drums, shimmied all the frippery of bangle-edged scarves and whipping fringes compassed round his bottom. She followed. So would you if you had been there. A great weight lightened on her mind.

"Hey!"

The boy looked back at her, she thought, regretfully.

There was another shout, the sound of a scuffle——

He pasteled, became rainbows on the spray of a wave, heat over the desert, nothing. Min, in his wet jeans and jersey, stepped back, elbows hooked from trying to grapple the evanescency. Her fingers clutched on the slipping book. She was facing the wrong way so it was to her left, now, that the black volumes of taffeta separated into two people: Tik spun, crouched, with her hands out.

The wizard shrieked something, purple-faced.

"Tetik!" the girl cried, and kicked him.

He hopped one-footed.

As Skylla pivoted, slowly, against the drag of heavy magic, the white falcons hied over rooftops and swooped into the square. The wizard signaled to them hysterically. Tik saw them. . . . Skylla slogged a step, The Book of Time simulating the dead weight of a star under her arm, the lodestone of the wheeling universe. Black robes flapped; a baritone voice declaimed. *Mother of dreams,* she urged, *rid your daughter of this baccalaureate jackanapes!* Behind her came the braking clap of wings. A spell impacted—a scream tore above her—her whole right arm flamed, charred, withered to the bone. Another scream mingled with a yell of rage from Tik, who launched herself at the wizard, ripped the paperback from his hands and hurled it through the gate.

Stock still, Skylla looked down at her arm. It had not hurt at all. But it had been meant to. She shifted the book across the constellations of her loins to her left hand.

She curled long blackened phalanges round her dagger's hilt.

The wizard looked in her face and ran.

Limping.

Tik screamed a deplorable phrase after him. Shadows of wings blew over her like leaves——

The thief's head cleared. She felt palm's flesh against metal and leather and let her blade slip back in its sheath.

The guard got off his stool and stepped to answer the telephone.

With no more ado the thief walked out between the gates of ebony. Unlike most cities, this one stopped right at its walls. She was in a country lane flanked by meadows, really little more than a dirt track for farmers' carts on market days. Borders of evergreen formed the horizon. Cornflowers, black-eyed Susans, and tiger lilies crammed the ditches.

Slowly the thief opened the book.

Looking at her in the most natural manner in the world, from the oval of mirror, was a woman. Her cheekbones were flat, she had a dished nose, a neat chin, and thoughtful dark eyes. A fair likeness, the thief decided. The woman gave her a rarified, serious smile.

"Look." The voice beside her was hushed; Tik stared, but not at the book. The falcons spiraled a point in the meadow, descending. White bodies elongated, toes stretching like alighting egrets to the earth, white feathered arms curved powerfully. The smaller one stumbled, recovered. The other one collapsed.

"Hey, there's . . ." The girl took a step, alarmed. "I think something's . . ." She ran a few steps, balanced a second, jumped the ditch. Going over the broken place in the honeysuckle-whelmed fence, Tik waded into clover that closed again behind her overalled knees.

In the gateway, the guard, gazing from under a corrugated brow, shifted from foot to foot and held his hands out from his sides a little. Min brushed his fingers along the stone of the gate-pillar. "Here, you!" The guard grabbed, but Min ducked away, his sneakers skipping on gravelly dirt. He looked up and around: he was outside. After a leery glance back at the futilely weaving guard, he slowed. He bent to pick up something from the weedy verge.

In the meadow, Tik had come up to where, shaking out white clothes, one of the albinos had knelt down. She bent. The two of them stood up supporting a third figure between them.

The thief looked into the mirror. Tugging her hat from her belt she put it on with a flourish. The woman in the book cocked an eyebrow.

Smiling, the thief closed The Book of Time.

Min came up leafing slowly through the pages of a rumpled, grass-stained paperback. He paused at one illustration and said, "Gosh." Skylla plucked the book from his fingers.

"This," she pronounced, scanning the table of contents, "will get you into trouble." She riffled back to the middle and, after a brief search, tore out a page. "Ask them if you don't believe it." She nodded at the albinos with Tik negotiating the broken fence. "There's nothing in it from one end to the other that will make you wiser." She tapped the paperback against his chest. Diffidently, he took it. Most of his color had come back. "Trash. Sheer trash," she repeated, and tucked the page into a special inner pocket of her jerkin.

Adaja and Tik got Tasneem through the ditch and lowered her to a big rock. Over her own clothes the boy's jacket was tied by the sleeves. Her thin white curls straggled. Sweat beaded the pinkened skin of her face, the hands she wiped on her slacks trembled and her lips moved in pronouncements of a hissed intensity. ". . . *kill* that eft-sucker . . ." Skylla caught, and the steamy whisper went on. Her steel eyes searched for something, struck Skylla, moved on. The kneeling Adaja used a handful of his hair to smear the tears running his cheeks (a gesture that, for the thief, pinpointed his northern home village within a radius of fifty miles) before he fumbled out of his brocaded belt pouch a large red capsule. He broke it open under her nostrils. Tasneem coughed. Skylla went and braced her when she tried to pull away.

"Breathe," she ordered. The girl coughed again. Her eyes focused.

"This is only thaumaturgic shock," the thief explained to Tik, who stood by wringing her hands. "They'll be all right."

"I'm going to kill him," Tasneem said with impressive sincerity. Adaja inhaled the capsule's last fumes and dropped the pieces into his pouch, coughing.

"She caught the center of that pyrergon." A shudder

hunched his shoulders. "He sent us in—we would have had his damned book for him. . . ." He threw it a glance of loathing where it flattened the grass by her feet. "Then that cross-warp hit us."

Skylla saw Min move his fingers gingerly to the edge of the paperback, looking as if he would like to get rid of it.

"I saw it," Tik whispered suddenly. "She was all fire. She went up. Flames fell off her wings. . . . Then she changed back and I thought it was all right. You flew over the wall." Her fists relaxed. "You were flying. . . ." Across the yellow empyrean of her irises the thief clearly perceived a soaring, tawny hawk, with remiges of ruddy-gold.

Tasneem twisted around. "We had to try to get the book away from you." She looked up at Skylla apologetically. "Our contract. No hard feelings, I hope."

"Not at all. You could have used claws."

Adaja shook his head. "No rough stuff," Tasneem confirmed. "We put that in *all* our contracts. We still owe you a favor."

"It was nothing," the thief replied, with that modest good breeding she had been at some pains to acquire. She picked up the book. "I believe I should be on my way." The guard had disappeared from the gate.

Tik trailed after her into the lane. "But—you're going?" She squinted with disappointment. "Can't you stay?" Min stood behind her with big sorrowful eyes.

Skylla shook her head. "My exit from the Rotunda was less inconspicuous than I could wish."

"I guess," Tik said disconsolately, "most of the time when people steal something it's not so involved with politics and stuff." The thief looked noncommittal. "A lot of people are going to be pretty mad." She dimpled.

"One thing. Didn't you tell me the book would reflect

the face of the person 'who will steal it'? 'Will,' in the future?"

Tik nodded. "Of course, tenses get a bit loose here."

"Hm," said the thief.

"Where will you go now?"

"Home." Skylla smiled to herself.

"And what will you wish for first?" The girl made half a gesture toward the book.

The thief laughed and looked down the road that lay like a long blissful animal in the sun. The trail wound up over the first hill. "Transportation," she said.

From the city came the thin plaint of a siren. They all turned toward the gate, except Skylla who strolled to the road's edge, shed The Book of Time among thick weeds, and strolled back, her hands clasped behind her.

"Really . . ." she murmured.

"Run," suggested Tik.

"Won't you ever come back?" It was Min, incarnadine, desperate.

"No." Skylla looked through the gates into the city, thinking on the nature of time and theft. "But this world is not so very wide. I would not be surprised if we met again."

The siren blared loud. Through the gateway trundled a dazzling equipage, a sort of motorcycle resplendent with chrome and blinking lights and innumerable rear-view mirrors, piloted by a man in a form-fit uniform of scarlet and gold; his gold-chased helmet sported a black plume. On the cycle's panniers were painted glittering lightning bolts.

The miniature pageant flanked them with a swagger, parked, and killed its siren.

There was a moment's silence, during which Skylla favored the vehicle with a look of resigned skepticism. Its driver debarked, hooked his keys on his belt, and faced them.

"Captain Frank Strong," he announced. "Ranger Patrol."

There was a sob of sound. Over on her rock Tasneem had hidden her face in her hands.

"I've been handed a complaint about a stolen book," said Captain Frank Strong. As by instinct, he settled on Skylla. "I'm afraid I'll have to ask you to come with me."

"Certainly," Skylla replied with politeness but no special enthusiasm. He looked extremely trim in his stretch uniform and he had a little curl right in the middle of his forehead but he was not her type. Then Min, trembling like a yearling aspen, extended the wizard's paperback.

"What's this?" Captain Strong strode up and took the book. "This," he said after a study of the cover, "will get you into trouble, young fellow. It looks like the one, all right." He bent a stern but kind look on the boy. "Where did you get hold of this?"

"I found it." Min gestured woodenly. "Over here." He led the man past the abstracted Skylla, back along the road's edge. "There." He pointed out a random weed.

Where they meandered together by the Ranger Patrol cycle, Skylla said to Tik ruminatively, "In a way, it all seems too easy." She cited the remarkable level of ineptitude common to the museum staff. With modestly lowered eyelids, Tik supposed that even certain relatives of her own must have performed with less than their usual acumen.

They heard Captain Strong admonish, "Well, son, you should have turned this in right away. Next time you'll know better, eh?" He reached out and ruffled the boy's hair. Min showed terrified teeth. The Captain started to turn.

"*I* have a complaint!" Tasneem, wild-eyed, breathless, pulled him back. "Someone just almost killed me!"

Captain Strong frowned. "That's a very serious charge."

Skylla, as she lugged The Book of Time over and dumped it in a pannier, saw Tasneem point to the wizard's volume, then press her wrist to her forehead. Tugging her hat down firmly, the thief bestrode the bike's waist and surveyed the controls. With a wave like a magician's she produced the ignition key.

An eyebrow raised like a question mark, Skylla tipped her head at the pillion seat. But far down in the deeps of Tetikte's pupils she saw the flash of sun on bronze wings. They both looked back.

Tasneem reeled, flung out her limp hands to the classic posture, and fainted away into Captain Frank Strong's arms.

Skylla inserted the key. "I suggest you join them, for appearances' sake."

"Goodbye," Tik blurted, backing away. "And—and thanks."

The thief winked. Then she turned her attention to gear-shifts.

"Mama mia," she murmured reprovingly, but by a turn of the key brought the sumptuous machine to throbbing, pulsing, fulgent, pinballesque life; and spurting stones under her rear wheel, with a swerve, with wind in her sleeves and lit like a carnival, and to the familiar startled cry behind, she pointed her hat toward home.

The Old Organ Trail
by
Bridget McKenna

About the Author

Bridget McKenna, First Place winner in the fourth quarter, lives with her husband, artist Doug Herring, their son, Jesse, and seven cats, well off the beaten track near the California/Oregon border. She credits her membership in SCRAWL, a writers' workshop and support group, for much of her success. We think she deserves some of the kudos too.

At Norwescon in March, 1985, Bridget was in the audience for a panel on Writers of the Future that we conducted at that major regional SF convention. Also, dropping in on our hospitality room afterward, listening to professional writers chat about their own early days, afterward, she formed a determination to submit a story each quarter, as she puts it, "for the duration. It was a good way to keep myself turning out stories. Winning First Place is more than I ever hoped for."

It was, in the opinion of the judges, no more than she deserved. And it was also a delightful surprise, since the judges see the manuscripts without authors' names on them. Only after the stories in each quarter have been voted into place do we learn who their authors are. When it's an old friend—even as new an old friend as Bridget—we can't escape a certain feeling that we're doing something right. As is she. . . .

My Uncle Pewtie was king of the liverleggers back in the days of the gaseaters, when it took balls and brains to drive a car (as Pewtie tells it), and the 'leggers in their firebreathing, gaseating hotrods would tear up the blue highways between pickup points and delivery drops, waxing Smokey's ass with their souped-up Camaros and Zeecars with their igloos full of livers and hearts and whatnot tucked snug between the front and back seats.

I wouldn't know what half that stuff means if I hadn't spent so much time hanging out with Pewtie and listening to his stories after I lit out from the Tahoe met and went looking for the family's legendary blacksheep. Camaros and Zeecars, in case you haven't been to a museum lately, are those steel dinosaurs on balloons like you see pictures of on greeting cards, and Smokeys were people who used to drive around looking for other people who went too fast (you could do that back then) and make them pull off the side of the road (you could do that too) and make them pay money to the state.

'Leggers were folks who found organs other folks weren't using—no questions asked—and ran them to places where doctors put them in folks who had worn theirs out. Pretty primitive, but that's the way they did it back when my Uncle Pewtie was a boy.

Pewtie started 'legging when he was seventeen or eighteen and there were still highways a man could drive. He had a souped-up Dodge Dart he'd inherited from his daddy, who used to drive dope up from Baja to the Bay. His daddy had high hopes of a regular family tradition of doperunners, but then they screwed up his plans by making the stuff legal. It just about killed the old guy, but it didn't bother Pewtie at all. He never did care much for dope, and by that time he'd discovered livers anyway.

He found a place—The Co-operative Community of the Sons and Daughters of Heaven—that he never told another soul about until he told me ninety-odd years later. Those happy young folks were the best and fastest sup pliers of fresh healthy organs—no questions asked—that an up-and-coming young liverlegger could want. They made Pewtie's reputation, those smiling Sons and Daughters of Heaven, and he was and remains grateful for that.

Pewtie plied the blue roads for twenty-nine years, supplying better organs faster than any of the competition. Even Turlock Taunya, the best driver and Smokey-waxer from San Diego to Susanville, didn't have Pewtie's gift for procurement on demand. He probably should have married Taunya and settled down—they always were sweet on each other—but he flatly refused to marry any woman who was a better driver than he was. He was awfully old-fashioned that way. As it was, Taunya went out crashing a roadblock on some dark stretch of Highway 395, and Pewtie never married anybody.

After folks began making organs from scratch instead of buying used ones, the bottom sort of fell out of the liverlegging business. There were a lot of jobs opening up growing organ cultures, but Pewtie said be damned if he was going to turn into a farmer, so he retired on his savings and bought a cabin overlooking that fatal stretch of northbound 395 so close to his heart. He built a garage for the Dart and devoted his days to memories and the companionship of a sorry-looking dog named Dave.

Eighteen years passed before he knew it, what with polishing the Dart on Sundays and firing it up on Tuesdays and Fridays. He never drove it anywhere, since by this time gaseaters had been outlawed and the freeways, once a heartwarming chaos of roaring engines and squealing brakes, were now lifeless strips of plastop underlaid with microchips that guided computer-brained cars along predetermined routes at predetermined speeds. There were no drivers anymore, Pewtie lamented, only passengers. And there was no such thing as an accident, or even a close call. They had taken all the joy out of it.

It was about this time, with Pewtie not sure if he was bored or just contented, that everything changed. The brown armored truck rolling cautiously up the gravel drive that Friday morning was the first break he could remember in his routine since the day Dave wandered in off the road.

The truck stopped. Its gun turret made a whirring hydraulic sound as it scanned a three-sixty around the clearing, and an electronic voice came from the loudspeaker.

"Pewtie Marshall?"

"That's me, all right," Uncle Pewtie replied.

"Voice print accepted. One moment, please, for package delivery."

The back of the truck irised open and two skinny metal arms poked out of it and deposited a good-sized package on the side of the driver. "Thank you for using U.P.S.," said the truck, reversed its body on its balloon tires, and crunched back down the driveway.

Pewtie got up and stepped over the shaggy form of Dave, who had slept through the whole thing. He nudged the dog with his foot. "Still breathin'?" Dave opened one eye and groaned. "Hard to tell sometimes," Pewtie commented, and went on down the steps to retrieve his package.

It was bulkier than it was heavy, and he managed to wrestle it up onto the porch without disturbing Dave's sleep. Under the wrapper were two boxes, the smaller one containing a pocket voicecoder, and the larger one a fancy, hermetically sealed, chrome-plated Igloo.

Pewtie thumbed the switch on the 'coder, and the voice that emerged was that of Angelo 'The Eliminator' Angelini, one of Pewtie's best organ customers from the old days.

"Pewtie. Pewtissimo, old friend. We meet again."

"No kidding," said Pewtie, sitting down hard.

"That's me there, in the fancy box. The part that counts, anyway, heh? Hey, we been through a lot together, you and me, in the old days. Maybe you think I forget you, but Angelo Angelini don't forget a friend."

"And I ain't forgot all the times I been shot at on account of you either, you old canneloni." He dropped the 'coder onto the porch and frowned at it.

"I've used up a lot of livers and hearts and a few odds and ends over the years, but it don't do no good no more, Pewtie. So, a couple of years back, I go on Lifesupport."

Pewtie shook his head. Even 'The Eliminator' didn't deserve that.

"Lifesupport, it's okay, I guess. I mean, I like being alive, considering the alternative. In a lifewagon, it's all been taken care of, you know? You're never tired or sick or nothing. *Or nothing.* You know what I mean? I mean, I miss some stuff. Walking down the street on my own two feet. Spaghetti dinners. Making love. I want to be young again, Pewtie, eh? You understand?"

"Course I do, you old scallopini. How do you think *I* feel about it, and I'm still on my original liver?"

"So there's this hotshot doctor up in Ashmed, just over the Oregon border. He says the brain is still pretty good and he can get me a body—no questions asked, eh, Pewtie—thirty years old, tops, in perfect health. So I say to myself, 'Angelo,' I say, 'why go on this way when you can be a young man with another seventy good years ahead of him to run this family the way it should be run.' But Angelo Angelini, he can't get a pass out of Bay met without running into an extradition order from 'Vegas, so I come to you without surplus parts. And that's where you come in, Pewtie. This box here, it's all fitted out with gyros, shock absorbers—I'll have a real safe ride—but nothing this big can go through Oregon Customs without they want to open it, you know, so it can't go by 'Ports or tubes or by the freeway. You get my drift, Pewtie?"

"Yeah," said Pewtie, mentally figuring how much gasahol he had on hand, "I guess I do at that."

"What I'm trying to say is, I know you're not getting any younger neither, but you're still the only sonofabitch I know crazy enough to take this job, and good enough to get me across the Oregon border on the blue highways."

Pewtie sat and stared at the two boxes long after the little one had stopped talking to him. Angelini was right about one thing—in spite of the amount of money being offered, he was crazy even to be thinking about taking the Dart out on the road, up the blue highways to Ashmed. On the other hand Benito, Angelini's youngest son, would be awaiting the delivery at six o'clock tomorrow morning, and the Family had real long arms. After noting the place where he would be dropp [illegible] he cooler, he ground the tiny 'coder under his heel an [illegible] ded for the garage.

The Dart shone i [illegible] ter-yellow stripes where the sun came through the sl [illegible] nd touched its glossy fenders. Pewtie turned the key a [illegible] ecked the gauge, then loaded the trunk with gasahol c [illegible] "Hey, Dave!" he yelled across the yard, "We're goin' [illegible] trip!"

His only roadma [illegible] s in his mind. Every one of those blue lines that m [illegible] a back door into Oregon was etched on his memory l [illegible] n an antique circuit board. He pulled out on the dirt [illegible] that led to 395 and gave the Dart its head. He fig [illegible] his best chance was to haul ass through the day w [illegible] the high summer heat off the old blacktop would m [illegible] he heat signature of the Dart's exhaust from the wat [illegible] infra-red eye of CHiPsat.

CHiPsat was th [illegible] Highway Patrol backup system that spotted speeders, [illegible] ater illegal gaseaters, from orbit and radioed their wh [illegible] outs to Smokeys in the vicinity. When asked, it could [illegible] a warning shot across your bow, or put a few neat ho [illegible] your engine block to slow you down for the ground [illegible]. When the state pulled off the blue highways, CHi [illegible] stayed up there with nothing to do, and occasionally [illegible] ould get a little bored. For years afterward you could [illegible] etimes spot a crater melted into the blacktop, with m [illegible] a handful of twisted metal parts scattered around it.

These blue h [illegible] ays, the old two-lane blacktops that criss-crossed th [illegible] pty spaces between the freeways, were badly neglecte [illegible] tally uncontrolled, and completely unsafe for this trip [illegible] -filing generation of cowards who called themselves d [illegible] s, but they were the only roads left you could drive wit [illegible] r hands and your feet and the seat of your pants, and feel like you were at least as smart as the car you were driving.

It was into this last free space between the freeways that Pewtie drove in the high noon sun, looking for the backest of the backroads going north. He figured to be within a few miles of the delivery point by midafternoon. They would hole up just over the border, deliver Angelo into the hands of his loving son, collect their money and be home by dinner Saturday. *If* they could stay clear of the emcies.

Emcies were gangs of mean, nasty folks on two-wheeled gaseaters they called 'hogs' (the real word was 'Harleys'), and they ruled the blue roads with an iron fist in a dirty leather glove. Since every citizen had the choice of living in the mets, which were climate-controlled and violence-free, the state didn't worry a whole lot about what went on outside. As long as the emcies stayed out of state-controlled territory, they were free to ride their hogs, party, and brew gasahol to their hearts' content. Few citizens ever strayed onto their turf, and fewer still ever came back to talk about it. Pewtie kept watch, scanning the side roads for dust clouds and the rearview for glints of chrome. Everything was peaceful.

The black and yellow warning sign hung askew on its rotting wooden post. It said 35, which any fool knew meant 50, and which to a driver of Pewtie's ability meant 65 or 70 with one eye shut, but that's because he wasn't figuring on the cat sitting in the middle of the road. He swore at himself as his hands automatically jerked the wheel to the right, and again as the Dart sailed off the blacktop and down a short incline where it came to rest in a rocky ditch.

The dust settled and Pewtie got out to check the damage, a bad scrape on the right front fender. At least it was on its wheels, and Angelini's ice chest was still safe in its seat belt. The cat was nowhere in sight. Dave clambered out the window and took a whiz on the tire. Pewtie sighed and set about trying to push the Dart back up on the road.

When he had pushed and sweated and strained the car about a foot up the slope, Pewtie began to feel distinctly middle aged. At sixty-five, and still sporting the heart he'd been born with, he probably was, at that. He set the handbrake and reached in around Angelini's gleaming igloo to his own cracked red plastic one and got out a couple of liverwurst sandwiches and two bottles of Henry's. He unwrapped Dave's sandwich and poured one beer into Dave's old Puppy Chow water dish, and they sat and watched the sun go down together. It was strange, Pewtie reflected, how he hadn't seen any sign of crazy old CHiPsat or the emcies. He guessed they were all getting old and tired, too.

It was solid black night before the Dart was back on the road, with Dave asleep in the front seat, and Pewtie none too sure he was ready to go on. Sagging against the Dart's rear bumper, he felt a distant rumble through his feet. Then it reached his ears—a low, growling, snarling kind of sound—and when he looked back the way he had come there was a glow on the horizon like a 12-volt false dawn, and he knew they were coming.

Over the last rise, the glow of a hundred Harley headlamps split the darkness. There was no place to run, so Pewtie just stood there, cussing under his breath and wishing he'd have flattened that damn cat.

The hogs slowed and stopped, forming a ragged half-circle around Pewtie and the Dart. One figure—maybe a little taller, a little heavier, a little greasier than the rest—got off his bike and walked into the pool of light.

He was big and he was hairy. His beard was long and

black and his eyes were little and red, and he wore a sort of leather vest all sewed together out of little patches with little hearts and stuff that said 'Sue Forever' and 'Mama.' He had a belt buckle the size of a porkchop that read 'Skullbusters M.C.' Pewtie smiled and nodded. It was Jimmy-Bob 'Roadkill' LaRue, war chief of the Skullbusters, the most feared emcies in this part of California by a long shot. Pewtie knew him by reputation only, which had suited him fine up 'til now.

"Hey, there, Roadkill," Pewtie ventured.

The big man growled.

"*Mister* Roadkill, I mean. Hope I didn't slow you down none. I'm just on my way up to the border. Name's Pewtie Marshall. Anybody seen any sign of CHiPsat?"

A low murmur went through the emcies, and they all looked up with the same cringing motion—a denim-and-leather wave of slinking shoulders and craning necks in the dark spaces behind the headlamps.

Jimmy-Bob made a circular motion in front of his chest, then turned his attention back to Pewtie. "This is our road, citizen, and we got things we like to do to citizens what can't resist taking they Granddaddy's gaseater out for a free spin in our territory." He grinned widely, resembling a piano keyboard.

Pewtie's eyes flashed. He spat on the road. "Watch who you're callin' citizen, *citizen.*"

Jimmy-Bob growled. Pewtie glowered. They stood there for a long moment on the way to something really awful happening when a sound emerged from the Dart, starting out kind of low and rising in pitch as it went, so as to make the hair stand up on everybody's neck at once. It went on and on until you wanted to clap your hand around your ears, and ended in a truly amazing yawn.

"What in Mother CHiPsat's holy name was that?!"

Illustrated by Art Thibert

Jimmy-Bob exclaimed, his voice shaking just a little. He grabbed a flashlight from one of the emcies and shone it in the car window. Dave looked up, blinking.

"Crusher?" Jimmy-Bob inquired, kind of low and wondering. Dave howled and leaped through the open window into Jimmy-Bob's arms. "Crusher!" Jimmy-Bob shouted, hugging Dave's furry body to his chest and turning around in circles. "I thought you were dead!"

Pewtie scratched his head. "Crusher?"

"Where'd you get this dog, Marshall?" Jimmy-Bob demanded when he'd stopped dancing. He was still holding Dave clasped against his middle, and Dave was licking his face like it was braised liver, so even though he was trying to look mean, it wasn't too convincing.

"Wandered in off 395 one day with a busted leg and a mess of cracked ribs," Pewtie said. "I took care of him. We been takin' care of each other ever since." He felt sort of dazed by the events of the past few minutes. He had never given a thought to Dave's life before he had found him, or what it might be like not to have him around. He watched silently as Jimmy-Bob put the dog down and Dave just sat there, then lay down and got comfortable at the emcie's big booted feet.

"I took a near hit west of the Nevada border riding alone with Crusher on the back," Jimmy-Bob recalled. "Woke up after dark and went callin' this sonofabitch for hours. Finally figured he must've crawled off to die. Gee, Crusher, it's sure good to see your ugly face." Dave looked up kind of contented from between his paws, like he'd just been thinking the same thing. Jimmy-Bob turned back to Pewtie. "Thanks for taking care of my dog, Marshall." He extended a hairy hand.

Pewtie shook it, muttering "I sort of thought he was my dog the whole time."

"Well, now, Mister Marshall, what can me and the Skullbusters do for you to pay you back for what you done for me?"

Pewtie sighed. "I'm a 'legger, Mr. Roadkill, on my way up to Ashmed with a cargo. I'm just a little worried about driving at night on account of . . ." He glanced at the emcies, then pointed straight up.

Jimmy-Bob circled his chest with a thick middle finger and said "She's done changed her ways, Marshall. Can I call you Pewtie? I seem to remember that name from the good old days: Pewtie Marshall. You can call me Jimmy-Bob. She ain't claimed a rider for over a year now. For a while there we thought she'd forgot us entirely, but about six months ago she fried half the Bonesmashers and most all the Bloodletters while they were havin' a firefight over a stretch of Highway 36 between Rosewood and Red Bluff. And we just got back from the funeral of the Berserkers, who were shootin' it out amongst themselves for the job of war chief. She plugged every mother of 'em that was firin' a gun. It don't bode well for wars of succession."

"I'm mighty sorry about your friends," Pewtie offered, "but you say she's leavin' gaseaters alone? I should be able to make it up to the border, then."

"Like as not," Jimmy-Bob agreed. "What you got in there anyway? I didn't think anybody hauled livers anymore."

"It's the brain of the war chief of a kind of business conglomerate. I'm meeting his son over the border at sunrise. This is gonna be my last run, then I'm going home. Alone," he added, looking pointedly at Dave, who was watching him with one eye.

"Well maybe you won't mind if we go along, then. Just in case you run into some *mean* mothers."

A mass of dark, wet clouds piling up on the horizon marked the Oregon border, and Pewtie and the emcies drove across as the sky was lightening in the east. Far, far ahead, you could see the squat gray dome of the Ashmed met, but out here it was as beautiful as ever—rolling hills, dark clumps of oak, and the tule fog slithering across the road like the ghost of a lazy snake. Pewtie could hear the muffled rumble of the Harleys a ways behind him. People like that couldn't live in a met any more than he could, Pewtie thought. Some people just had to be free, no matter what it was they were being free to be.

A shiny black aircar bounced into the middle of the road and hovered. Pewtie jammed on the brakes and went sideways, skidding to a stop a few inches away. The doors hissed open and Benito Angelini stepped out, accompanied by several associates in identical dark suits, carrying identical automatic weapons. They glared at Pewtie and the crowd of emcies beginning to pull up behind him. Pewtie got out of the car.

"Here I am, right on time," he said, reaching toward the back seat to unstrap Angelini Senior. The tiny click of a safety catch made him straighten up and turn around.

"You don't understand, 'legger," Benito said. "Papa's trip ends right here. I'm head of the family now, and my first official act is gonna be to eliminate 'The Eliminator'." He smiled, pleased with the joke. His friends smiled.

"Well, it's just a suggestion, Mister Angelini, but I really wouldn't fire those guns out here in the open if I was you."

Benito's smile became a snarl. His friends snarled. Pewtie began to back away from the car, slow-like. Angelini opened the back door of the Dart and took up a point-blank position with the other gunmen crowded close around him. They opened fire. Clouds of refrigerant boiled out of the car as The Eliminator's igloo was blown to smithereens.

Pewtie and the emcies went flat. The smell of ozone soaked the air as a cluster of hot red beams hit the road, the Dart, the friends of Angelini, and Benito himself, searing precise holes, large and small, in everything. It got very quiet.

Pewtie raised his head and saw Jimmy-Bob looking back at him. "Well, you told 'em not to," Jimmy-Bob said, standing up at last and gazing up at the sky, where patches of blue were beginning to show. "She's done spoke again about the evils of firearms." He shook his head sadly. "Looks like we're going to have to get us some lasers."

Pewtie got up slowly and dusted himself off. He limped over to the Dart, stepping around the mess in the road. The Dart looked like a giant swiss cheese between Benito's bullets and CHiPsat's lasers. "And we weren't even in her goddam jurisdiction," Pewtie muttered, sticking his fist into a hole in the fender whose angle led to and through the old cars's brave engine.

Jimmy-Bob came up and put a huge arm around Pewtie's shoulders. "Tough luck, buddy."

"Yeah," Pewtie said. "Even tougher for old Angelo, I guess. He wanted to live forever."

"Sounds like a real stupid idea to me," Jimmy-Bob said. "Let's head on back to California. I'll pick up a sidecar and take you home."

Pewtie waved goodbye to Jimmy-Bob and Dave as they rolled down the drive. When they were out of sight he walked across to the garage, looked inside, closed the door. He could hear the Harley idling for a long minute down on the highway, then a roar as it went into gear and doppplered off into the west. He leaned against the garage door for a time, feeling a whole lot older than he had yesterday, then straightened his shoulders and headed back for the house. Dave was slinking up onto the porch, wagging his shaggy tail from somewhere between his legs.

"Hey, there, Dave," Pewtie acknowledged casually, "how about a cold Henry's?" He held the screen door open and they walked together into the house.

Click
by
Ray Aldridge

About the Author

Ray Aldridge is a potter and stained glass designer. "Click," his first fiction sale, arose from his speculations about future art forms, stimulated by three years of his experimenting with computer art.

He lives in Florida, where one of his long-term projects is a series of stained glass windows, The Alien Lightscapes. *We've seen samples and they're wonderful. There are eight in all now. Aldridge's project is to craft the effect of a long series "discovered on various backwater planets, apparently the work of a single itinerant craftsman. . . ." He hopes someday to create an anthology of stories inspired by the windows and has provisional commitments from several noted SF authors he admires, including Gene Wolfe, but is looking for a publisher.*

In other words, like many other writers and would-be writers, he is a various person with many artistic interests. Like most successful artists, he is also single-mindedly energetic when pursuing one of his objectives. He has been "writing with determination" for a year and a half after twenty-five years of SF reading that he describes as his only classroom. Winning Third Place in the fourth quarter, he says, "strengthens my resolve to persevere in the business, to keep my nose to the grindstone 'til it hits bone." Hopefully, further validation of his considerable talent and growing skill will arrive before that point is reached. . .

The click booms along my circuits; reality floods in. It's late afternoon. The Museum is almost empty, and I stand in my niche, bathed in the fading skyshine. It's the daily lull, when the faint rattle of weapons outside the fortifications dies away. My eyes track away from the hallway, settling on the two middle-aged tourists who watch my display. Their lips move, spelling out the words that describe me. They wear light body armor, as is usual for tourists these days, but their holsters are empty; no personal weapons are allowed in these sacred halls. The armor is a fashionable make, but a little scuffed and scarred as if from a tough trip through the Pale. They've kept their helmets on.

When they look up, I've already shifted my gaze to a neutral corner. I'm not supposed to frighten them immediately.

"Would you look at that!" the man says, his face shining with sweat. Since the air conditioning expired for good, I've liked the climate better; not so the tourists. "You'd think it was real; I mean, you really would."

"Jon." She frowns, a short woman gray with dissatisfaction. "It *is* real. It hears everything you say. Didn't you even read the display?" She glares, annoyed; an Art Lover saddled with a Philistine. "I don't think you've really paid any attention to anything we've seen today!"

He flushes, assumes a practiced hostility. "Sure

I have." Resentment curls his lip. "You're a real expert yourself, is that it?"

He looks at me with small piggy eyes, and he addresses me in a loud, careful voice. "You can talk, that right?"

I answer politely, as my programming directs. "Yes, sir, I can speak."

They're both startled by my voice. The booming undertones are disquieting to the human ear. The woman draws back slightly, her wattles vibrating. Then her chin juts out, and I imagine that I can hear her thoughts. This is ridiculous, she is telling herself; how can I be afraid of a statue, even if it *is* a Nacama?

"What are you thinking about, right now?" she asks.

She asks one of the Two Questions. The other is: Do you know you're a statue? I answer truthfully, as I must. "I was thinking about your fear of me."

The mate tugs at the Art Lover's arm. "I've seen enough of this. I won't be right until we're back in the Pale. And it's a long trip, so let's go."

"Please, Jon, be quiet." I admire her tenacity. She still wants her money's worth, despite the fear and repugnance she feels. "I didn't ride all this way in the hardbus, I didn't put up with being shot at by Rads, and sneered at and ignored when we got here, just to turn around and leave."

From long experience, I expect her to ask me to say something in Afei, my native tongue, as the display so unimaginatively suggests. Thus I'm surprised by her next question. "What," she asks,"do you think about when no one is here?"

She penetrates to the heart of the matter. My response is curious. Despite my programming, despite the fact that she is more polite than many others, I cannot keep my anger private. "Nothing. I'm nowhere and I think of nothing."

My voice grows mighty. The man pales, and his shaking hand darts for the button.

The Museum is dark. In the dim green glow of the safety lamps, I see my friend, Sergeant Bush. He has clicked me, as he does each night. Sergeant Bush is an ancient black man, the night security guard in this wing.

"How's it hangin'?" he asks, his archaic false teeth glowing cheerily in the dark. For some reason, he refuses to get a set of new buds. His round dark face is scribed deeply with age and good humor. I am overwhelmed for a moment with affection for him, my only friend, Sergeant Bush.

"About the same, Sergeant Bush." I smile, an expression that could be misinterpreted. Sergeant Bush smiles back. I can only suppose that he has seen worse things.

"Well," he says, hitching up his gun belt, "you jest wait right here while I make the rounds, hear?" He cackles at his little joke and teeters off down the hall.

I cherish Sergeant Bush, with his baggy uniform, his antique prosthesis. I squat down on my plinth, luxuriating in the sensation of unwatched movement. I hope that Sergeant Bush never suffers for his kindness to me, though I cannot imagine how anyone would ever find out. He is alone here at night, his job a sinecure left over from before the Museum was a fortress. The Museum softens from the walls in, all its defenses on the outside, so that in these echoing halls there is little need for guarding.

I am grateful for the opportunity Sergeant Bush gives me, to be alive without spectators, without their questions and remarks, their eyes.

I think my own thoughts. I scratch my toes, even sing

a little, "... When the droon fruits take wing, then will I come to the bonepits of the People...." I sing a song of homecoming. But I have a poor singing voice, a rare failing in Nacama's last and greatest work. Yet, I love to drone tunelessly the traditional songs of my people. Perhaps the voice is no error. Great art requires paradox, or so say some of the critics who come to stand before me. These are the braver or more contentious critics; the majority, I believe, shut me down before they begin to expound on Nacama's philosophy, the deeper meanings of his work. I understand their caution; I am in a position to contradict them. But they need not fear deflation from me. I am stringently programmed against self-analysis in public. Nacama believed that to dissect a work of art was to destroy it. Therefore I am seamless.

Sergeant Bush doesn't give a damn about art, so he tells me. He takes me at face value. I think he really just believes, at least at night, when he is with me, he really just accepts the lie that I came from another world, a world of lavender sands and sluggish red seas.

Some nights we talk for hours, he about his worthless grandson, I about Home. The memories seem so fresh, so real to me. Of course, I know that Home existed only in the fevered imagination of Paolo Nacama, and now, in my memories.

I hear Sergeant Bush now, returning from his rounds. He reappears and sits heavily on the low bench before my plinth. He takes out a gray handkerchief and swabs at his forehead, hard and shiny as a turtle's shell. "Damn if it don't get harder ever' night, Curly."

He calls me Curly, for reasons he has never explained. My real name is Klatu—Klatu the swift.

"You shouldn't work so hard." I am trying to express sympathy, and he laughs.

"Don't worry, Curly. This is the easiest job I ever did. I'm just in the habit of complainin', I guess." He extracts, lovingly, a flattened silver flask from his shirt and takes a healthy pull. "Stuff'll be the death of me, iffen I'm lucky." He stoppers the flask, spirits it away. "Wish I could offer you a snort, Curly. You strike me as a born drinking man."

"Your company is sufficient, Sergeant Bush." I wait for him to speak again. My programming does not allow me to initiate conversation without great effort. Sergeant Bush claims to enjoy our talks for just that reason. If he wants to talk, then I will talk, or he can choose the exclusive sound of his own voice. He calls me a boon to a talkative old man.

"You not bad company, either, for a guy looks like a screamin' fiend, ten feet tall an' covered with scales. Not like my goddamn grandson, the defective. The blood's runnin' thin." He laughs again, a thick, cheerful sound, free of malice.

They are not scales, really, just a skin corrugation. My blood would run warm, had I any, and red. I could, in a poor light, pass for a very large and muscular and somewhat deformed human, were it not for my hard skin plates, and the semi-retractable claws at all four extremities. I am longer of limb and bigger in the chest than a human; I am of a coursing species.

But I don't mind if Sergeant Bush jokes. To show my amusement, I smile, bearing twelve-centimeter canines. I would laugh, but Sergeant Bush says it makes his hearing aid whistle. He clings to that grimy artifact out of mulishness, and so our friendship is made possible. This decrepit hearing aid functions so crudely that the fear-inspiring nuances of my voice are filtered out. I bless his cantankerousness.

He takes another long pull at the flask, which

appears and disappears like magic, before launching into a relaxed account of the grandson's latest misadventure. I settle back on my claws, only half attentive. I grunt with disbelief at the appropriate intervals, and that is all Sergeant Bush requires of me. Occasionally Sergeant Bush pushes my button. The Museum decided, in the name of conservation, to install an automatic timer to my activation circuitry. If my button is not pushed every fifteen minutes, I shut off. My circuits are irreparable, should they decay, and they will, someday. The Museum wants me to last as long as possible, of course.

As always, my thoughts are of home. It seems only yesterday that I roamed the bright dusty plains with my packmates. We revelled in the release of movement, the great game of the hunt, the joy of the kill after the long dry chase. In my memories, the blood of the food beast still fills my mouth with its sweet steely tang. I shake myself. Synthetic memories are always fresh and hot with life. Even the great Nacama could not build into me the ability to forget. That is reserved for real beings.

Now I remember, as I do each night, the first time I was activated.

I woke hunched on a pillar of black stone, in a cavern of strange pale lights and unfamiliar stinks. A small pulpy-looking biped stood before me, watching me with with frightening intensity. I had no recollection of coming there and I was afraid. I attempted to leap down, to make my escape. To my horror, I couldn't force my body beyond the edge of the pillar, though I could feel no barrier. It was as if a globe of invisible glass held me. I shook in a paralysis of terror for long minutes, until Nacama shut me down.

When he reactivated me, I was calmer, an artificial calm, and Nacama explained.

At first I thought I'd go mad, but of course my

program does not allow for aberrant mental states. There is a limit to my matrix capacity and so I am as I am. Still, it's hard for me to accept that I am nothing more than a very fine work of clockwork art. I didn't understand the meaning of the word *art* then. I still don't.

As those first days passed, Nacama withered visibly. I of course began to seem less real to myself. "But that is not true," he would lecture me intently, "you are as real as I, except that you can be deactivated with a button. You will never know how much I wish I had a button like yours, Klatu."

In the foundry, on the last night, he seemed no more than a fading mockup of a man. When he activated me, he sat in an old wing chair, cradling in one arm a large sonic chisel.

"Klatu," the great man said, "I want you to understand. Why I made you, for example, though I am no longer very clear on that myself." He slumped slightly in the chair, looked down with eyes full of confused disappointment. He looked for a moment as if he would speak again, then he deactivated me.

Dawn filtered through the high windows when he woke me from the dreamless sleep of my holding circuits. Nacama was still sitting in the chair with the sonic chisel, looking both shrunken and exalted. "I worked blindly when I made you," he said to me. "That's nothing to you, I know, but I meant no cruelty." He smiled, a terrible sight. "So now I will sum up, for the last time, your situation, Klatu. There is no Home. You cannot hope to return. 'To return.' Home was my finest creation, not you, I regret to say. To make you, a puppet of plastaflesh and sensors, dancing in a pressor field; why, a lesser artist might have done as well, but I, I made a world in your memories!"

I was silent. He had explained this to me in a

hundred ways. It had been fortunate, he said, that my circuits had proven flexible enough to absorb this knowledge, else I might have spent my life in a zoo, unaware of the circumstances of my captivity.

"Still," he continued, "don't hate me for what I've done. I meant no harm, my goal was creation, and I didn't look past that. But I am tired, now."

"I don't hate you," I said, "I wouldn't exist, but for you."

Nacama moved as I spoke, a gesture of pain and pleasure, as he listened to the power of his work. "I am too proud of this, too proud to destroy it," he murmured, as if to himself. I drew back to the limits of my plinth, eyeing the chisel. I had no wish to die, in whatever limited way was possible for me. But all of Nacama's attention was pouring inward at that last moment of his life. He put the tip of the idling chisel, with its little bubble of displaced air roiling around, into his mouth, and thumbed the vernier to full power. Small bits of his head pattered softly to the floor, and the blood that geysered from the stump of his neck dyed the wing chair in a graceful crimson pattern. An artist to the last.

It was four long days, while I watched the blood lose its brightness, until his ex-mate got a court order and broke in, to find us. That was the longest period of time I have ever spent activated and unobserved, and now I look back upon that time with some nostalgia. When they found me, they almost shot me before they realized I could be shut off. I did not wake then for a long time, I'm told, not until the court awarded me to the Museum, over the agonized protests of the ex-mate.

I force myself to cease remembering. Sergeant Bush is nearing the end of his nightly narrative, and of his shift.

The time seems to move with such swiftness on the nights that Sergeant Bush works in my wing. I get to my feet, and position myself so that no one will notice I have moved in the night.

"I enjoyed it," I say as he reaches for the button. Sergeant Bush gives me a cheery wink and pushes.

I wake to a class of schoolchildren and their teacher. The teacher is a gaunt woman in bruised armor, nervous without her stun rod, and determined to maintain control.

All eyes watch me. Children interest me; childhood is not a custom on Home. They resist fear, children do, and their unskeptical belief lets me forget what I am, sometimes.

"All right, now, children, have you all seen the display? Would anyone like to ask Klatu a question? Remember, he's really not a person, but he thinks just like one." A forest of small arms wave, bright predatory eyes gleam. She calls on a boy with red hair and a missing front tooth.

"Do you ever get tired, just standing there all day?"

"No. I don't ordinarily feel fatigue."

A child with a pinched, sly face asks, "How come you speak such good English, if you're supposed to be from another planet?" He sniggers, looking to his classmates for approval.

I grin and flex my claws. They all draw back as I answer. "So that I may answer foolish questions like yours." My programming allows me to respond to frivolous or hostile questioners in kind, so long as I am truthful. Nacama was no abstract artist.

"How long have you been here?"

"I don't know, but if you will tell me the date, I'll be able to say." They chorus out the date and I tell them.

"Thirty-four years, eight months, and eleven days."

"Do you feel safe here? They say there's no Pale-runners here."

"Yes, I feel safe." I do, but if I were real I might be worried. The thump of explosions can be heard more clearly every day through the thick walls of the Museum.

They grow familiar with me, and there are many more questions. They ask about Home. What was the weather like there; do I miss it? Nacama was a great artist; after a while one stops noticing that his work is only a complex illusion. Even I forget.

Lost in my memories, I allow the children to lead me on. When I begin to speak of the flesh-sharing of the pack, my libido circuits are triggered. In my species, the sexual organs are internal in both sexes, until stimulated. The teacher reaches for the button in a flurry of high-pitched giggles.

It is night in the Museum. To the reverberation of the click along my circuits is added the tremor of arousal. Sergeant Bush grins in a noncommittal manner. I am intensely embarrassed.

"Uhmhm," he says. "Looks like you need a friend. And I ain't that good a friend, Curly."

He laughs, and says no more. Except for the occasional covert look of pity and calculation from Sergeant Bush, the night passes comfortably.

The click fires me with life and I see Sergeant Bush in civilian garments! Nothing can match my astonishment at this sight. It's daytime in the Museum, and I have never seen Sergeant Bush by daylight, the cold light that spills down from the skylight above me. He wears a spangled jumpsuit which I recognize as the height of fashion thirty years ago. In his ear is a new, barely visible hearing aid. On his frail arm is a remarkable female. She towers over him, and she looks like nothing I have ever seen before.

"Lucy," Sergeant Bush says in formal tones, "meet Curly. He can't help being naked."

She extends a long hand in an unmistakably coy manner. Not knowing what else to do, I take it as gently as possible for a moment, then let it drop.

She is unusual in more than size. She is over two meters tall, almost chest high to me were we both on the same level. She is a big woman, but not fat; the flesh just packs deeply on her long limbs. Her body is shaped much like any human female's, but exaggerated in scale, and her head is bald. She wears no personal armor, just a brief tunic of some shiny black material, and she is dyed or tattooed in a pretty reticulated pattern everywhere her skin shows. It gives her tight smooth skin the look of pink frogskin. Her scent rises light and uncomplicated. There is an empty scabbard at her shoulder, shaped to carry a shocker.

She has large green eyes and an ugly ragged scar along her jaw. She looks very little like the females of my pack; on Home they would tear her to pieces as an oddling, but I am entranced. It is my first social occasion.

"Pleased to meet you," I say, and both Lucy and Sergeant Bush wince a little. It is difficult, I find, to project courtesy with a voice that makes the skin crawl. I resort to whispering, which robs my voice of the most unpleasant nuances. "I'm sorry," I hiss, "it's not intentional."

Sergeant Bush cocks his eye at me. "How come you never whispered to me, Curly?" His eyebrows twitch.

"I didn't think you would approve of whisperers, Sergeant Bush."

"Well, I guess you were right. But it's different in

your case, Curly. Why don't we just whisper in the future, and then I can wear my new hearing aid to work. Lucy here, she's a big girl, isn't she? She likes 'em big, too, she tells me." He winks and wanders away, pretending to look at the art, as if he hadn't been looking for thirty years, leaving me alone with Lucy, the first human to whom I have been formally introduced.

She studies me without embarrassment, but without that panicked intensity I associate with those desperate humans who have made sexual overtures to me. Some were unbalanced, I think; others were seeking publicity. None succeeded in arousing more than my pity.

"So. Bush tells me you don't care for your work." She speaks in a rich tenor. "Me too." She stops and looks at me, as if she is wondering whether I am an elaborate joke played on her by Sergeant Bush, or if she is crazy to be talking to a statue.

"Well," I say, "things could be worse. I'm not complaining."

"Why not?"

I flounder. "I don't know why not."

She arranges herself comfortably on the low bench. "Bush said I'd find you entertaining, Curly. Or do you prefer Klatu? Klatu the swift. . . ." she says as if savoring the barbaric ring of my given name, graven on the side of my plinth.

"Curly will be fine, Lucy." I smile but Lucy shows no sign of fear. "Let me tell you about Home, Lucy. I know many fine legends. I'll tell you how Bhagg the Dry God tricked the pack queen Kepela."

I am entertaining with all my might. My whisper works well for delivering the lines of Bhagg, dry and sinister enough to be convincing. She is charmed rather than horrified.

She thanks me politely when she leaves, promising to come again, as if I were real.

She comes several times a week, and though I don't know why she comes, I am grateful. She sits with me by the hour, pushing my button and pretending to be a student of art. The day guards don't move her along as they might once have done. There are fewer visitors, for one thing, and then there are the constant emergencies on the perimeter that pull the guards away, to return with new lines on their faces.

The time passes easily when she sits with me. I have a store of strange memories, and so does Lucy. Her stories are hardly less bizarre, in human terms, than are mine. She works as an entertainer, in a bar called the Slick Pit. She is paid to remove her clothing, if I understand her. It seems an odd profession to me.

On her third visit, Lucy makes a startling revelation. She is a Pale-runner! Or at least she does live Outside. When she tells me, I gaze down at her in amazement. I'd always envisioned the Pale-runners as subhuman and monstrous, certainly not people you'd discuss your ancestors with. They constantly attack the Museum and the convoys of tourists from the Pale.

"No," Lucy says, "I'm not political."

"But, isn't it dangerous, living Outside? I've overheard some terrible stories; what happens to people there."

"To tourists," she says. "That's the difference, Curly."

I mull this over.

"It's like Bush. Now, Bush is a Citizen, but he goes outside all the time. A lot do, and they have a good time if they can blend in like Bush. You know, Curly, your buddy Bush is a woolly old man. You wouldn't think it to look at him, but it's so. Oh, it's true; when I take it off he stomps and hollers just like the rest of the old punkers."

I'm dazed. Apparently Sergeant Bush has forged an entry permit for Lucy, and I fear for him. He would lose his job, his Citizenship, possibly his life should he be caught. He reassures me, saying that he's thinking about retiring anyway, if the Museum doesn't fall down first. He's not optimistic about that. Let the worthless grandson support him, he says. About time, he says. Sometimes I feel a little sorry for the grandson, with such a headstrong ancestor to contend with. On Home, the custom was to eat ancestors before they reached such an obstreperous age. I'm glad that is not the custom here.

"I'm very grateful that Sergeant Bush introduced us, Lucy," I whisper.

The softness of human flesh is no longer so strange to me; Lucy's is firm with muscle beneath the smoothness of the alien skin. The pink pattern was a temporary dye, a passing fashion outside the Pale, replaced now with a spiderweb moire in silvery sepia. Lucy's love of patterned skin pleases me. It makes her seem less human.

"I, too," says Lucy. She smiles her pleasant smile. "I've always liked big men."

I don't know what to reply, for I am not a man, yet I know her statement is directed at me. I think that Lucy, my second friend, is a different sort of friend.

At night Sergeant Bush wears his new hearing aid and I whisper, and my existence is good.

Before me stands Dr. Harvey, the chief curator in this wing of the Museum. The Director is with him. Dr. Harvey is speaking in that tone of submissive cajolery he always uses with his superiors. "It is the last Nacama, after all. Many visitors come here specifically to see it."

His incurious gaze slips across me. "Hello, Klatu," he says absently. I do not dislike Dr. Harvey, because he treats me like everyone else; as if all were just complicated puppets. There's no discrimination in his disinterest.

I do dislike the Director. He has a sly and unhealthy smell.

He is a sleek, well-dressed man in early middle age. He frowns, looking studiously at a spot twenty centimeters to the side of my right eye. "I'm not suggesting that we dispose of the piece. We're not quite that hard up yet. But, it's been on display for a very long time, eh, John?"

"Well, you're right, of course."

I listen with growing unease, although I detect no obvious scent of danger.

The Director gazes on Dr. Harvey with paternal eyes. "I'll tell you what," he says, "we'll store the piece for two years. Then we'll have a Nacama retrospective; it's about time for another. You'll be in charge, John."

All I can think is: Will the walls of the Museum stand for two more years?

But Dr. Harvey is gratified, as is the Director, who likes to wield his power with finesse. They prepare to walk away arm-in-arm; Dr. Harvey reaches for the button

The click sings through me and I live. I'm in a tiny alcove of raw grey concrete, lit by a single yellow bulb. I crouch in shock. My life, that portion I think of as real, had been spent in the Museum, under the northern skylight.

In the corridor two anonymous maintenance men fold their dolly. "Looks just fine to me, Bill. It probably sounded worse'n it really was, it only dropped a couple inches. What do you think, Bill?"

"Ain't my problem, Eddie. I just want to get out of here before the loonies break in. I'm quitting before it's too late, and you ought to do the same."

"You're right there, Bill. It's been close a couple times this week, I hear."

"You know I'm right," says the other, reaching for the button.

It is Sergeant Bush who wakens me. I thank the Gods —Nacama's false pantheon and whatever real gods there may be. But I am still in the alcove.

"Hey, Curly. Surprised to see me?" he asks with a broad yellow grin.

For me it is just seconds after the Director pronounced my sentence. I struggle to collect myself, despite the artificial adrenaline currents sweeping through me. I straighten up with an effort, remembering the words of the maintenance men. But I detect no obvious damage.

Sergeant Bush looks concerned. "Hey, Curly, you look a little ruffled. You okay, boy?"

"I . . . I am all right, Sergeant Bush." I shudder with the stimulation. "What is the date, Sergeant Bush?" This last I force out, over the threshold of my programming, easier under the stress of the moment.

Sergeant Bush pats the hard ridges of my foot. "Calm down, Curly, it's only been two weeks since they moved you down. Hey, why do you think I've snuck down here, where I ain't supposed to be?"

He rolls his amused old eyes at me. "Lucy made me. She don't understand how it works, I guess."

Sergeant Bush interprets my reaction in his own way. He chuckles tolerantly.

"I mean," he continues, "how you ain't gonna notice how much time passes before they put you out for the tourists again. But Lucy, she's not so patient."

He sits on a packing crate and fishes out his flask.

"You been a good friend to that girl, Curly. She just in a state since they moved you down, you know. She say it just ain't fair, what with you two getting along so good and all." He had a good belt of his antique poison. "I'll tell you 'bout Lucy. She say to you how she likes big men? Well, she's found more than one of 'em who weren't big enough. Ever' one of them, one day he'd go down to the corner for a bag, you know what I mean?"

"No."

He looked at me. "Well, don't matter," he said. "The thing is, this time she got it in her head that she had her one she'd always know where he was. . . . Are you following me any better?"

"No."

"Okay. But Lucy's a good girl, a little wild and set on her way, but good as gold, Curly. We all hate to see her disappointed."

He rubs his hand across his head, and falls silent, giving up. There is a long silence as I wrestle with Sergeant Bush's words.

Finally, I say, "I don't much like it here, even if I won't know anything about it."

"Well," Sergeant Bush says slowly, "what I came to tell you, Curly, is I'm gonna retire. It just ain't the same without you there, and I'm tired." He takes a long pull at the flask. "But I ain't dead, Curly. How'd you like to bust out of here?"

I am shocked. But I'm willing.

This time Sergeant Bush has brought Lucy. She reaches up to me, and I take her hand, hold it delicately so I won't mark her with my claws. She is armored and carries a spitter in her other hand. She has a purposeful air.

I don't know what to say, but Sergeant Bush, wearing an uncharacteristic look of worry, begins to tell me of the plan. As he speaks, I sense movement, and a half-dozen men move closer, into the light from my alcove. I find it difficult to match them to any of the human types I have observed in the Museum. All bear the scars of age and other scars as well. They are dressed ludicrously in the uniforms of the Museum maintenance crew, pulled hastily over their own outer garments of poorly cured leather. They are armed; I catch a glimpse of a splinter-gun under one flapping smock. For some reason all are wearing cheap wigs in the current style. The air smells of fear and anticipation.

The plan is simple. I am to go out with the trash. It is an eminently practical plan, Sergeant Bush assures me, and I reluctantly release Lucy's hand. I will depart my home of thirty-four years stuffed into a plastic sausage of garbage. There will be no trouble, he tells me, but we must hurry. Several of the less intrepid of the conspirators nod heartily. They are consumed with impatience to get me, and an adequacy of garbage, into the giant tube that they are unfolding. I stand straight on the plinth, while Lucy reaches for the button.

Success! The geriatric raid on the Museum has succeeded. In rigid oblivion was I carried through the intestine of the Museum and deposited into an autobarge. The autobarge was boarded by elderly pirates, and so now I am outside the Pale, stashed in Lucy's flop two doors down from the Slick Pit. Outside is different. I thought it was gray desperation Outside, but such is not the case. Few wear armor here, unless they go to raid the Pale. There seems little malice in these raids; they are just entertainment to the raiders, but they will burn the Museum, and that is sad.

The first thing that Sergeant Bush did here was to find a buzz to disconnect the timer on my button. The buzz trudged in, a small, angular man in a dirty coverall, bearing an immense instrument rack. He laughed when he saw the timer. Lucy switched me off for the removal of the timer, but she later told me that the buzz required nothing more than a pair of clippers and a pocket fuser to set me free. After he woke me he welded a lock plate over the button, keyed to my palm signature. He never acknowledged the strangeness of the situation or asked any questions.

It is a strange world here after the sterility of the Museum. I welcome Lucy's company, but she spends many hours at work most nights, and these are long, not as pleasant. But still, I'm alive.

The change in my circumstances is too great for me to absorb yet. Day changes to night and again to day, and I am still here. It's far beyond remarkable, for me.

Sergeant Bush visits often. He becomes a different man here, but still I admire him. He says the Museum has not noticed my departure from storage, and I think that they won't notice before the museum falls to the Palerunners.

The people who live beyond the Pale are nothing like those who came to view me in the Museum. There are the abject, in great numbers. But also the mighty prowl, predators who live beyond the Pale for the freedom to reave. And between these two extremes are a greater variety of people than I would have suspected could exist. I am by no means the most bizarre of the dwellers Outside.

I crave the oblivion of the button sometimes. This only happens when Lucy is at work. I ask her to call back

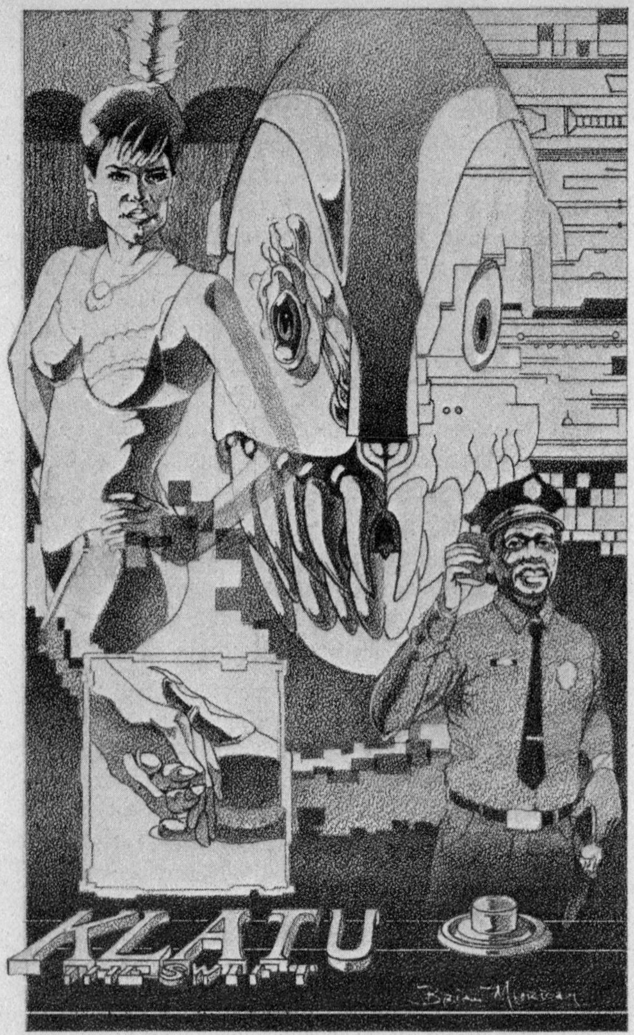

Illustrated by Brian Patrick Murray

the buzz, and I ask him to reconnect the timer and modify it to my control, that I may sleep and awaken when I choose.

I have gained employment. The Slick Pit has need of a doorman; the last one succumbed to religion. The work is within my capabilities, for to enter, the patrons must edge by me in the narrow hall inside the door, one at a time. No one gets in free on my shift.

The pay is not bad, for a being with my handicaps. In order not to alarm the customers, Lucy glued zippers artfully to my hide, dyed me a lurid color, and dressed me in shoes and gloves. I am regarded as a somewhat stale publicity device. The owners of the Slick Pit believe that I am a very large man obsessed with a costume. They did wonder why I never step down from the powered plinth that I ride everywhere. Again the buzz was invaluable, mating my plinth to a floater power unit. Now I have mobility, another freedom. Lucy tells everyone that I am crippled, that my legs are artificial, that the plinth is an eccentric prosthesis. She is an artful improviser, and no one is very curious.

The old men who rescued me from the Museum are devoted to Lucy, and no rumor of what really happened that night has escaped their tightly clamped lips. They are all regulars at the Slick Pit, like the majority there, small elderly men who wear their hair in unusual shapes and colors. They dance with each other, not because of strayed biological impulses, but because few small elderly women frequent the bar. Lucy says the bones of women become brittle with age before the bones of men, and the dancing is too energetic for the wives and companions of the old men.

Others do come to the Slick Pit, in particular heavy young women, wearing a guise of exaggerated femininity.

Most of these are there for no reason that I can guess, but I have learned the smell of a similar group, less well-groomed, more aggressive. These dance too roughly with the old men, sending some to the bonesetters. When one of these appears in my doorway, sweating with anticipation, I bar her way.

I enjoy employment. My time is more interesting, and I can gradually repay Sergeant Bush, who advanced me the money to pay the buzz for my modifications. And I am proud to be able to contribute to our living expenses.

My time with Lucy is sweet to me, though she resembles the females of my race only in size. Sergeant Bush built us a bed, hung to the wall so that with the plinth parked beneath it, Lucy and I can lie down touching. What we do there is strange, but satisfactory to both of us.

Today I called in the buzz for the last time. I no longer want the button; I have him weld a permanent cover over it.

I've learned to sleep. Lucy tried to discourage me from this course, because I will wear out a few decades sooner if I am active all the time. I do not wish to outlast her, in the first place, and in the second, well, I have learned to sleep, something that my creator never intended for me.

In time, I will learn to dream.

An Idea That . . .
by
Gene Wolfe

About the Author

Gene Wolfe is a Texan, a veteran of Korean combat, a former editor on a plant engineering trade journal, and, now, a Midwestern suburbanite father and husband whose office is down in his basement rather than at the other end of a commutation ticket. In his mid-fifties, he holds most of the major awards for SF writing, is also the author of considerable prose in many other fields, and is one of SF's major poets. To read his work is not to see the muddy-booted infantryman at first; it is to see the man who married his childhood sweetheart and still holds her hand unabashedly in public.

But the soldier is there, as well; so is the man who graduated in engineering from the University of Houston. In a career that has already enriched SF with such ornaments as his Book of The New Sun *tetralogy and many a short story as elegantly constructed as a Swiss chronometer, he has deployed all his aspects in the service of his art. He smiles sweetly and readily; he also snaps out short answers to foolish questions. You may take it as given that down in his basement he is ready to smile at his latest creation, just as soon as he is done being ruthless with it.*

No further ado is required. What follows is a masterpiece of telling you the difference between a piece and a masterpiece:

Dear Contestant,

I was one of the judges who read your story; the editor has asked me to write you and explain why it isn't here.

Let me begin by acknowledging that I am not an infallible judge. Nobody is. Only time, the accumulated judgements of thousands of readers, is infallible. And time is infallible only because we declare it so, having chosen it as the standard by which all stories are to be judged. I've read forgotten stories that seemed excellent to me, and I've read "classic" stories that seemed like limping failures.

Nevertheless, there's some consistency. I picked the three stories I thought best in one quarter's entries, and you'll find all three of them in this book. Unfortunately, as I said, yours isn't among them.

I'm sorry it isn't. You had a good idea there, you have a way with words, and you worked very hard. You probably felt you *deserved* to win; and in a very real sense, you were right. But there were other writers—the new writers whose names and stories appear in this book— who deserved it more, including many who deserved it in a way you didn't. These were writers who entered stories of professional quality, and not just good, solid, amateur fiction.

(Have *I* ever written an amateur story? Oh, yes indeed! Dozens of them. No doubt I'll write more, if I'm not run over by a truck soon after I complete this. I don't think there are many of us who don't produce a good, solid, amateur story now and then. You've sent me a note occasionally to let me know I let you down, remember?)

Acquaintances are always giving writers ideas for stories, and sometimes we get letters—and unfortunately, phone calls—from people who have an absolutely great, sure-fire, world-shaking idea they'll share fifty-fifty (or maybe sixty-forty), if we'll just do the writing. "And that'll be a snap. It'll practically write itself."

Most of us stopped listening a long time ago. The fact is that it's very easy to get a good idea for a story. The world is full of them; there's an idea in every dust mote and every broomstick, and there are scores if not hundreds in every man, woman, and (especially) child you pass on the street.

What about style, then, which I called "a way with words" a moment ago? And what about all your hard work? Terrific, both of them, and I loved you for them. They made your story a whole lot better than it would have been otherwise. And yet, strictly speaking, neither was absolutely necessary. Good stories have been written by people who were barely capable of putting them down on paper. Much better ones have been written by talented people who sat down, dashed them off, and sent in the first draft.

Do you know anything about costuming and masquerades? I judged a masquerade a couple of months ago in which all the contestants had filled out forms asking how long they'd worked on their costumes. We judges were given these forms when we retired to decide the awards. Since we had the forms, we tried to correlate the time needed to create each costume with the quality of the costume we had seen.

And we found we couldn't—there was no correlation. Some costumes had taken six weeks, and one, if I remember correctly, six months; the grand prize winner had been created in less than ten days. Stories can be like that, sometimes.

Just about every conceivable way of making a costume was represented, too. Some of the costumers had worked in cloth, some in plastic or rubber, some in papier-maché, some in fur. Most had combined two or three materials when they felt they were appropriate.

Ideas were significant, but not especially so. The grand prize winner had used a fantasy idea that's been around at least since the Middle Ages. The prize for the best science-fiction costume went to a contestant who'd taken his idea from one of my books and made no secret of it. What matters, you see, is what masqueraders call the "finish" of the costume—what is done with the idea, the time, and the materials. Would it be good enough for a Broadway show or a big-budget film? Really, now . . . is it professionally done and professionally exciting?

Perhaps your trouble is that you're used to approaching stories (including your own) like a reader. The first thing that strikes you is the idea. If it's a good new idea, that's great. But if it's a good *old* idea, that hardly matters. (I used to work for a man who would read post-nuclear holocaust stories, and nothing else.) You may or may not also notice the style, and you certainly notice the effect the story had on you—whether it made you want to call up some friend and tell him all about it, for example. Now that you've written some stories of your own, you may speculate about the amount of work the author put into the story, though if you're honest with yourself I think you'll admit you can seldom come to any firm conclusion about that. But you've had too much fun just reading the story to notice what was actually going on in it.

When you write a story of your own, you start with a good idea. You try to get the style right for the particular story you're writing (because no one style is right for every story). You work hard because you notice that the harder you work the better the story gets. Then you discover that your story doesn't have the effect on others that you know it should and you don't know why. I'm going to tell you—watch my lips.

You didn't really *do* much with your idea. You unconsciously assumed that because it was such a fine, strong, sleek, and even potentially dangerous idea, it could run the story by itself. Let's change the metaphor. There are tigers in zoos and there are tigers in circuses. The tigers in zoos are strong and sleek and beautiful, and potentially quite dangerous, but they don't do anything. The tigers in circuses are no stronger, no sleeker, no more beautiful, and no more dangerous, but they do things that surprise us and perhaps even frighten us a bit. We see them in action. People pay to get into circuses, but zoos are free. Now do you get the picture?

If I could give you just one piece of advice for the story you're going to enter in the next contest, it would be this: Think of yourself as a wild beast trainer and your idea as a big cat in your show, walking out onto the stage and saying, "Hey, look at my lion," isn't going to cut it. So what show—not what *kind* of show, that's amateur talk—are you going to put on? Is your idea going to jump through a hoop of flame? Is it going to climb onto the shoulders of two other ideas and roar?

Well, oil up your whip and make sure you've got a good, stout chair, because somebody's going to have to make it do that, and that somebody is you. You've got an idea in your head, and that's good; now let's see you put your head in the idea's mouth.

Faithfully,

Gene Wolfe.

A Sum of Moments
by
Laura E. Campbell

About the Author

Laura Campbell says: "I entered the contest because everyone in my writers' group had. I hoped to win some desperately needed money (I did, just when I was at my most desperate!) The payment for the anthology should get me through another desperate time."

Not to sound melodramatic, but also not to gloss the truth, desperation is hope's handmaiden in the arts. Some even hold the theory that desperation is needful to creativity. We doubt that latter proposition, but few are the writers who are not thoroughly familiar with fear. They are not, in that aspect, any different from anyone else who has to step up before an audience and not make a fool of themselves. The thing about writers—and illustrators, and other forms of artists/craftpersons—is that they volunteer for this excruciating position. And by definition, when they are just beginners, they are stepping up with very few defenses and not too many surefire ways of bedazzling the audience. Many a seasoned professional, looking back, stares in wonder at his younger self and realizes that only naiveté prevented him from realizing how hopeless it was.

If it's any comfort, Laura Campbell, it doesn't get any better. It does get different. The desperations occur on different sorts of scales, and there are sophisticated evolutions in the ingenuities with which the world and the artist conspire to mutually enmesh themselves. But it's the same old thing, really; it's always the same question: Am I going to carry it off this time? And then there's: If I do, will they appreciate it? Will they pay me; will they show they're not just nodding polite agreement . . . will they applaud, and, if so, how loud?

Lonely. They say it's a lonely profession, and it is; all you have, in the end, is your own resources and the hope that your mind can still use them, some how, some way. Rather like the hero of the story that follows. Rather like both the heroes. . . .

When I was six, my parents sent me to a monastery. There was little else to do with me. I had four elder brothers, so it was not likely I would ever inherit. I had absolutely no talent they could make use of, and I was just another mouth to fill. They might have sent me to Broadens, where I could have come home to visit on holidays, but they decided to make a clean break of it and instead sent me to Gildard, which was within sight of the Capital and far enough away so that even my letters would have taken weeks to get to them, had I chosen to write.

At Gildard I showed no more ability with animals than I had at home, and I was just as bad at deciding which was weed and which was crop down there at the end of my hoe. My voice was no better than the croak it had been, my arm no better at cutting wood, my mind no better at learning history. But the Brothers continued to look for worth, as they did with everyone, and discovered I had a steady hand for small things within an arm's reach. I was apprenticed as a scribe.

Being close to the Capital, Gildard did the King's parchments: his formal proclamations, awards, gifts and summons. Unlike the government papers in the far away Port cities where, it was rumored, like-copies were made by the hundreds and not one of them could be told from the other, tradition required of our work that each piece be individual and at the same time beautiful and perfect. It was a skill that took years to master.

It was during my time of apprenticeship that I met Idzik, up in the dayroom with its rows of desks under bright windows and its warm smell of wet ink and new paper. To us, the young apprentices, he seemed a thousand years old. His body was thin, his face lined, his almost translucent white hair wispy and scraggly. His hands were huge, ink-stained, and all bones and ropey veins. He had no beard, though it would have been appropriate. His nose was long and the only straight line on him. His face was long to match and the eyes dark and very deep, almost hidden under unruly white brows.

He moved with a slowness and carefulness that seemed, to us, dreamlike. The paper appeared to come to his hand, so slow was the reach, so anxious the vellum. The ink almost put itself on the paper, the pen hanging over each letter for separate small eternities. The end results were always magnificent, and furthermore, somehow, any given page was done in little more time than it took any other master. How this could be was a mystery to all of us boys, but no more so than the man himself.

We talked and whispered of curses and enchantments, though the Brothers told us there were no such things. Yet *something* had obviously happened to Idzik. Talk to him one day, assuming you could get his attention, and he would talk as any other man with somewhat limited experience. He could follow a conversation even to the point of coming back to the beginning, and he would make sense. But speak to him of the day before and you met with a blankness as complete as if someone had wiped a slate.

He did have his fund of constant knowledge. He knew his lettering, he knew where to go to sleep or eat or rest in the sun. Sometimes it even seemed he could learn certain things, for if you presented yourself to him steadily, day after day, he eventually came to recognize you—though not always your name—as if repetition might force some kind of pathway to his brain. This, though, was a rare thing.

Idzik was not required to teach the apprentices, but because of his Master status, we had, each in turn, to serve a number of periods as his assistant. We were to bring him his paper, refill his inks, bring water. In between, we were to study the manner in which he made each stroke, the way he held his pens, the way he cut them when a tip was no longer suitable. Generally, this meant long hours simply standing at the ancient master's elbow.

Occasionally, however, Idzik would stop his work and move his gaze to one's miserable self, studying carefully, just as Brother Laine does his bugs and worms. The eyes that looked were clear, and so deep they seemed endless; they were not the rheumy eyes of an old man. What they saw, he never said, and I could not tell if they were searching my soul or his own.

This often frightened the other apprentices, as it did me at first, but nothing more than this ever happened. For myself, I found that I was intrigued by his existence. The rest of us can look to events a year back, many years back, and see how we ourselves fit into them. We are not the moment, but the sum of our moments, and Idzik did not have that. He gathered no history behind him, and therefore I wondered how he had gathered a Self.

In time I discovered I enjoyed being in his company. He made no demands in exchange for his companionship, either in the present or for the future, and this was more to my liking than were the ways of the young men of my own age. He was comfortable, constant, and his attentions,

Illustrated by David Dees

though strange, were always tender, his words seeking to know you, if only for the instant.

For Idzik's part, he seemed to like it best when I took him for walks outside the gates, especially in the spring when the area around Gildard burst forth in an ecstacy of color beyond which I had never seen elsewhere. He would stroll about for hours—to the point of *my* exhaustion—muttering, "Yes, yes . . . ah . . . yes," as if the new spring growth meant something beyond what we could see. Brother Laine said this was simply the change in the angle of the light that fell upon us (though Brother Staphon implicated the flower perfumes, too). Didn't we all become a little crazy then! Indeed, work generally got done, but sleep did not, then. Appetites varied with the change in the wind, and prayers evolved into song as often as plowing did into dance.

And so life had been in the monastery, I was told, for generations before. So we expected it to continue—until one year the Army marched through our fields just as the new shoots were coming up.

When the thunder, the ground shaking, and the sea of bodies had passed, there was left across the hills a wide swath of muddy dirt on which nothing grew the rest of the year. Eight days later we had word that the Capital had fallen, and the work we scribes had been trained to do was, for the time being, not needed.

It was a swift change: from a King and a Government which had wished to protect us and our ways, to an Army which wanted our people to come to a new age by way of making our Capital a Port. The King had been opposed to this, for, he had said, while there were good things that could come from off-worlders, that which would come with a Port would bring evil, too. But he had evidently not been strong enough to defend his view.

The Brothers waited for further word about the conquerors while the planting and plowing went on, the cleaning and airing continued, and we scribes helped where we could. Criers came through, then, declaring that as long as no one bothered those in control of the Capital, nothing would be done to the rest of the country. The tensions we had pretended not to feel disappeared, and Gildard went back to ignoring the politics of the lay people.

The first day I took Idzik outside again, he stood for a long time, gazing thoughtfully at the dark brown scar which slashed across the fields. Finally he walked to the pocked earth, and, bending closer, asked, "What was it?"

"An army," I explained, knowing he had no memory of the noisy passing.

"An army?" he said, standing up. "Did they want me?"

"No!" I laughed. "Should they?"

He merely shrugged and walked away.

The next day he found the scar again and examined it as closely as the first time. "An army," he mumbled to himself when I explained it for a second time.

We did this again and again until I gave up repeating and he gave up asking, though he would touch the hardening earth and look to where the mark led.

In between, we celebrated spring nights. We were allowed to dance outside the walls of the monastery. Brother Timor would play his Owda, his fingers flying over the strings of its wide belly. We would dance in lines or in pairs, arms on each other's shoulders, feet stomping the ground in joy, our free arms and our faces lifted to the heavens.

Idzik danced that spring—the first and only time I had seen him do so. It was a strange dance with many dips of the knees, done slowly and in so studied a manner that it seemed almost as if the information to his muscles was coming from somewhere else. He danced on and on, each of us expecting him to stop from fatigue, but on he went until we could do nothing else but clap and ululate in appreciative response. We cheered Idzik when he finished; he simply walked away.

A bit later, when he seemed to have come out of the almost trance-like state he had walked away in, I asked him where the dance came from. He sighed. "The body knows, not I," he told me. Then he smiled suddenly. "The body knows everything, but it doesn't often tell."

A few days later, soldiers came marching back up the hills, led by their be-medaled officers and bringing with them men who moved and dressed differently from any I'd seen. This was my first look at off-worlders.

None of these people looked like pleasant beings. None of them sounded or acted like people I had grown up with or had lived with in the monastery. Yet they must have been the sons and brothers of families somewhere. I wondered, then, what there was about soldiering that might change a man—if, indeed, that was the case.

They were brusque with us, marching in our gates without leave or ceremony, and then they demanded in loud voices that our men must go back with them to the Capital. They needed help to build the Port, they shouted, and they were gathering workers from every village and other establishment.

"It's called conscription," Brother Staphon, our most worldly Brother, told us.

An off-worlder turned to face him. "If you like."

"That means you have no choice," Brother Staphon continued.

"We will take volunteers first, of course," the off-worlder answered in a growl. "If there are not enough . . ." He waved a well-muscled, well-fatted hand toward us.

High Brother Mickel told them we would be happy to send a few men now, and more later when the spring work was done. He offered ten, and perhaps ten more in a week or so. . . .

A command was shouted, the army made a loud and massive show of arms, and when they left they took half our population—almost all the younger men—without our being able to do anything about it.

We didn't dance that night, but sat huddled in groups. Fear sat with us and we didn't know what to do with it. We prayed, but underneath we were not calm. Even Idzik was infected, as he moved about constantly, muttering to himself, until I, at least, came close to becoming angry with him.

Brother Timor must have noticed, for he came over to me and put a hand on my shoulder. "He does that when he has attacks of memory," he commented, looking at Idzik. "Poor man. What a time to have memories."

I understood the gentle rebuke and huddled next to Tuan, the only other one of my age who had not been taken. I was small and thin. Tuan, as a child, had fallen off a cliff while tending his father's flock. His left leg was bent and twisted, and though he could walk, it was not well nor fast. No doubt the off-worlders had not wanted defective men.

With our depleted number all of us had to work at two or more jobs, many of which we had not done before. It was true that most of our experience and expertise still remained at Gildard in the form of our older Brothers, but the backs and arms to accomplish the labor were severely limited. Everything went slowly. We prayed for our

Brothers in the Capital.

Idzik had to know, day by day, that something was wrong, if only for the small number of people around. But he didn't ask. At the same time, I heard one of our older Brothers comment that Idzik was not sleeping well at night, and during the day one could find him constantly in motion, muttering soft nonsense to himself.

A week from the day the army had invaded our gates, Brother Aimes stumbled into the courtyard and collapsed in Brother Staphon's arms. He was bleeding and badly bruised. His clothes were torn and filthy.

The work was hard, he moaned, but they could do it well, given the time and a few safety precautions. But the off-worlders and the army wanted it done fast and their way only. Anyone who protested was beaten in front of the others and then beaten in a cell. Two of our Brothers had already died in an accident which could have been prevented with a little extra scaffolding. But no one would listen to him about this. No one! he cried.

Brother Staphon held the poor man and rocked him there in the dirt of the yard. "Some low-bidding, two-bit outfit," he snapped. It didn't mean anything to me, but Idzik was suddenly stooping next to him.

"Not legit, you think?" he asked.

Brother Staphon looked up at him for a long moment. "Not likely."

Idzik got up and wandered away, twisting his thumbs in alternating grips as he obviously tried to pursue some thought. We let him go and took Brother Aimes away from the courtyard to be washed and ministered to.

In the middle of the night a hand shook me roughly, and a voice hissed at me. When I managed to bring my mind from some far-off dream place to the dark world of my room, I saw a face peering at me. It was a mask of shadow and light in unreal combination, and I drew in a squeaky breath. The hand which had been on my shoulder covered my mouth.

"If you bite me, you make a mistake," a voice whispered and I recognized it as Idzik's. I nodded and moved away from the hand. "Dress," he said. "I need your skills."

I did so quickly, not questioning the demands of an elder, even if he were not an ordained Brother. We stopped and roused Tuan too, he seeming to wake more quickly than I. We both followed Idzik to one of the old buildings left over from a time when the monastery had been larger. The main room echoed eerily as he led us to a corner piled with blankets and lit with an old lamp.

Tuan and I gratefully tumbled into the blankets, shaking not so much from the chilly night but from the excitement of an unprecedented happening. Idzik, meanwhile, arranged himself in front of us slowly and with great dignity. We waited, not speaking. When at last he was settled, he reached to one side and brought out a battered wooden box. From this he withdrew, one by one, many small scraps of paper with bits of writing on them. Some were old-looking and dirty from handling, others were fresher, crisper and unwrinkled. One almost in front of me bore the words Brother Staphon had said in the courtyard that afternoon.

When the box was empty, he looked up. "You," he said, looking at each of us, "keep your important thoughts up here." He touched the side of his head with a large, boney hand, then gestured to the paper around him. "I keep mine there . . . though . . ." He stopped and smiled wistfully. "Though . . . I could not tell you at the moment just why any of them *are* important."

He stared at us in the dark as if he expected an

answer, but neither Tuan nor I moved. Idzik's smile faded and he sighed.

"Sometimes I'll have a thought ... out of the fog ... unconnected," he whispered. "A taste of another time."

He held up a piece of paper. "Sometimes this happens—memories happen—more in the spring. Brother Laine said it might be the angle of the sun . . . or a shift in, uh, magnetic fields . . . or . . ." Idzik tossed the paper aside with a shrug. "He might have said more, but I must have had only a small scrap."

Hidden under the blankets, Tuan poked me in the ribs with an elbow. I ignored it.

Idzik's face had suddenly gone blank and we sat for some moments until Tuan leaned over and whispered in my ear, "We could grow cobwebs here."

Idzik stirred, then sat up, bristling. "You will not let me sleep!" he demanded, shuffling the papers together again. "*You,*" he said, pointing to me, "will go to sleep now! *You,*" he directed Tuan to pens and paper near the wall, "will write! *I* am going to look for a thought."

Though I did curl up in the blankets with my head on one arm, I was too excited and curious to drift off to sleep just then. I watched as Tuan sat against the wall, pen in hand, apprentice-quality paper on a board on his lap. Idzik, in his place, leaned over the litter of scraps and mumbled to himself. The scraps went into different piles, the piles were rearranged. Occasionally he would indicate that Tuan should copy something.

Eventually I did fall asleep and it was late morning when Tuan woke me and told me to take over for him. He handed me a list of seemingly unrelated thoughts carefully lettered on several sheets of paper. In my turn Idzik added more to these, some apparently from his papers and some which seemed to come solely from his own mind.

We stayed in that small corner, which Idzik had supplied with food, for a day and two nights, venturing out only to relieve ourselves and stretch a bit. If anyone was curious about what we were doing, none showed it.

Idzik stayed awake all the first night and all the next day. The longer he stayed awake, the more he talked without benefit of his notes and the more he had us write down. Still, there were relatively long pauses where he would sit and say nothing. During one of these pauses early the next evening his eyes slowly shut and he slipped into a light sleep. Both Tuan and I knew we should rouse him, but we were reluctant to handle an elder. By the time we had decided that perhaps we had better, no matter our fears, he had awakened himself.

He straightened and yelled—the first time I ever heard him do so—"YOU MUST NOT LET ME SLEEP!"

Tuan performed a meek, seated bow. "One must sleep sometime."

Idzik glared at him for a while, but finally sighed and agreed that, yes, he did need to sleep a little. But only for an hour at a time, and *only* when he told us that that was what he intended to do.

So we set up a new schedule. Idzik would sleep his hour. He would read what he had had us write down earlier. Then we would continue as before. By this time he had begun revising, too: crossing out some of what he had written, condensing, regrouping certain thoughts, and at times going so far as to grab the pen out of our hands and scribble words himself, even though he said having to letter slowed down his thinking.

He kept no information having only to do with living in the monastery. Yet Tuan and I heard and remembered.

We learned that he must have been there an incredibly long time—perhaps as long as forty years—which meant the current inhabitants had, in a way, inherited him. He had apparently come in his present condition, already an old man with no past but his name.

Before that—Tuan and I sat in stunned silence when we heard—before that, Idzik had been an off-worlder! And not just one who had come to live here, but one of those who had carried the others in ships that never landed. He had gone from star to star and had watched, he said, the worlds age before him, as each return trip passed more than a generation on the planet and only months in the stars.

This made no sense to us, nor did his explanation of it, with its strange words such as "time dilation" and its strange "fact" that apparently when things travel at a great speed, time is different for them than for those not so traveling.

Idzik went on to insist that it was this "fact" which made travel between star systems possible at all, for without it, crews would need to repopulate themselves as they aged, too, and even what could be transported would then be limited. When he finished, however, he continued mumbling to himself about the problems inherent in the situation, and how every freight company and governing body constantly sought ways around them.

I was not sure I understood anything any better after his explanation, and from the here-he-goes-again look on Tuan's face, it seemed he did not, either. Speaking of this had done something to Idzik, though, because he became lost in thoughts he did not seem to want to share with us or have us write down. He remained that way until it was my turn to sleep. I settled down in the blankets, surrounded by an unnerving silence.

I awoke around dawn to see Idzik reading and rocking back and forth, while Tuan slept hunched over his writing board. Idzik seemed alert and well, but my own body ached and protested the condition of too little sleep and too little physical activity.

Idzik looked up at me as I pushed the blankets off. "I need a guide," he said. His voice sounded vaguely different; less hesitant, perhaps. "Dress for walking."

He got up then, slowly, carefully unbending folded limbs, but once he was upright he hurried off with surprising speed.

"I suppose that leaves me with this to clean up," Tuan grumbled, eyes open now, his back against the wall. It was a good-natured complaint, however. He didn't like leaving the grounds.

I went to wash and to put on traveling clothes. I went to the kitchen too, twice, coming back to the courtyard each time, but it was late morning before Idzik arrived leaning on Brother Staphon's arm.

Brother Staphon looked down at me as I rose to meet them. "You must take care of our Master Idzik," he said. "Do as he says, but take care of him."

"Yes, Reverend Brother," I bowed, looking from one to the other. "But where are we going?"

"To the Port," Idzik said impatiently, taking my arm and practically pulling me along. "Where else?"

Where else indeed? We could have wound up almost anywhere, as I had been down to the valley so few times that I was often unsure of the way. But Idzik walked so slowly, reading over his notes, adding to them and rearranging as we went, I had plenty of time to puzzle out the way.

Idzik had had his hair cut that morning so that it was

half a finger's length at its longest on top and very short on the sides and back. So light and fine was his hair that this almost made him seem bald. I carried a bundle, besides our food, which contained an odd-looking garment some of the Brothers had hastily made that day. Few words passed between us until our midday meal.

We ate at the junction to the main road. Idzik drank sharp-smelling liquid from a dark bottle, not passing any to me. "To keep me awake," he said. I could have used something of the sort myself, but did not say anything about it. Instead I found my mouth asking, "Is it sleep which takes away your memories?"

Idzik leaned forward and touched my arm with one long hand, the nails of which were black around the cuticle. "Good reasoning, young fellow!" he smiled. "Though it needn't be sleep. Any lack of concentration can do it."

He shook his head. "Even daydreaming can be a real thief."

"Were you cursed?" I asked before the hand which I clapped over my mouth could keep from letting those words out. The Brothers forbade such talk.

Idzik stood up creakily, having apparently finished his meal. I crammed the remainder of my food in my mouth, embarassed that I had actually asked such a question, embarassed at the long silence. I hastened to put the odds and ends back into the pack.

"Not cursed as *you* mean, little Brother," Idzik suddenly said. "Though some would say certainly cursed."

"I do not understand," I went on timidly. I was immensely curious and had never before dared to say these things, but I also feared to offend.

Idzik put his hand on my shoulder in preparation for walking. "I don't entirely myself," he said. "But it should be interesting finding out."

The usual journey of a long day took us almost two, Idzik catching his hour of sleep before and after my night-long one. I was too tired to notice what he did with himself while I slept, but he looked better in the morning than I felt. My body did not enjoy the ground as much as it did my narrow bed.

As we approached the Port I decided I wouldn't have minded a journey of a week, however, if it would have kept me from seeing what we did. What had once been a pretty, if not particularly productive minor valley had been turned into something ugly; great masses of ground covered over with some gray, dead-looking material. Here and there skeletons of buildings rose from this barren waste and everywhere small figures of men, unreal and ant-like, swarmed over the structures. I do not know what I expected Idzik to do—lodge a formal complaint, I suppose—but instead he steered us in a wide circle so that we were not seen by anyone at the growing Port. He found us a tiny hollow, over-covered with brush, and had us stop there and take our dinner. Again, as at each meal, he drank the dark liquid, offering me some that time. I tried a small cup, but the stuff was horribly bitter and strong. I did not finish what he gave me.

As the sun went down Idzik grew restless. He still moved slowly, but so constantly he reminded me of one of the busy field rodents. Finally, he pulled the garment I had carried from out of my pack and began to dress himself in it.

It was a fitted piece of clothing, though loosely so. It was completely unlike our draped robes, and though it would not have stood close scrutiny, I knew it was supposed to look like one of the suits the commanding off-worlders wore. It was a silvery blue—several shades darker than the real thing, but not so noticeable in the darkness—with painted markings on the sleeve and over the left breast. Most I did not understand, but the one on the breast spelled out I.D. Zickman.

"Is that a name of renown?" I asked, pointing.

He looked down at himself. "More of infamy, I think. But it might save our Brothers." He put his hand on my shoulder again. "Come now, find me the Port."

We stumbled along until the greater moon rose. It was not quite full and gave us fairly good light. The walking was also easier once we left the slopes, but we were stopped in a bit by a wide ditch filled with what must have been broken glass and some nasty-looking wire.

Without a word Idzik handed me heavy gloves and some short-nosed shears from a pouch he had been carrying. I took them, holding them for him, until he gestured toward the ditch, making clipping motions with his hand. Unhappily, I climbed down into the pit, going very slowly and carefully. We both wore heavy boots, but a fall would have been extremely painful. Idzik sat himself on the edge and waited, while I cut and pushed my way through the wire.

"Guards!" I suddenly heard him mutter, with what almost sounded like a tone of delight. I straightened quickly.

"Guards," I whispered.

I thought I heard him chuckle—a strange sound from what I had known as a quiet, serious man. "There's no guards!" he called to me, while I cringed at the noise. "They didn't even *consider* that someone would try to get in!"

No one had come to investigate the area by the time I had reached the other side. I tried to peer through the dark to see exactly how far we were from the buildings, but the light was deceiving. I worked my way back to Idzik.

"Wait for me here," he said, taking the gloves. "Right here, nowhere else!"

"Yes. Of course." I sat where he pointed.

"Here!" he commanded again. I nodded.

He walked across where I had gone through. Every so often he would turn and pull some of the cuts back together so that one did not notice the damage that had been done. Perhaps this was to make me appear innocent of anything should someone happen by. Perhaps it was neatness.

When he climbed from the pit on the other side I could just barely make him out by the glint of the moonlight on his silver clothing. He did not walk or even run from the ditch, though, but moved along as if he were dancing! A mocking, juvenile dance it was, too. What had happened to the slow-moving, feeble man at whose elbow I had stood for so many years? I wondered.

I lost track of him in the dark, even though he was bobbing and skipping enough to attract much attention. My fears kept me from moving from where I had been ordered to be, but the quietness of the night and the boredom of my duty may have caused me to doze off, even sitting in the open like that. Suddenly the noise of frightened, perhaps even dying animals filled the night, almost causing me to fall off my ledge. Moments later a figure appeared on the other side of the ditch, descended, picked its way through the wire, opening false obstacles and closing them behind him. It was only this sight of Idzik, coming grinning toward me, that kept me from bolting.

"Haven't had so much fun . . . in . . ." He giggled! ". . . longer than I can remember!" Idzik reached out a hand for me to pull him up.

"What did you do?" I asked.

"Woke them up!" He waved his arms, still grinning, still panting a bit.

"Is that the noise off-worlders make when awakened?" I said, still wondering at the wail.

"Sirens, my young one! Mechanical sound to arouse the unaware to arms."

Who knows how long I might have stood there, my mouth gaping, if Idzik had not turned me around and indicated we should move on. I expected, then, to go back to our hollow, but Idzik directed us around to our left instead.

I looked back as we went along, seeing the now well-lit buildings beyond the ditch moving with life, searching vehicles having been put into motion at their bases. No one seemed to be coming toward the fence. Perhaps Idzik had been right; they hadn't thought someone might disturb them from the outside.

We wound up in a shanty town made partially of new buildings and partially of old construction sitting where once the slums of the village had been. The area seemed to have decided to cater to the Army and the off-worlders, as many taverns and gambling places were in evidence, and even late as it was, noise and loud voices drifted into the streets from most of them. We walked past them all, Idzik now striding along without help from me.

Some of the men on the streets wore garments much like Idzik's was meant to be. Most of the rest wore uniforms, with a few in village clothes wandering here and there. Idzik and I walked in silence, while I tried to behave as if I belonged.

Suddenly Idzik walked directly in front of a large, very drunk off-worlder. The man had no time to stop, and the two met with a loud thump.

"You space-blind, vacuum-brained idiot!" Idzik

growled in such an ugly voice I was not sure, at first, that it had been he.

"Who says, you dreck-mouthed droid?" the other snarled, while eyeing Idzik's name plate.

Idzik let him peer long enough to read it, then barked back, "*I* say, you syntho-bred sumper."

The man puffed up, much like an angry bird. At the same time Idzik crouched and then sprang at the man, striking him with his open hands in several locations and in a highly offensive and pain-causing manner, though the last location may have been an even more offensive pull rather than a poke.

In less time than it takes to tell it, the man went to his knees, moaning, and Idzik began walking away without me, muttering something about something ". . . taking less strength than skill. . . . Good thing."

I caught up with him as he rounded the corner into an alley. Rubbing his fingers, he looked up at me. "I do not think that that conformed to Brother Staphon's idea of nonviolence," he said, then grinned that grin at me, "but I will have to check my notes."

"Why did you do that?" I asked, still feeling shaky.

"Trying to let them know I'm here," he said as he turned another corner into another street, thereby heading us back the way we had come.

"Is that what we came to do?" I think I sounded disappointed.

He took my arm and stopped us. "*We* haven't the means to fight them. So I'm trying to get someone here who can."

"Who?" I demanded.

"Anyone who might be still looking for me."

"Why is anyone looking for you?" I asked sullenly.

"Because I made them mad. Do you have any money?"

The two sentences made no sense together, but when I started to protest, I saw he was looking over my shoulder, beyond me.

"A little. Brother Staphon gave it to me for food."

Turning, I followed Idzik's gesture toward a small boy sleeping on a pile of rags near us. "Wake him and give him whatever you've got," he said.

When I started to say something, he simply nodded at me. I went over and shook the boy, standing back as he sat up to look at us. Rubbing his eyes, he said tiredly, "It'll be a five-piece."

That was all I had. Taking it, he began to climb out of his rude bed, but Idzik waved at him. "Go back to sleep. Tomorrow you tell everyone that Zickman gave you that five. Just gave it to you."

The boy looked from one to the other of us.

"Zickman," Idzik said.

The boy repeated it, looking as confused as I felt. Idzik had him say it again, a couple more times, then turned away, heading back up the street. The boy called after us, asking why we wanted him to do this.

"I'm running for office," Idzik called back over his shoulder.

As soon as we were out of the village, he stopped and asked me what that had meant.

"Running for office?" I asked.

"If that's what I said."

I couldn't tell him. Though I knew all the words, they made no sense together.

"Write it down," he told me, but I had nothing to write with. I told him I'd remember it and would write it down on one of his papers when we got back to our camp.

He began to fairly dance about. "Damn, I wish I could be as sure as that!" he cried. "If I don't catch an idea and tie it down immediately as it comes to mind, it . . ." He fluttered his fingers outward, then shrugged.

"But," he mumbled to himself as he went back to walking slowly, "I am getting better with practice." He was silent, then, all the way back to the hills. At the hollow, he told me to lie down and get some rest. What he did and where he went while I slept, I do not know, for I slept deeply despite the rocks and pebbles under my blanket.

Late in the morning he came and ate with me, twitching and moving as if his skin itched. He snatched at things quickly, but in between would often sit and watch, seemingly contemplating everything he did.

Before leaving again, he insisted I keep out of sight, doing whatever moving around I must very carefully. He went away then and I gathered some brush to lay in the hollow. I spent the day in boredom, watching clouds, insects, and what few birds flew over, while in between, falling often into a light doze. Idzik appeared again for a late dinner, more animated than ever.

"You are going to kill yourself if you keep this up," I commented.

He looked at me in surprise. "Do you think so?" he said, looking down at his arms and legs. "I have had a few pretty sore muscles, but . . . well . . . altogether I feel so good!"

He leaned forward in a conspiratorial manner. "I have memory of four full days and nights now, plus partial memory of a few days before." There was a sparkle in his eye and a mad sort of smile on his face. "Besides that, a lot of old memories are cropping up and then *staying!* It seems I was reading the scars correctly."

I didn't think I had reacted to this but, looking at my face, Idzik unfastened some closure in his pant leg and pulled off a boot. He pointed to several lines of raised scars along the outside edge of his foot.

"A boyhood code I can read as well as lettering. I knew what it said before, of course, but it was never important to me. I was happy where I was."

I looked closely at the purple marks. They were like animal bites more than anything. "What does it say?" I asked cautiously.

"Mostly it says I was right. That I did the right thing."

"And what was it you did?"

"I escaped." He stuck out his chest, then stood up. In an instant, he had disappeared into the twilight shadows.

He came back later that night and we did much the same as the first night. This time there appeared to be mobile guards within the fence, but somehow he got past them, returning to the tune of sirens again. We moved along faster than the previous night and were a long way away when they got to exploring the area of our cuts.

When we reached the village, he attacked no one, however. Instead, very late, when the river fog had come in, we walked into one of the barely lit taverns. We stood in the doorway—or rather he did, as I was behind him—until the crowd inside turned in growing silence to look at us. Then he stepped out, shoving me first, and we slipped into the mists.

I slept through the rest of the night and awoke in the morning a few times to hear Idzik prancing from rock to rock. He wouldn't come down to eat when I asked him, but darted here and there constantly, manic in his activity. I dozed throughout the day, bored with sitting, bored, I regret to say, even with my prayers. We were running out of food and what little we had was stale, so meals, too, had become uninteresting. I nibbled at a midday snack Idzik did not even appear for.

I was dozing again, I suppose, when suddenly the brush above me was yanked away and large, strong hands hauled me from my niche. I struggled and yelled until someone kicked me in the small of the back, then found myself dangling by the armpits between two very tall uniformed men. It was dusk, a difficult time to see in, but the face that came around and stopped in front of me was clearly angry and tired. The man stared at me a long time, and may have been about to say something when behind him, up the hill, a voice called down a very dirty name.

The man whipped around so fast I jerked back despite the hold my captors had on me. I looked up then, and of course it was Idzik, standing on a prominent rock, looking quite cocky. From that distance no one could have guessed it was an old man who stood there. The man to my right raised his free hand and pointed a weapon at Idzik. It produced a loud, high noise and when I dared look again Idzik was gone, but not his funny, taunting laugh. Three of the uniformed men took off up the hill after him, but he appeared in a moment a little higher up and to our left. He waved.

"Don't worry, little one. You're doing just fine," he called.

I didn't think so, as my arms were hurting rather badly, but I didn't want to say anything in front of these men.

The officer turned away from the chase, leaving his men to do what they could on their own. I didn't have much concern for Idzik at the moment. Whereas he had once lived much slower than other men—not even keeping up, really—he was now moving so fast I had my doubts that any ordinary man could catch him.

The men marched me down and around the hill, where, to my surprise, a machine waited for us. I had not heard it coming and should have, even if I had been dozing. I guessed it was some special, silent, off-world invention and I was not going anywhere near it.

I dug in my heels and when they tried to yank me forward I threw my weight back instead, pushing against them, screaming. I fell free, landing rather hard on the ground, knocking the wind out of myself. I turned over somehow and began scrambling in the dirt; hands, feet, knees determined to get up that hill. Suddenly, however, a pair of well-muscled legs appeared in front of me, and feet shod in heavy-soled dark boots. One of them came at me and slammed into the end of my chin.

I woke lying on the floor of a small, gray, dimly lit room with nothing in it but a door and a hole in the roof. My face hurt terribly, below my mouth and in the jaw hinges. My head seemed fuzzy and full of mushy sounds. I crawled into a corner and lay down again, putting a cheek carefully on the cool floor. I slept and woke intermittently while the gray light got brighter and the room uglier.

By and by, I had to relieve myself. I got up carefully and looked around the cell until I found what must have been meant to be used—a stinking hole with a sloping floor around it. It was disgusting and degrading, but I assumed no one watched.

Shortly after that a man came in, followed by another with fewer marks on his uniform. The first man tried to talk to me as if he were my friend. He asked politely about the monastery, having searched me no doubt and found my relics, and he asked me about my friends, my family.

I didn't answer, partly because I had no wish to say anything to anyone who held me captive, and partly because I had no wish to move my mouth.

He persisted, moving into the subject of Idzik as anger crept into his voice. Finally he stopped talking and stared at me for a long moment. Nodding to the second man, he left. That one then proceeded to beat me with his fists and, when I could no longer stand, kicked me until I passed out.

I woke in semi-darkness again, unable to move at all, as each time I tried the abused muscles of my body went into spasm, causing excruciating pain. I lay as still as I could, my face in some sticky substance, and listened to the noises around in the growing dark.

Somewhere nearby many men were coming into an area, individual voices standing out once in a while with some complaint. I listened hard—the only thing I could do without pain—but as the light faded the room also quieted. I may have slept, or it may have been only a short while, but I began to make out whispered conversation between men who seemed just on the other side of the wall. Suddenly I noticed that the name Zickman was a major part of what I could hear!

By listening carefully I gathered that these were some of the "conscripted" workers. They seemed well acquainted with Idzik's exploits; they chuckled over his setting off the alarms, his ghostly appearances in the village, his beating up of the off-worlder (an account much embellished from the original).

After a bit, the talking stopped and I assumed the men slept. In the morning, cold and numb, I tried to move again, but my muscles screamed in protest and I let it be. I was too sore to even shiver properly and I was sure I would die there, alone and filthy. I felt deserted and depressed;

the only thing I could do was pray silently.

The two men from the day before came back, one of them prodding me with his toe as if I were some half-dead creature he had found in his yard. I could only whimper, and they left without saying anything.

As the day warmed up, I slowly regained the use of my body, managing to take myself back to the foul hole in the corner. I passed no blood, so I knew my injuries were not likely to be the cause of my death after all, but I later discovered two loose teeth and a badly misshapen lip.

Someone had left some food, which I could not have eaten even if I had been hungry as it was too putrid for even a scavenger animal. I did drink the water, however, bitter as it was, and felt the better for it.

When the men came back to the nearby room in the evening, I sat against the wall, my ear pressed to the stone to catch every word. They talked of the army still searching the hills for this strange man, Zickman, while the ghost-man seemed to be regarding it as some kind of game, leading the searchers here and there, taunting them at will. The men in the room quietly cheered his every deed, both in the hills and in the compound, though it hardly seemed possible for one person to be in so many places. He seemed to have become some kind of hero to them, doing what they could not, though wanted to.

Someone laughed just on the other side of the wall from me and was shushed. Then two men whispered back and forth in Catalanese, a peasant dialect from the north and one close enough to my own childhood language for me to understand most of it. It seemed a certain amount of the sabotage going on was not being done by Idzik, but by the prisoners themselves, with Zickman being given the credit! Furthermore, the longer I listened, the more it became clear that what they didn't actually know about

Idzik's deeds, they simply filled in with what seemed credible. He had become, in just a couple of days, a legend to these people. He, a man who only a few weeks back would have gotten lost if he had wandered very far from the monastery.

Yet, I was beginning to worry about him. How long could he keep this up before he damaged his body irreparably? Or went crazy from lack of sleep? Or was caught? I doubted his frail body could have taken what they had done to me, and it was certain they wanted him more than they wanted me.

I spent a bad night, the alarms awakening me only to send me back once more to a constant stream of nightmares. In the morning I was stiff again. Examining my bruised body, and particularly my tender and purple abdomen, I cried. In addition, no one brought food or drink; no one even came to look at me.

About midday a horrid rumbling grew in the distance and rose to such a volume I was sure it was a tremendous earthquake rolling our way. I remembered them from when I was a child and I acted as I had then—screaming and scratching at the walls to be let out. Then something shook the cell for an interminable time, rattling the very bones within my body. It mercifully stopped before I had torn my nails out completely.

When I heard the sounds of distant fighting, of a number of weapons being fired, it slowly occurred to me that the people Idzik had been expecting might have arrived. The terrible rumble might have been their ship landing outside. Their soldiers might be rescuing us. No one came for hours, though, and I had collapsed into a corner by the time they did.

It was apparent, immediately, that these were very different people, whoever they might be. Their clothing fitted well and was cared for, unlike those of the earlier soldiers I had seen in that place. Their bearing was upright and controlled, meant to intimidate. Yet they spoke to me gently in a language I didn't know, while they carefully helped me to my feet.

I was taken to a large room filled with other men—peasants, Brothers, farmers, etc.—though my personal guard never left me. There I was examined, as others were, by a man with many instruments. My wounds were washed, my lip pricked and then ripped open only to be reclosed with many tiny stitches, my abdomen pressed and listened to, my head looked at with some kind of box.

Next I was taken by my guard to a slovenly kept office where it was immediately apparent that the man who stood in it was not its usual occupant. If I had thought the men who had come to fetch me were impressive, this man exceeded anything I might have dreamed up.

He was older than the others, but very fit still, his uniform showing that his body, too, was well muscled and hard despite the gray in his hair. His eyes were steady and his bearing one which indicated he was used to having his words obeyed.

"Please sit down," he said. Then he offered water, bread and cheese, not with a pretense of niceness as the other man had, but as common courtesy. I was happy to accept, though I would have liked better to have been able to wash, but that was not mentioned.

"Hello, pup," a voice said behind me and I turned around quickly. There, in the back of the room, sitting in a chair he had managed to prop on its rearmost legs, was Idzik. He was very dirty, what I could see of him at least, but he smiled, and under the dirt his skin glowed with a ruddy flush.

He was not a free man, however. They had wrapped

his upper body in some heavy material so that his arms were held crossed over his chest, hands trapped at his sides. His feet were taped together at the ankle and his boots were gone. Yet under all this restraint, his body was still trying to move. Muscles twitched all over his face and the long muscles in his thighs were visibly spasming. He must have been very uncomfortable despite his smile.

I was too stupid to say anything but, "Idzik!"

"Zickman, Isaac Daniel," he bowed his head. "Late of Earth by way of Daedalus, Darham and . . . damn!"

He was still Idzik of the faulty memory.

"I was worried," I stuttered, finding my lip not particularly painful, but rather stiff. "It was so long . . ."

"Just coming to my peak," he grinned.

I looked back at the officer, and he was studying Idzik carefully. He noticed me then, and, nodding formally, introduced himself as the Commander of the special forces that had landed a bit earlier. His knowledge of our language was good, his accent slight. He took a more casual attitude after the introduction, half-sitting on the front of the desk. "I take it your part in this was incidental," he said to me.

"I needed help early on," Idzik answered him.

"You do not know who this man is, do you?" the Commander asked, ignoring Idzik. "Nor exactly what he has done."

"He is one of our Masters," I said, "and he came to rescue our Brothers." When the man waited as if he expected more, I went on. "We are not allowed to use violence, and we were not great enough in number to stop what was happening at this Port. Master Idzik told me that he thought there were others who might wish to find him and who could possibly stop these people." I hoped I had gotten it right.

"You do not know why anyone would want this man?"

I shook my head.

The Commander crossed his arms. "Do you know what time dilation is?"

I looked back at Idzik. He had had his eyes shut tightly, against the twitching, I suppose. He must have felt me looking at him, for he opened them again. "Go ahead," he nodded.

I parroted back Idzik's lesson on time going slower for things going fast, then added, "But it makes no sense to me," feeling I was betraying something by saying that.

"I know it doesn't appear to," the Commander answered, "but we are talking of speeds far greater than you could imagine. And your 'Master' is correct in saying that it is what makes long-distance travel even possible. He is also correct in saying that people are trying to get around the limitations that even this imposes."

The Commander looked past me toward Idzik. "This man, Captain Zickman, is the only person who may have succeeded."

"I did succeed," Idzik broke in. "Unfortunately."

The Commander cleared his throat. "Service reports describe an experiment in which the Captain was a pilot and co-experimenter on a ship designed and almost entirely outfitted by a Dr. Peter Colbert. Tracking records indicate this ship disappeared from Service screens at one point, and then reappeared near another star far distant from the first after such a short length of time one could call it negligible.

"Unfortunately, Captain Zickman was not lucid upon arrival and Dr. Colbert was dead. Drugs did not seem to bring the Captain around. Furthermore, he seemed to be suffering from some kind of ongoing amnesia that made him unable to remember what had happened to him even a short time before.

"Reports indicate that the Captain may have been purposefully uncooperative, however. This was never confirmed, but the Captain did disappear, implying, of course, that this may have been true."

The Commander paused as if he expected someone to say something. As I knew nothing of any of this, I kept silent. Idzik, too, said nothing, and I somehow was not comfortable with the idea of turning to look at him.

"The Service, all the services, cargo and human, for that matter," the Commander went on,"need this alternative means of travel. They need it to relieve the strain that the current method of travel imposes on societies, on the individual crewmen, on the intercourse between different planets."

The Commander frowned. "At this point, Captain Zickman is our only clue to this alternative means. With Dr. Colbert dead, with what few notes he left behind almost worthless to us, and with the equipment and the ship . . . well . . ."

"I blew it up," Idzik said.

The Commander nodded. "It was, evidently, the one thing he would admit to, even in his amnesia. He was picked up in a lifeboat with none of the equipment or design plans with him."

I did turn around then and looked at Idzik. He seemed to have brought his facial muscles under control.

"Is this other . . . method . . . really a good thing?" I asked him.

The Commander spoke instead. "If one of your Brothers were ill and the only medicine was in a town normally gotten to by walking along a certain road for two days, but which you could reach by a shortcut in two hours, which would you take?"

I felt as if I were back in a novice class, responding to one of the exercises the Brothers had us do. "I would wonder," I said carefully, "why the shortcut wasn't used more often."

"Exactly!" snapped Idzik, making me warm with pleasure at having given the correct answer.

The Commander shook his head gently, as an older Brother often does when exasperated by his student. He looked at the floor for a while, saying nothing, until a shadow appeared in the doorway. He nodded in response to some signal.

"I'll leave you to say goodbye to one another," he said. "I am sorry this happened to your people, to the people of this area. It is just the kind of thing that a trip such as Captain Zickman's might possibly have prevented. These criminals, as it stands now, can move in somewhere and complete a job before we would have any chance of reaching a planet. Your Brothers and the rest were simply fortunate that our unit happened to be licensed to another part of this world and that we were nearby just now. Other places have not been so lucky."

He opened the door, then looked back at Idzik. "You used the fact that your name is well known in the Service to get us here. Perhaps you will reconsider helping *us* when you think of your friends."

He left then, closing the door. I crossed the room, sat near Idzik.

"Is what he said true?" I asked.

Idzik had his eyes closed again, but opened them at the sound of my voice. He was obviously trying to slow himself down from his earlier fevered pitch. "Every word of it," he answered.

"Then why won't you help them?"

He raised his head and looked at me intently. "Because," he said slowly, "because I was there. I watched Colbert screaming and trying to tear himself apart until he died." His voice was very strained, very bitter. "I—I almost did the same. There has never been anything so painful, so ugly, so completely vile in this universe. Never."

He spoke through clenched teeth, his jaw muscles knotting. "No one was ever meant to be in a place like that. There are not even words in any language—*any* language—to describe it."

"They know that?"

"Sure," he said, putting his head against the wall again, visibly releasing the anger he had just held. "But they think that with all their other advances in technology they can take care of this, too."

"Perhaps they can," I said, not wanting Idzik hurt because of stubborness.

"Maybe," he said slowly. He watched me for a moment. Finally he sighed very deeply. "You know, this is what they want you to do. Play the Devil's advocate."

I started to speak, but he shook his head.

"It's all right. When an idea's time has come, there's nothing that will stop it. Not you, not me. Colbert was a crazy man with crazy ideas, but they did not come from a vacuum. Whatever led him to his conclusions will probably lead someone else some time. Unfortunately." He stopped for a moment.

"Unfortunately, because besides making shipping and passenger traffic easier, just as the Commander said, it will also make it a hell of a lot easier to carry on war, too. War," he repeated. "Bombs. Dirty waste. Mass death. I don't want to be any part of that!"

"But you just said——" I broke in.

He shut his eyes and nodded. "Yes. It is just a matter

of time. So I made sure I took care of it this go-round." He opened his eyes to narrow slits and looked sideways at me.

"First, I tried checking things on my own. You know, who had come how far. Didn't seem like much was going on—I'd always thought Colbert was a man centuries ahead of his time, but it's hard to tell these days. I couldn't find out much in this backwater area, even sneaking in and using their information sources here." He sort of smiled apologetically.

"So I went to the next step." He leaned forward a little. "I used their own communication system here, as well as a couple of the old King's semi-defunct ones, to send sealed information with everything I know to every civilian, religious, lobbying, and peace organization I could find a listing for. Ran up a mighty big bill for the monastery, I'm afraid, but at least it won't be anybody's military secret much longer."

"They still have *you,*" I pointed out. "You might know something you haven't remembered yet."

"Maybe." He shut his eyes again and hummed to himself a moment.

"Though it's really not going to be very long before I'm not important. And I've got time on my side, as they say." He grinned.

"Caught sight of myself in a mirror as I was wandering around passages here earlier. I'm the same handsome fellow I was years ago. White hair—born with it—craggy face. Born with that, too. Only a mother could love. Lots of people aren't going to believe it's me anyway, it being so long."

"I don't understand," I said.

"Simple," he said slowly. "Walk like an old man; people think you're an old man. Get me a suntan and a loincloth and people would think I'm thirty years younger than you do."

I looked at him closely, beginning to doubt what I had always known.

He rubbed his head against the wall, moaning gently. "I should, don't you think, look like somebody's great-grandfather. I do look like somebody some vague age of forty or more. Maybe." His voice came in a low whisper.

"It's stasis, you know."

"Stasis?" I asked.

"My mind has been in some kind of stasis. Body, too." I could barely hear him.

"Had no beard in the monastery, did I? Never shaved. Look now."

He had a definite growth. What I had thought, from across the room, to be gray dirt, was a well-developed stubble.

"There's no way I'm goin' to let 'em in on that," he chuckled. "Don't need a bunch of ageless amnesiacs around."

His joking didn't make me feel any better. He was still a prisoner, full of knowledge, even if it would be only a matter of time before everyone would have that knowledge, too. Besides, I wanted him back in the monastery with us.

As if reading my mind, he clucked gently. "Couldn't go back with you, anyway, little Brother. It jus' wouldn't be the same." He paused, breathing heavily.

"Besides, when things start movin', I wanna be there. Even if I don't understan' right away." He grinned sloppily. "I know . . . I'll know . . . it's all right. . . ." His mouth went slack and he snorted. No, it was a snore.

I let him be. Little enough sleep he'd get when they started questioning him, I thought. Waiting, I found myself nibbling at the food, and had made a sizable inroad upon the bread and cheese by the time the Commander appeared.

He stood in the doorway and looked at Idzik. Despite his military bearing, there seemed to be compassion in his face. "I suppose this is really too much for the old man," he said quietly.

"Are you going to hurt him?" I asked.

The Commander turned to me. "He's a very valuable man," he said. Two of the soldiers who had come with him moved to Idzik and began hauling him out of the chair.

I stepped forward, reaching out a useless hand to those men. The Commander put his own hand on my arm gently, but signaled the soldiers with the other. "Handle him carefully," he ordered.

Idzik mumbled as they untaped his feet and tried to get him to stand. I strained against the Commander's grip until he finally turned me firmly, but not without care on his own part. He walked me to the door as I watched the soldiers decide to lift Idzik by the shoulders and knees in order to carry him.

"I'll have someone escort you out of the valley since your Brothers have already gone ahead," he said, as I tried to keep an eye on what was happening behind me. The Commander stopped at the doorway, looking deep into my face. I looked back, wondering what he wanted.

"Don't worry about your friend," he said, gripping my shoulder momentarily. "I can see what this has done to him. I'll make sure he gets a good long rest before we reach the base."

I took in a quick breath, then had to turn to keep my face from betraying me. "Yes," I said, thinking there was no way he could know, after all. I went out the door, not daring to look back. "Yes. That's exactly what he needs. A good long rest."

All You Can Eat
by
Don Baumgart

About the Author

Don Baumgart is an old hand: worked on a morning daily paper in Spokane, moved on to Seattle and the Associated Press, and from there into public-relations writing for the telephone-company. (It may or may not be significant that one of our contributors to 1985's Writers of the Future Volume I, *Michael Miller with "Tyson's Turn," writes telephone-company public relations copy, but on the East Coast.)*

Baumgart, in any case, has moved on. For a time, he wrote for The Fabulous Furry Freak Brothers *at the Rip Off Press, San Francisco's famed comic-book publishers. Now, however, he has emigrated to the quiet town of Nevada City in search of stories that are all his own. It had occurred to him after several years' bus trips to New Orleans and Mardi Gras, that he had at least one. This became "All You Can Eat," which is his first completed science fiction story. It won Second Place in the third quarter, and now it's included here. He says:*

"The fame, success and money are all wonderful, of course. But what blew me away was judges like Pohl and Zelazny liked *my story. That's the reward. I thought the story should work; humor is so rare, especially in science fiction. But it's very hard to tell if your own humor is*

funny. So, now I know. And now all those half-begun stories have a purpose . . . and a future."

Which implies that he plans a career as an SF humorist—indeed a rare thing, and one the field is always short of. So we wish him the very best of luck, and if "All You Can Eat" is an accurate example, we wish him a great deal of it.

Driver smacked the big bus down onto a deserted stretch of dark rain-swept Lousiana highway in a hard wet kiss. Over his shoulder he shouted to his wakening passengers, "Red-beans-and-rice stop! All you can eat! Everybody into human form!"

In the darkness behind him his riders began to rustle and rumble as he flipped switches for diesel emission, running lights, headlights, license plates, windshield wipers and a hundred miles of scan in both heat and motion sensing. The heat blip of the roadstop café glowed like neon on a small dashboard screen.

"Awright, now," Driver called loudly, "this is your first food stop. You're not at Mardi Gras yet, so no weirdness! Get your groceries and we get out. No biggie."

Lights flickered on over seats as passengers stirred, stretched and reached for their party lines. A long thin tube dropped from the ceiling over each seat, ready to supply ups, downs, mellows and madness by the sip. Sucks and grunts filled the bus as riders gulped big hits of leaper, trying to regain consciousness. The party had started a long way back. The starship was built like an old silver-and-gray parlor diesel bus registered in the state of Montana and sporting a country-western band sticker on the rear bumper. The bus had begun collecting passengers for Mardi Gras on a small world circling a star hidden from Earth behind the Milky Way.

In the front seat across the aisle from Driver, Vrandi and Dreex leaned forward, peering into the wet night. Vrandi was a tall woman with straight blond hair. Her body moved in the seat with grace and relaxed power as she turned to the side window where dark trees flashed past. A smile never quite left her lips, a little smile that said, "I know the nastiest thing you like to do." It was a startling smile, jarring. Captivating.

Dreex was a talker. He talked about everything, rubbing each subject smooth, like nervous fingers on a rosary. His hair was dark; his bright electric eyes flickered constantly.

Vrandi and Dreex were Melleron. Lovers. Like most of the riders, they had boarded on the other side of the Magellanic Clouds.

Alone in a double seat behind driver, Morrow still dozed, black cowboy hat tilted down over his eyes. Morrow was Texii. His home circled one of the four stars that Earth called Pegasus constellation. His lanky body, now folded into the seat, was like his hidden face: lean and as well worn as his faded jeans. When he got on, Morrow had told Driver he was going to Mardi Gras to fall in love with a Beautiful Stranger. He was also, he said, running away from a love affair that had become about as interesting as singing "99 Bottles of Beer on the Wall."

Alone and awake in the seat behind Morrow, the Thief watched the night for opportunities. A very successful trader in antiques, his specialty was objects removed illegally from quarantined cultures, like Earth. He had no name, and Driver thought of him as a shadow with hands.

Jondeaux the Magician weaved down the aisle offering to make passenger's wads of Earth dollars disappear. The riders he disturbed were horrendously hung over and a giant slug from Fornax offered to make him disappear.

"Here, fool, make this disappear!" A hand thrust a transparent flask at him. Its contents seemed to boil as Jondeaux drank. The magician teetered off down the aisle, a long multicolored silk scarf dripping from his sleeve, his shirt lumpy with birds and flowers out of control.

"Good shit!" he mumbled, falling into an empty seat and losing human form completely.

A creature with the body of a slim woman and the head of a purple chicken danced with her wine bottle as Hank Snow sang "I've Been Everywhere," Driver's favorite song.

The usual gang of happy drunks, Driver thought, leaning over the big steering wheel. Demon alcohol—intergalactic ambassador. It wasn't mathematical equations that were the language of First Contact, it was a good stiff drink. It's amazing how clear and wonderful two martinis make everything, he thought. And throughout the explored universe the one quality shared by an enormously different range of intelligent life is a fondness for alcohol.

One Mardi Gras, in the scuzzy men's room of an off-Bourbon Street bar, Driver had written the chemical formula for alcohol above a crude star map that looked like a stick man. Under it he scrawled "First Contact" and the date. Hours later, when it took his eyes a long time to focus on the wall in front of him, he saw that someone had received his message from the stars. A penis had been added to the stick man and a drunken scratch said "Yo Mama!"

First Officer Vike stood beside Driver, trying to push back the night with his eyes, getting no farther than the gusting rain flying at them through the headlight beams. Vike was in his human form of a short, balding lecher. In his true shape, he was composed almost entirely of fingers and lips.

Driver wore the shape of a big Oregon logger and no one had ever seen him out of it.

The Saurians were the last awake, of course. There were two of them on this trip, Groont and Harvey, both fat, both with rough yellow skin well on the way to turning bright green from alcohol overload. They shifted their swollen bellies on their laps, piping, "Eat, eat!"

Driver liked the Saurians. These two had made the Mardi Gras run with him three times now and they were almighty fierce drinkers. "My little lizard buddies," he called them when he got what would later be called "pig drunk."

Night that had been much darker than interstellar space flared with a neon nova and Driver wheeled the bus off the highway.

Inside, the little diner was almost deserted except for the men with shotgun eyes and bib overalls who sat drinking coffee at the counter. Real aliens, Driver thought.

Talk too loud cracked through the room as the riders swarmed in and all tried to order at once from the single waitress.

The Saurians were still really drunk and the smell of spicy food made Groont sick immediately. As he ran for the men's room, he was losing control over his shape.

"Vike!" Driver called, nodding his head sideways after the fleeing lizard. Vike sighed and followed Groont into the toilet.

He was back almost at once.

"It's bad, real bad," he said as he slid into the booth across the table from Driver. He's completely lost human form."

"Hey, waitress!" Harvey shouted from a nearby table, his mouth sputtering and clacking. He still looked

whined on the drying cement as Driver put the bus onto a curved ramp off the freeway.

"To make the bus on time," Vike continued, "*do not get arrested!* You have several pieces of equipment that will prevent arrest. Carry them and don't get too drunk to use them." Music drowned him out. "Be on the bus!" he shouted, then gave up.

The exit ramp touched ground and they were in New Orleans. As they crawled through city streets flooded with people, Driver watched his dash where the bus computer rotated a three-dimensional image of the giant RV parking lot ahead.

"Plenty of room!" he said as an empty Dixie beer can bounced off the barely moving bus. Groont slid his window open and gave a terrible roar at the crowd.

"Eat beer, lizard!" a man shouted back and hurled a nearly full can at the window. Groont caught the speeding can with his tongue and whipped it inside the bus.

"Hey, *awright!*" the woman clinging to the beer-thrower cried. "Mar-dee-GRAW!"

Inside the chain link fence of the big lot, Driver pulled the bus into a roomy space beside a green bus of stone freaks from California. A naked young woman leaned out of a window and passed Morrow a joint. Driver cut the engine noise synthesis program and the sudden stillness was strange.

"Ladies, Gentlemen and Things," Vike said, standing in the aisle, facing back toward the riders, "Welcome to New Orleans and to the best party in the explored universe! Welcome to Mardi Gras!"

Music roared. Slinky-hot fire-mating music from Xicacor pulsed through the bus. Riders were up and moving around, gathering their toys—image generators and sonic pleasure pulsers, blue fog capsules and lust beam pistols.

"I'm *ready!*" shouted a spider-creature from a world that was mostly radio pulses. A jolly couple followed it off the bus, the male dressed in striped double-knit pants, flowered Hawaiian shirt, grotesque necktie and screaming sport jacket.

"*Mister Polyester!*" he yelled as he jumped down onto the crushed shell parking lot, both arms upraised. His mate smiled, shook her Texas high school band uniform into place and stepped down.

Tipping his crushed straw hat back from his forehead, one rider quickly inhaled several lines of flourescent blue powder from a table top. Snorting loudly, he reached up, punched a button. The music shifted and the Grateful Dead boogied out with him singing ". . . come join Uncle John's Band. . . ."

Groont and Harvey lumbered down the aisle. "Nice costumes," Vike said, as they crowded past him. The bus rocked with their departure.

Morrow resettled the dented black hat on his head, grabbed his thick warm coat, and headed down the aisle. "I probably won't see you again," he said to Driver and Vike. "I came to Mardi Gras to fall in love. Unmasking is the magic moment and by then it'll be too late to make it back to the bus. Y'all have a good trip back."

"What'll you do if you miss the bus?" Vike asked.

"Try to stay in love," Morrow said, tipping his hat and stepping down.

No one had seen the Thief leave.

"Come on, Driver, we'll buy you a drink," Vrandi smiled at him.

"Maybe later." His teeth clamped down on a toothpick.

"Come on," Jondeaux urged, much revived by the prospect of a fresh audience. "Free drinks anywhere if you're with the magician!"

"I didn't come here to party," Driver said around the toothpick. "I came here to drive home."

The bus emptied past Driver until he and Vike were alone.

"Goin' out, Vike?"

"Oh, yeah, guess I'll walk around and check out the ladies. Always fine ladies at Mardi Gras. They come here to get wild because if it happens at Mardi Gras it's okay, whatever it is. Maybe have a drink. It's early . . . what time is it?"

"Where?"

"Exactly. Mardi Gras!" Vike called as he swung down and closed the door.

"Well, two more trips," Driver thought, alone now in the silent bus. "Two more Mardi Gras runs and I'll have my planet paid for. Then I can hang up my hat." A long arm tugged at the bill of his Ed & Tom's Truckstop cap from Gila Bend, Arizona. Driver owned, nearly, a planet rich with forest and water out on the fringes of explored space. It was peopled with his lady and a few friends. When he bought it, he immediately tossed out its official letter-number designation and named it Oregon.

Standing up, stretching, he decided to set the security program and go eat. Driver liked his parties smaller than the block-wide crowds at Mardi Gras, liked a simple drink without wading through a swamp of fools. But he could always eat.

Outside, the shells crunched underfoot and the abandoned, slowly decaying Jax brewery buildings loomed like a dark cliff.

A trio of hefty after-dinner drinks changed his mind

about Bourbon Street and soon shoulders dug into his chest as he worked his way through the crowd. Too much of it was uncostumed men who had spent good time and money to get to Mardi Gras and were grimly determined to have fun, no matter how drunk they had to get.

Driver thought he was the first one back to the bus until he saw the blue glow leaking out of the big bedroom at the back. The streets around the parking lot were nearly empty now. Iron balconies were empty. No crowds stood beneath them chanting for a tossed string of beads or a quick flash of flesh.

He coiled his big frame into the pilot's seat and fished a bottle out of the map bag. "Playtime," he said quietly to the bottle. He sat sipping until, with a flickering crackle, the blue light reached a bright peak and then faded to a restful glow.

When Vrandi and Dreex at last glided down the aisle, they were arm-and-arm with a beautiful golden-haired girl. She was wet with exhaustion and wore a smile that would stay for a long, long time. In her eyes Driver saw reflected pleasure that she had never before imagined.

Vrandi leaned over and kissed him on the way out.

Another sip and the Thief was there, standing in the doorway. Floating outside were several hundred pounds of iron.

"Got a few sewer lids to stow in the cargo hold," he said softly. New Orleans sewer lids were decorated with an ornate design as rich as the city itself. In the gas nebula, they were priceless.

Driver was alone again for a long time. When Vike came back to the bus, Driver saw him about to put his palm on the key plate and opened the door.

"Well, get laid?"

"No, but I made love to a hundred women with my eyes," Vike answered. "Ran into some other travelers. There's a load in from Centaurus A. Big ship in orbit and two Winnebago shuttles. There's a lot of talk about an invasion."

"Invasion?"

"Right. Lot of rumor that the Vritt are going to hit Earth. Open a door into New Orleans during Mardi Gras. Perfect place for an alien invasion. Who'd notice? Those creepy-ass insects will send through two scouts who'll go skittering down the street gorging their uncommon appetites. Then back they go with a feeding report and next comes the swarm."

"Aw, crap!"

"Exactly. BUQUAR will shut this scene down so tight there won't be anybody left on the streets from farther away than Texas. They'll get the Vritt, but they'll also toss us offworlders out, and if we have to lift off before Fat Tuesday the passengers are going to want their money back."

"Aw, cripple crap!"

"So, what you have to do is stop the invasion. Save Earth from an alien invasion. Stop the space creeps and keep New Orleans safe for good, dirty, profitable fun."

"Why me?" Driver groaned.

"Because you have a mortgage payment due. Simple, honest motivation."

"Oh, how I hate banks."

"Look, you've got time to think of something. It's only Friday night. They won't make a move until Sunday at the earliest. That's when the costumes really start showing up. They'll wait for that to get maximum cover."

After an uneasy night's sleep in the big back bed, interrupted by drunks banging the side of the bus and the all-night game of Win-or-Die in the front, Driver woke with a headache and a plan. While the bus slept he went out for dark coffee and pastry exploding with powdered sugar in the French Market.

"It's save the world or get a job," Driver said when Vike joined him. "And I'll be damned if I'll push a garbage barge around the worlds of some industrial system."

"What are ya gonna do?"

"Get 'em drunk. When the scouts don't report back . . . no invasion!"

"Great plan. One minor obstacle—Vritt don't drink alcohol."

"Even better!" Driver roared. "They'll have no resistance. We'll get 'em blotto. Crash and burn!"

"Well, maybe," was Vike's enthusiastic response.

"Look, spotting 'em quickly is the hard part. We need to be on 'em as soon as they materialize. They'll start feeding immediately."

"Of course. And what they like most is microchip circuitry. It's like Mexican food to them."

"Right. So, first we alert all of our riders. Have 'em watch computer stores, stereo shops and video game parlors. Get the Winnebago wimps from Centaurus A and all the other offworlders in on it too. How many of us do you think there are in New Orleans right now, Vike?"

"I'd say there's probably five hundred."

"More than enough," Driver said, slipping the first toothpick of the day between his jaws.

It wilted visibly at the news brought by the purple chicken-woman. "They're here."

"Already?" Vike asked excitedly.

"I saw them walking down Canal Street," she said,

daintily snapping up a half dozen pastries.

"Well bite my fungadoon!" Vike said, shaking his head. Driver held his head in both hands, his temples silvering with powdered sugar.

"The Jack Schofield Task Force," Purplecluck said, swallowing.

"What?" Driver bellowed.

"I'm sure it's them. Bureaucrats always take the same form. Six of 'em wearing three-piece suits and carrying briefcases." Driver's moans were becoming embarrassing.

"You told me you weren't going to do that this trip!" Vike's voice was loud and angry.

"I just called home," Driver said lamely.

Several trips ago he had found a way to avoid the killer communications charges for calls between galaxies. By billing the calls to his favorite bank in the name of Jack Schofield, he had used the lines free until an outraged Astronomical Telephone & Teleporting security staff had formed the Jack Schofield Task Force to track him down.

"I didn't even use their system this time," Driver explained. "I cut into the defense network."

"The military!" Vike groaned. "We're all doomed!"

"First things first," Driver said finally. "Get the bugs."

By Sunday they were set. Nothing happened.

On Monday the network of watchers started to fall apart. Tuesday, Driver took to the streets to try patching it up. Pirates with beer cans swaggered and staggered. A half-dozen revelers dressed as beer bottles marched in six-pack formation. A gorgeous woman wearing only a pair of blue jeans and strings of Mardi Gras beads danced with a tinfoil robot. Neon Dixie beer signs glowed only half as brightly as the red-sequined crayfish who strolled past.

Feathers and leather and platform shoes, Satan in sneakers, painted faces and bare bodies.

Beer trucks pushed through the packed streets to thunderous cheers and garbage men were hailed as heroes as they loaded their trucks with mountains of empties.

In the thick of it, Driver ran into Jondeaux and the straw hat cowboy. They were quite drunk, singing ". . . Commies from Mars are jamming the bars. . . ."

"Hey!" Driver shouted, pushing aside a gorilla to catch up with them. Not far away, Vrandi and Dreex sat at an upstairs bar sipping pink hurricanes and occasionally stepping out onto the tiny black iron balcony to look down at the crowds. They saw the gorilla make an obscene gesture as he recovered from Driver's shove. They also saw two tall skinny green insects materialize in the doorway of a porn shop across the street.

When the alarm was sounded, it caught Vike in an old Victorian house far from the city center, where two college women from Baton Rouge were spending the day exploring the sensual possibilities of his true shape. The Thief was gathering his second hundred-pound batch of Mardi Gras beads, removing a heavy rope of strands from the neck of a fat man from New Jersey. The fat man felt only a slight absence of pressure and saw no one. As best they could—and some couldn't—the riders drew their circle closed around the invaders.

"Look at those things," Mister Polyester said. "They look like pickles on stilts."

A skinny girl with a fancy automatic camera called, "Hey, look over here!" and took a picture of the aliens. In a blur of speed one Vritt reached out, snatched the camera and ate it. The other one whipped the digital watch off her wrist and gulped it down.

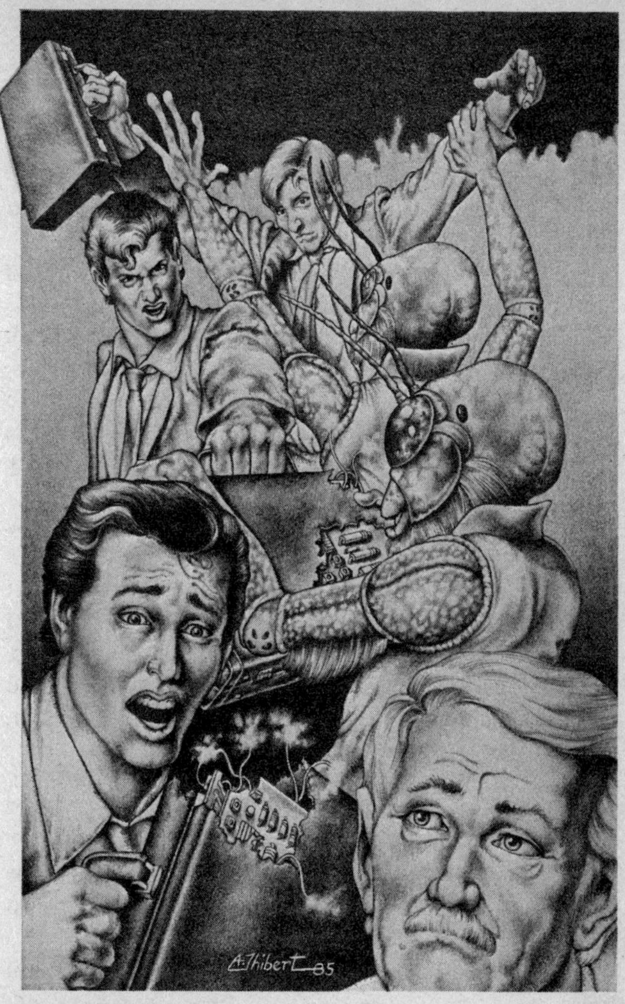

Illustrated by Art Thibert

"Come, we eat," it said.

"Want real eat."

As they stood chirping to each other, the riders jostled them into a handy bar. Inside, Harvey and Groont sat on the floor amid the smashed wood of what probably used to be a booth. Drinks were ordered. The Vritt declined. Groont insisted with a rumbling roar. The Vritt sipped, cacked, spit and chattered, "Nononono!"

"They won't drink," Vike said. The two women with him smiled and ordered another round.

"No biggie," Driver answered. "We'll just squash 'em." Harvey thundered his approval.

It was Mrs. Polyester who solved the problem. To her, the answer was obvious. She crowded her way to the packed bar and came back with two tall green foamy drinks.

"Here, boys," she said, handing the drinks to the invaders. "Grasshoppers!"

The party went on for hours and from bar to bar. At about their fourth stop the Vritt invented a new drink—a grasshopper in a mug with a garnish of pocket calculator. Their legs had grown rickety and their scratchy speech had become punctuated by rasping belches as the riders taught them to shout "Mardi Gras!"

"Well, V . . . uh, Vike, ol' buddy," Driver beamed, "saved th' worl' din I? Save th' farm, too. Good groceries!" The Vritt had not, of course, been drinking alone.

Vrandi stood on tiptoe and kissed Driver's ear. Or seemed to. "They're coming down the street," she whispered. "The Jack Schofield Task Force."

"Aww shit!" was all he said, but he said it several times.

Nobody knows whose idea it was, although nearly everyone claimed it during the long ride home. It didn't take much, really. The drunken Vritt were led to the door and pointed toward the advancing squad of men, each of whom carried a briefcase full of the most sophisticated electronic tracking gear in the universe.

"Transistor gumbo, little buddies," Driver said. "All you can eat!"

The task force won, of course. They were a higher life form, had better weapons, and they were sober. But it took time. Enough time.

The bus sat idling in the dark drizzle just inside the parking lot gate. Driver sat behind the wheel wearing a grin as big as the Crab Nebula. Behind him the riders continued to party. Bottles and burning sticks passed from hand to claw.

"Everybody on, Mister Vike?"

"Two missing. Got five minutes yet."

"Who's not here?"

"Morrow and the Thief," Vike said, peering out the open door at the wet night. Finally it was time.

"Midnight," Driver called over his shoulder as he set the bus rolling slowly toward the street, the door still open. With a thump a shadow became a form and the Thief was standing on the steps.

"Go! Go! They're right behind me!"

Outside the moving bus, the streets were deserted. Once the tradition had been: Lovers unmask and show their faces to each other. Now it was unmask, show the cop your ID, hotel key and a hundred dollars or go to jail. Broken strings of beads lay embracing crushed beer cans in the gutters.

Picking up speed, Driver moved onto the freeway entrance ramp. Vike stood in the stairwell watching the raindrops become flaming meteors as they rushed toward the big headlights. They both saw the flash of white at the same time but it was Vike who cried "Morrow!"

Coat collar up against the gale, hat down to his eyebrows, Morrow was nearly invisible. What had caught their eyes was the white dress. Standing beside him was The Beautiful Stranger, a smile on her face and love in her eyes. Her mask dangled from slender fingers.

They boarded the bus to ringing cheers that were only briefly silenced as Driver called over his shoulder, "Next stop, Narcosia Four! Dream melons and skiv, all you can eat!"

They That Go Down to the Sea In Ships
by
Marina Fitch

About the Author

Marina Fitch entered the W.O.T.F. contest because, she tells us, she loves science fiction and fantasy and writing, and she figured, "Why not?"

A very high percentage of our winners tell us essentially the same thing. Why not, indeed? What is there to lose? Oddly enough—for the benefit of those who, unlike Marina, need to hear this—there is a great deal to lose . . . the safety of never having tried, the self-assurance that comes from submitting to no tests but one's own, the splendid knowledge that what other people feel and respond to is of importance.

Putting it conversely, the person who prepares a manuscript and mails it off to be judged by strangers is performing a brave thing. This is also, of course, the only person who stands a chance of winning, as distinguished from not losing. What is winning like?

Marina, who has been trying to become a fiction writer since childhood, and who is currently an editor and nonfiction freelance writer in California, has entered contests before. The best she had done was second place in a Christmas short story contest sponsored by a local weekly *paper. When she heard she had won a $500 prize in our third quarter, and received our offer for the right to publish her story in this book, she wrote us as follows:*

"Winning this *contest is wonderful, too incredible to fully comprehend! It won't seem real until the book is in my hands and I see my name on the Table of Contents."*

Go look, Marina. Why not?

Mike had Toby pinned with a knee to the bladder. Toby shifted slightly, careful not to wake Mike, and sat up a little so she could watch him sleep. She tugged at the St. Christopher medal around his neck, unraveling the tangle of chain and hair.

It wouldn't seem that long, Toby promised herself. Sure, the outer-galaxy expedition would take fifty years, but she and Mike would only be awake for a decade. He and the rest of his crew would be awake periodically, as the expedition needed them, but she would sleep the last forty years in one stretch here at the Space Exploration Institute, in the Sleep Center down the hall from their apartment.

There was a knock at the door followed by footsteps repeating and fading like an echo. Toby shivered, then bent over her husband's ear. "Hey, Columbus. It's time to discover new worlds."

"What did I promise you?" Mike said, holding her while they waited for the sergeant. "When I get back we'll have a baby. No, two."

"One and a half," Toby said. "Let's see how we like the first one, okay? Besides, who wants to have a baby in their eighties?"

Mike laughed. "God, I'll miss you."

"I hope so."

The sergeant leaned into the room, smiling apologetically. "Preston—time to go," he said. Mike nodded.

Toby later wondered why there hadn't been more to say.

"Mom, when Dad died, did the house seem too big?" Toby asked. She frowned at the onion she was slicing, brushing tears away with the back of her hand. "I found one of Mike's socks today under the cushion of that recliner. He's been gone three months and I'm still picking up after him."

Her mother looked up from the cookbook. "I was reading one of your father's books the other day, and I found a photo he'd taken of us. He didn't like it, said it made him look stupid. I always thought he'd thrown it away."

"Mom, does the house always echo when someone dies?"

"Toby, he's not dead. Mike's not dead, and he'll be back. He sent you that video-letter on the computer just last week."

Toby slashed at the onion. "I know, Mom."

"Mike's only been gone a year," her friend Robert said. He handed Toby the freesia, one stem at a time, as she arranged the bouquet. "I used to get a lot of those 'One Lifespan' nuts when Karen first left. After five years, they've forgotten about me."

"They still pester me," Lisa grumbled. "They keep trying to cure me with God. I'll be glad when I go to sleep next month."

Toby crimped a purple flower into place. "But this guy followed me home from work, yelling the whole way. I wanted to turn around and bash him a good one. You know

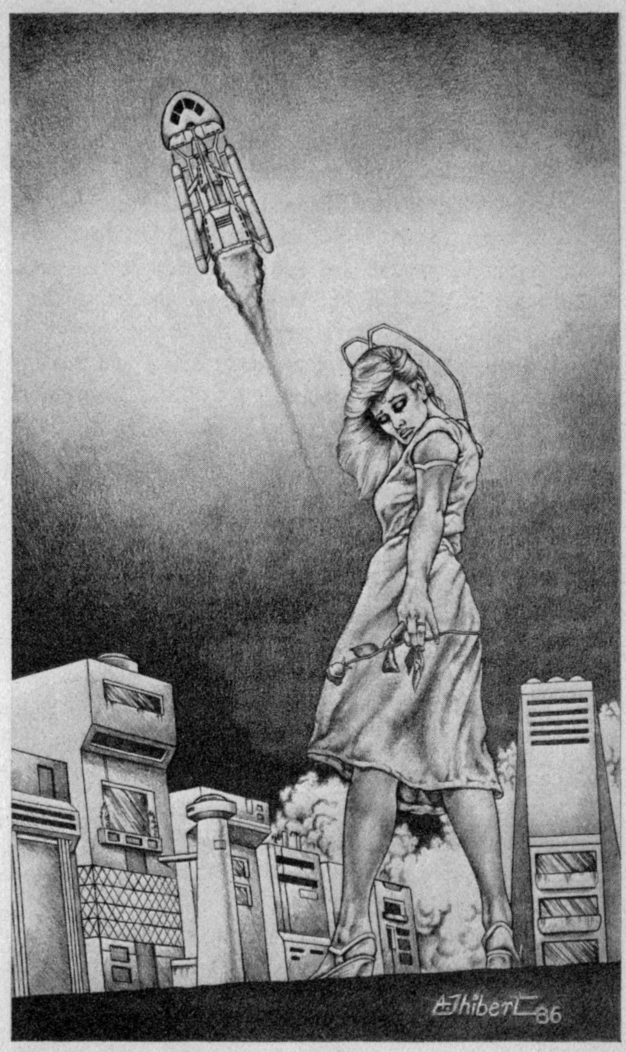

Illustrated by Art Thibert

those slogans they always chant: 'One life, one lifespan,' 'God will choose the time.' So I stopped and said, 'Look, I'm not hurting anybody. I love my husband. All I want to do is be sure I'm still alive when he gets back, all right?' "

"They'll forget about you soon enough," Robert said.

"Sure," Lisa added sarcastically.

Toby looked at them, Robert with his ferret-lean face and dark curls, Lisa with her sour smile. Years from now, Toby wondered, would she, too, befriend young Earth-bound spouses? And if she did, would she bring them Lisa's weariness or Robert's weekly flowers? She glanced around her living room at the roses, daisies and heather that sprouted from jam jars and juice bottles. Some were on their last petal, but she couldn't give them up. They were such a treat. Mike had never had time for flowers.

Toby stared at her hands, watching her fingers entwine like a tangle of lovers' legs in the morning. "Sometimes I feel guilty about wishing Mike hadn't gone," she said, "but then I think, if I'd talked him out of going, if I'd stopped him in some way, he would have been wanting to go all his life. He'd resent me, and then I'd lose all of him, not just ten years."

Toby heard Lisa's rasping sigh. She peeked at Robert and caught a quick wink. She smiled, self-consciously, and glanced back at her hands.

As they peered out the window, Toby poked her mother in the ribs. "Great weekend, huh? No chance of rain?"

Her mother shrugged, connecting raindrops with her fingers. "So we can't hike," she said. "Let's have the picnic here."

"Where did you leave the basket?"

"In the kitchen."

"And the wine?"

"In the basket."

Toby pushed herself from the windowsill and ran to the kitchen. When she returned with the basket and two wine glasses, she found her mother leaning over the computer console. Toby smiled. "What are you looking for?"

"I thought I saw a new letter from Mike."

Toby shook her head. "No. I won't be hearing from him for a while. He'll be asleep for the next three years."

"But it's only been a year and a half."

Toby pulled a corkscrew from her pocket and popped the cork. "I know. It's okay, Mom. A toast to Mike?"

"With wine? Mike would hardly approve. Let's wait 'til we can get a six-pack and do it right."

Toby grinned. As she savored the tart merlot, she raised her glass to the window where the raindrops hung like stars.

"That one over there, that's Venus, isn't it?" Toby pointed into the dark summer sky. "That one."

Robert squinted. A lock of gray hair fell across one eye. "Could be. It isn't white like the others. It's a planet of some sort."

"That's where Mike is. Somewhere beyond Venus."

"Karen's over there."

Toby watched the flutter of one thin hand as it swept at the stars. She wanted to catch it and press it to her cheek, to see if his fingers were as soft as his voice. A flush fanned to life in the heart of her womb, and her thighs tightened against it. She leaned away, unable to step back.

"What's the longest Karen's been asleep?" she asked.

"Four years."

"Mike's been asleep for three," she said, then frowned.

Would Mike's hair be shot with gray, too? She imagined him stepping off the shuttle to meet her, his hair spiked like a dandelion. He used to mash it down with his hands, tufts springing between his fingers. "Robert," she said, "do you ever feel abandoned?"

"Oh, sometimes." Robert stepped behind her and drew her to his chest. The brush of his fingers was soothing as his hands strayed along her neck.

Robert scooped at the water, splashing Toby as she struggled to the sandy bank. Sliding on the stones, Toby tripped and went under. Robert's arms locked around her waist and he lifted her from the river, dangling her above the grass. He rolled her over in the leaves. "There we are, Tobias," he said.

Toby made a face at him. "You and Mike. You're the only ones who ever call me that."

"What about my sister Katy and her husband? Of course, they won't be around years from now when you wake up from the big sleep—"

Toby sat up suddenly. "They won't, will they?"

Robert bowed his head, his curls a glossy bouquet between her breasts. There was hardly a curl now that wasn't rimmed with gray. He turned his face toward the river.

"It's a weird feeling, isn't it?"

"Robert, aren't you afraid of going to sleep? I mean, after next month, you'll be . . . unconscious for forty years. Everyone you know will be gone—"

"But I'll wake up and Karen will be standing over me."

And five years after that, Toby thought, I'll be waking to Mike. She wondered if Mike would kiss her, like Sleeping Beauty's prince, or if he would simply whisper in her ear. He might even pounce on her, tickling her awake. But Mike always woke after she did, and it was impossible for her to imagine. She rolled over on her stomach, the leaves crackling as Robert snuggled beside her.

"So, Toby, don't be a stranger," Katy said as her husband Cliff pulled her toward the subway entrance. "Just because that bum is dropping out of sight doesn't mean you have to do the same."

"We're having lunch on Thursday, remember?" Toby replied.

Katy stopped, hesitating on the top step. "Pleasant dreams, Robert!" she called.

Toby looked up. Robert's smile was as tight as the grip crushing her hand. His gaze followed his sister down the dark stairway and out of his life, probably forever. He released Toby's hand as Katy disappeared.

Toby locked her fingers in his, squeezing them gently.

"Let's go," she said. "My mom's waiting for us."

"Why so glum, Robert?" Toby's mother asked as she filled his glass with champagne. "Tonight you'll go to sleep and when you wake up, Karen will be there."

Robert shook his head. "I still can't believe it."

Gulping her champagne, Toby swallowed wrong and coughed. Robert patted her back until she nodded, his fingers tracing tiny circles on her shoulder. She swallowed another mouthful of wine.

"It's exciting," Robert said, "but it's sad—I mean, I'll be sleeping through so much. So many people will be gone."

"Dead," Toby's mother said softly.

"And you know, I just found out my sister Katy is going to have a baby, a boy. He'll be forty when I wake up. I won't even get to watch him grow."

"When I wake up, I can tell you about his first four years, " Toby offered.

The shatter of her mother's glass startled them both. As her mother knelt to pick up the shards of pink glass, her lower lip trembled. The fragments crossed her palm like scars. "I meant to set it on the table," she murmured, then lurched to her feet and darted from the room.

Thrusting the glass at Robert, Toby followed her into the bedroom. Her mother looked so small, sitting on the edge of the bed with her ankles crossed. Toby sat down beside her, taking one of her hands. "Mom?"

Her mother gazed through the watercolor on the far wall as if it were a window. "It will always be 'Mom,' won't it?" she said. "Never 'Grandma.' "

Toby's cheeks burned.

Toby rested her palm on Katy's swollen belly, a tiny kick battering her hand. She laughed, looking up into Katy's dark face. "He's pretty feisty."

"Bobby's going to be a real tiger." Katy's smile twisted bitterly. "Just like his uncle. The bastard."

Toby removed her hand. She started to hand Katy a tissue, then daubed at Katy's cheek herself. The tissue disintegrated with blotted tears.

"I'm sorry," Katy said. "I miss him, that's all."

Toby took a deep breath. "It's all right. I promise."

The man held out a hand, begging Toby to jump. She looked down. The chasm stretched like a leer below her, well-toothed with faces. They were all screaming, but she could hear each voice clearly: her mother, Katy, friends and co-workers, strangers. She stared across at the man on the far bank, squinting to see who he was.

He waved to her, gesturing that he would catch her. Toby hugged herself. Could she trust him? He stepped closer to the brink, his hair as frantic as dandelion fluff. It was Mike—awake, thank God, finally awake! She shouted to him, nothing more than his name, and crouched low to spring to him.

As fingers grasped her arm, the shouts below became cheers. She wrenched away, then turned, looking up into Robert's eyes. "Don't," he said. "They need us."

"But Mike . . ." she pleaded. Robert swept her into his arms and plunged into the chasm. They were adrift, gliding gently through billowing air currents. For the first time in years, she felt warm and peaceful and . . .

Toby hammered at the alarm clock with her fist. The tatters of the dream fell away.

It was true, Toby thought, dead people do look as if they're asleep. She leaned over Katy's husband and wondered if Mike was as still in his prolonged rest. His hair would be matted with sleep, his skin pale from years on the shuttle, his body a little soft. He was so lazy. . . .

An arm sled through hers, clutching at her hand. "Oh, Toby," Katy whispered. "You're here."

Toby pulled Katy away, steering her outside. There was an echo in Katy's hollow eyes. Staring at the crowd, Katy nodded and shook her head as people offered condolences. "It's so . . . unreal," she said, turning to Toby. "A heart attack! At least he got to see the baby. . . . But it's just . . . it's too much. Both of them, in one year. First Robert, now Cliff. . . ."

"Robert's not dead. He'll wake up—"

"And do you think I'll be alive?" Katy said. "Do you

honestly believe I'll ever see my brother again? Toby, he's dead. For me, he's dead."

Toby stepped back, releasing Katy's arm. She blinked at the overcast sky, at the dark crowd, at Katy's averted face. She began to walk away, slowly, then she ran.

The computer spit out the letter and Toby put it back in. Mike's face filled the screen. She recited the words as he spoke, nodding her head when he nodded, smiling at his jokes. It was only the twelfth time that day she had watched the letter.

The phone rang. She ignored it. It wasn't Mike; he was still asleep. On the screen Mike mimed tossing a coin. "Heads," she said.

The phone continued to ring. She wondered vaguely who it was, then turned up the volume on the computer. She had made her decision: it was unfair to be close to people and then go to sleep for the rest of their lives.

On the screen, Mike laughed at a passing crew member and Toby realized she'd missed something. She told the computer to go back a few frames.

"Ms. Preston," the sergeant said as he strode past her into the apartment, "we want you to help us— God, woman, look at you! When did you wash your hair last—or brush it? Jesus!"

Toby stared at him listlessly. She wanted to get back to the computer. She'd found a lost letter from Mike and had only had a chance to watch it four times.

The sergeant took her to the bedroom and sat her down. "Stay here," he ordered and left.

He returned minutes later with Katy. "She refuses to answer the phone, she won't come to the door, . . ." Katy was saying. "I haven't seen her in about six months, and I know her mother— My God!"

Toby ran her hand self-consciously through her hair. Her fingers caught in a snarl. With passive indifference, she let them fuss over her, brushing her hair and scrubbing her face, until the sergeant called someone on the phone and demanded a nurse. Within an hour her hair had been cut and washed, her clothing changed. The sergeant led Toby down the corridor to the Sleep Center while Katy called her mother.

". . . And we're hoping that having Ms. Preston there when he wakes up will help lessen the blow."

Toby stared at the wall as the sergeant explained to her mother in a deadpan newscaster's voice. Karen was dead. In her mind, Toby heard the crew's screams ruptured by an explosion as Karen's shuttle fell into the white-hot center of a pulsar. On another shuttle, in another part of her mind, she could hear Mike screaming, too. Her fingernails scored her palms.

Placing a hand on Toby's knee, her mother sat down beside her. "You've lost weight," she said absently.

Toby turned to her, then curled into her mother's arms. "Mom, it's too awful," she whispered.

Her mother rocked her. " 'They that go down to the sea in ships, that do business in great waters,' " her mother recited. "In God's hands, just like the first sailors."

Toby wriggled upright. "A lot of the first sailors never came back."

"The doctor says she's ready to wake him now," the sergeant said.

Toby rose and followed the sergeant to the Sleeping Center.

The room was stark. Along one wall were large drawers with combination locks and file cards. Toby glanced at the one nearest the door. In dot-matrix print, the card read: Lisa Gorbach. Toby shuddered. She hardly remembered Lisa.

One of the drawers stood open, revealing a cradle of wires and sheets. On a gurney beside it lay Robert. "He's in a normal REM sleep now," the doctor said. "Be gentle when you wake him."

Leaning over the sleeping man, Toby pursed her lips. The door opened behind her and she heard Katy ask the doctor if Robert was awake yet. Toby touched Robert's face, lightly, with only the tips of her fingers. "Hey," she whispered. "Robert, wake up."

The dark eyes opened slowly, blinking into focus. "Karen?" he asked, propping himself up on his elbows. "Toby! Did Mike get back first? Where's Karen?"

Toby opened her mouth, but her throat closed on the words. Robert's eyes widened with alarm as they searched the room wildly.

"Pulsar," Toby managed. "Robert—"

She felt herself lifted to her toes as he clutched at her, blanketing her in a desperate embrace.

Toby pointed her toes so that they just touched the muddy riverbed. Beside her, Robert sighed, his shoulders folded inward. Three months and he still dangled between two lives: the one he left, and the one with Karen he would never have. Toby tossed a pebble, watching circles explode across the surface.

"Was it worth it, Toby?" Robert said suddenly, unfurling his long legs. "All that hope? And if she hadn't died, then what? Ten years changes people. Hell, two-and-a-half years changes people."

Toby bit her lip. The glassy water reflected the cattails, as faintly as her memory reflected Mike these days.

She threw another pebble in the river. "I don't feel Mike sometimes," she said. "Robert, it was terrible while you were gone."

"Well, it's not so great now." He tore at the nodding cattails, then flung them into the water. They scattered, bobbing along the current. Robert shook his head, then looked at her: not at the far bank or some lost future, but at her. "Toby . . ."

She blinked back tears. "Robert, did you dream?"

"No, I don't think I did."

She nodded.

The sergeant stopped her in the hallway as she was leaving to meet Robert. "Ms. Preston," he began hesitantly, "I need to talk to you."

She stared at him, suddenly cold. "Mike? He's all right?"

"He's fine. No, this is something very different. Ms. Preston, do you remember Lisa Gorbach?"

All she could picture was a file card, then a bitter smile. Lisa had gone to sleep . . . oh, seven years ago. Toby said, "Yes, vaguely."

"Lisa died this afternoon. One of the circuits shorted——"

As the sergeant explained, Toby began to shiver. "I need a sweater," she interrupted, pushing past the sergeant. She walked stiffly to the apartment, her panic swelling, suffocating her. Lisa had died, at the Sleep Center, in a cryonic state. She wouldn't wake to a sweet reunion. No one would really notice or care until her lover came home because Lisa was just a file card, just as Toby would be. . . .

Toby locked the door after herself, leaning against it. She rubbed her arms, hugged herself, and wondered if she would ever be warm again.

"You never do anything with me anymore," Toby accused. "Mom, what is it? Are you mad at me or what?"

Her mother leaned forward and picked up a cup of tea. She sipped it, set it down, then picked it up again. "When you withdrew, it was so hard, and I started thinking, 'For eight years I've been waiting to lose her. . . .' " She put the cup on the table and scooted it from the edge. Leaning over, she reached for Toby's cup. "Remember when I used to read your tea leaves when you were little?" she said.

"They were always full of handsome strangers."

Her mother smiled sadly. "Strangers. . . . Toby, I've missed you, but it's so hard. Do you understand?"

Toby nodded, pressing her palms together as if in prayer. "What do the leaves say today?"

"Aren't you afraid of me?" Toby demanded.

Robert pulled the sheet over her chin, stretching it across her nose. "No." He pulled it down and kissed her.

"Two years," she said. Karen and Lisa trailed through her mind like comets and she shut her eyes tight. She tried to imagine Robert growing old, his face a history of every year she'd miss.

Toby wrapped her arms around her knees and rocked backward, her gaze fixed on the stars. The endlessness of star after star stretched before her like the sea melting into the horizon.

A cold thrill crept down the back of her neck. How did she know there was anything beyond those flecks of light? How did she know Mike was out there? She tried to find Venus but she lost her way as her mind wandered. Suppose Mike lost his way? It was possible.

She couldn't feel him . . . anywhere.

She tried to imagine him coming home. He would leap from the shuttle and sprint through the Institute until he came to the Sleep Center. With a wrench, he would fling open the door, grab the flowers from the vase in the waiting room and offer them to her as she woke up— No, that wasn't Mike.

He would brush away the reporters that followed him from the decontamination room, shouting, "Toby, I want to see Toby. God, if anything's happened to her, I'll——" He would stop before the Sleep Center door, peeking into the room so that he could watch her sleep— But that wasn't Mike either.

Toby sat a while longer. the stars seemed to wink at her as she rose and padded across the dewy lawn. How light she felt, as if she were a wind-fairy on a summer breeze. She went inside, leaving the door standing open.

Toby traced Mike's name with her finger before handing the letter to the sergeant. "You can still change your mind," the sergeant said.

Toby took a deep breath and shook her head. She glanced around the apartment one last time, tapping the computer keyboard. In a little box beside the console were her letters from Mike. She nudged them toward the sergeant. "Will you keep these here at the Institute for me?" she asked.

"Don't you want to take them with you?"

Toby shook her head. She picked up her suitcases and walked out into the hallway. The sergeant caught her elbow. "Ms. Preston—"

"No, I've decided," she said. "I'm not going to sleep. My letter explains everything, but maybe someone else could try to explain it to him, too. And tell Mike—tell him not to look for me when he gets back. If he gets back."

For the first time in years she pictured Mike clearly—shaking his head in disbelief as someone explained that she was no longer waiting for him. He faded and she realized she didn't care—not really—and hadn't for some time.

Hefting the cases, Toby said goodbye to the sergeant and hurried down the hallway. Her mother was coming to take her home. As the exit door slid open, the cool morning air frosted her cheek.

She stood half in, half out the door for a full minute. "Wake up, Toby," she said, and stepped outside.

A Thousand or So Words of Wisdom [?]

by Anne McCaffrey

About the Author

Writers of the Future contest judge and master storyteller Anne Inez McCaffrey, is today, SF's leading authority on dragons, lives in the Irish countryside, and enjoys gentlewomanly pursuits. A multiple award winner and—more important to her—with her stories beloved by millions of readers around the world, she has put her days of struggle behind her. But she has not forgotten what it's like to be young, determined to succeed as a writer, and not altogether sure of one's talent or how to mold it.

Her first sale, in 1953, was to Hugo Gernsback, founder of the magazine SF, *who was then publishing his last fiction periodical,* Science Fiction. *Her next did not come until 1959, and in the following essay she tells a little story about that. Although her magazine stories were thereafter well received, she did not begin to enjoy material success or general public admiration until the late 1960's. The advice she gives novice writers is hard-won wisdom.*

As a girl and then as an apprentice, she was inspired by great storytellers . . . Rudyard Kipling, Edgar Rice Burroughs, and Andre Norton are some she mentions from among those who have each made their mark on a generation. From the Golden Age, she recalls with delight the fiction of L. Ron Hubbard. She speaks of the rip-roaring adventure that bursts forth from his stories; their tumultuous opening of fresh gateways in her imagination. As she thinks back to such works as Slaves Of Sleep, *her voice resonates with the pleasure that only a memorable reading experience can instantly awaken.*

She hopes, it would clearly seem, that she has found a place beside those from whom she derived so much magic. And without pretension or nonsense, she passes what she has learned to those who would someday stand beside her. . . .

A basic commandment every writer should remember is to Tell A Story. Some aspiring writers labor under the delusion that it is the taut phrase, the witticism, the exhibition of a vocabulary, or the involved sentence showing a perfected knowledge of syntax, that maketh the writer. My friends, no. Double NO when the writer gleefully makes a deliberate show of his way with words, under the impression that he cannot fail to bedazzle his reader with his technical proficiency. Sure, sure, but *where is the story* beneath all that glitter?

A case in point is Edgar Rice Burroughs, who often wrote in a stilted and posturing manner. It didn't much bother us as kids because we were in the hands of a master storyteller and the sheer magic of the *stories* he told transcended his flaws in literary style. Even today, re-reading ERB and writhing at his defects, I can still get so caught up in his telling that I ignore the style for the story.

Myself, I'm not the least bit literary and have no pretensions to heightened style. *The Ship Who Sang* is actually badly *written,* but twenty-four years after its first publication it still makes people weep for its characters and what happens to them. "The Smallest Dragonboy" was a yarn I dashed off for an anthology, better crafted than *Ship:* purpose-written, you might say, but it *tells a story people enjoy reading.* These two are the most reprinted of my stories, with some sixteen reprints for *Ship* and fifteen for "Dragonboy."

The second story I got published, 1959's "The Lady in the Tower," required some tinkering, so adroitly done by Algis Budrys that, lacking the original copy, I can't spot the alterations—which means the alterations were not only deft but duplicated the original writer's tone. That represents a lot of extra editorial effort. Why did I, a novice, get that sort of attention? Algis, then Assistant Editor at the *Magazine of Fantasy and Science Fiction,* has since told me that "Lady" was such a good *story* that he and the editor, Robert P. Mills, were willing to work with its flaws.

So, tell your readers a story. Tell *yourself* a story. And if you start boring *yourself,* you can be certain-sure that you're going to bore your readers. Go back to the point where you're still interested in what you were writing and check out the story logic, or the people you're writing about.

And mind you, everyone I've ever talked with in the profession, has a different way of getting down to the nitty-gritty of writing. It's not how you do it, but that you are doing it. For instance, all I know about a story or a novel is its starting point: The initial conflict and the personalities involved in the conflict. I know a story is going well when all of a sudden I find the characters doing something that wasn't exactly what I had thought they should be doing; that will send the story in a new direction, or provide a different emphasis. I used to put a recalcitrant story to one side, until "they" learned to behave themselves. Now I've learned that "they" know who they are better than I do, and I'd better present them to the world properly. It's a feeling of power like no other to have characters take off on their own and become *people* to you and the others they are interacting with.

Sometimes you have to go back and rearrange earlier paragraphs or chapters to correspond to what actually happens later on. Great, that sort of spontaneity is a gift of the Muses. I rewrote the first chapter of *Dragonsinger* four paragraphs or chapters to correspond to what actually happens later on. Great, that sort of spontaneity is a gift of the Muses. I rewrote the first chapter of *Dragonsinger* fourteen times until I had it right. And that's after eight or nine rough drafts when I was experimenting with how to start off in the first place. (It's not always that much hard work. And these days, ain't word-processors the best things since sliced bread for that sort of tinkering?)

So, my first deathless advice-line is TELL US A STORY. My next is to learn how to spell and acquire some basic understanding of grammar and syntax. The best "style" emerges from simple clarity of expression, and that requires communicating in accurate language. After all, you wouldn't drive a car, would you, without gas and oil? Well, how could you expect to drive the vehicle of your imagination without consistent spelling and grammar?

You might think that such matters fall within the province of an editor/copy-editor. But you had better convince that copy-editor you basically know what you're doing, or you're in BIG trouble. And if you get changes in your syntax, wouldn't it be much better to *know* when s/he's wrong? I remember how incensed my old friend, Elsie Lee, was when she received back the galleys of a Regency novel and every single word of her carefully constructed period dialogue had been rewritten by a conscientious twenty-two-year-old editor who had never been exposed to the idea that people in historical times spoke differently. She made him change it all back.

So, the second deathless line of advice is to know how to spell and construct a sentence. It gives you confidence.

And that only makes telling a story easier to do.

But in the end, becoming a writer is more DOING than all the agonized inspiration, the grammar, the clever metaphors, the apt similes or polished, witty phrases. So often, brilliant ideas discussed in front of admiring friends die the death of the Doing. They get "talked away" and never reach paper. Writing in itself is a solitudinous life style. But it has to be *done.* All the talking in the world won't do it for you. As Charles Dickens put it,

> "I hold my inventive faculty on the stern condition that it must master my whole life, often have complete possession of me, and make its own demands upon me, and sometimes for months together put everything else away from me."

And he is still right!

So my last *caveat* is: Don't bother to show/send your story to admiring teachers, relatives, friends. *They* aren't buying it. They can warble delight and envy, approval and admiration. But they are not your audience, which cares naught for your tender ego and *demands* a good story. Your relatives are not going to pay you one ruddy cent for your carefully crafted words. Chance your arm: send the wretched thing to the magazine/book publisher of your choice. And keep sending it until it breaks through into publication on its own merits. Having the *story* bought is the only positive assurance that *you* have become a writer.

So, tell us a story!

The Trout
by
Marianne O. Nielsen

About the Author

Most professionals have mixed feelings about writers' clubs. This is because some of them quickly degenerate into venues for petty power struggles, while others turn into mutual-admiration societies. Neither sort does any writer any good.

The writers' club to find, if you can, is one in which there is a tradition of mutual respect for each other and for good work, and a habit of straight-from-the-shoulder but impersonal appraisal of each others' efforts. The most useful atmosphere is one in which judgments are made on stories, not on people, and the judgments on stories are functional. The situation that must happen in the end is that persons of reasonable talent and industriousness could, by dispassionately improving their technical performance, emerge with a professional ability to convey whatever stories they are moved to create. Anything else having to do with the club is persiflage.

From this, presumably we can deduce the nature of the two clubs Marianne Nielsen belongs to, one in Edmonton, Canada, and the other in Moscow, Idaho. Marianne is the fourth Moscow Moffia member to appear in one of the first two W.O.T.F. anthologies.

Unlike the other three persons, she is a Canadian.

She resides in Alberta, where she is a technical writer in an agency providing criminal-justice paralegal services on behalf of Native—what Americans call Indian—Canadians. Her B.A. honors thesis in Sociology was on outlaw motorcycle gangs. Her M.A.thesis was on the Royal Canadian Mounted Police. She has taken three writing courses at the University of Alberta, under the tutelage of noted Canadian writers Rudy Wiebe and Caterina Edwards, but "The Trout" is her first fiction sale.

This excellent runner-up story would be here no matter who had written it or where it came from. But it was sent in to us in particular because she had seen the success of fellow club members. As to how she came to be a member of a club some distance from her home, that appears to have something to do with Steve Fahnestalk, long active in the Moscow group. They were married in 1985 and now reside in Alberta together, although their visits to northern Idaho friends continue.

There's a lot to be said for writing clubs in some cases, and one should not always take a narrow view of their scope.

Lillian heard her daughter cry out in the shower. Unhurriedly, she pulled off her gardening gloves and eased off her wooden shoes. So Margaret's baby was early, just as the doctor had warned them it would be. Lillian found Margaret swathed in a towel, short brown hair plastered to her skull, dripping water onto the bedroom carpet. She was clutching her abdomen and staring fixedly at the half-filled aquarium on top of the bureau.

The sight of the spreading splotch on the green wool carpet prompted Lillian to push the reluctant girl back into the bathroom to dress. Slowly, Margaret dried herself off and pulled on a corduroy jumper. Lillian went downstairs to get their coats and Margaret's suitcase. When she returned, she again found Margaret in front of the fish tank.

"Remember, Mother," the girl murmured, as she stroked the glass. "You have to kill him at noon. Exactly at noon." Lillian glanced at the large gray fish and shuddered. It hovered almost unmoving, except for the faint ripple of its pale gray-green fins and the open and close of its pink-tinted gills.

"Of course, Margaret. I think I know a little more about these things than you." Margaret allowed herself to be led from the room.

The nurses were surprised at Lillian's refusal to stay at the hospital. There was no husband to pace and worry, surely it was Lillian's role now? She pleaded urgent business and asked one particularly attentive nurse to call her when the delivery had begun. Margaret smiled and said nothing, her gaze internal, the only sign of the contractions an occasional falter in her smile.

Once more at home, Lillian retreated to her garden. After a moment's indecision, she wrestled the aquarium down the stairs and placed it on the porch. The thought of that fish alone in her house, able to splash about, to make messes while she was in the garden, made her uneasy. The trout dashed back and forth within the tank but calmed down once the tank was settled in the shade. She grimaced at the scratch marks its metal corners had made in the clean white paint of the porch.

The steps needed painting again, and the plum tree was straggling branches. Jim had teased her about the garden, about her painting the steps every year, about "castrating" the fruit trees, about putting chicken wire along the top of the garden fence to keep out the neighborhood cats. But then, *he* had been the main offender, the main maker of messes in her garden and in her house. He had roamed around, leaving footprints in the garden, tracking grass blades into the kitchen.

She remembered him the evening of the wedding, drunk in the garden, swinging Margaret around by the waist, crushing the lobelia, knocking down the peonies. Then, when he had tried an impromptu minuet with Margaret, he had tripped and fallen in the strawberry patch, destroying four years of careful weeding and fertilizing. Margaret had just laughed at him. And at her, her own mother, when she had demanded that Jim get out of her strawberries, out of her garden, and, finally, out of her house. He had been a drunken, no-good, filthy man, and Margaret had pushed him into her clean, orderly world.

Lillian glared with hatred at the fish. It watched her, a few bubbles trailing up from its mouth.

She shook her head and marched back to the garage to get the pruning shears and ladder. It was three-and-a-half hours until noon, and the garden needed ordering. The funeral two weeks ago had interrupted everything. The potatoes needed hoeing and she should have planted the last row of peas on Saturday. Now the frost would probably get them before they ripened. A magpie watched her from the apple tree as she pulled the ladder up the walk. She had seen the bird scratching in the garden for worms; it and some of the robins. She stooped and threw a dirt clump at it but missed. It laughed at her as it flew away.

Jim's laugh had reminded her of a magpie's; harsh, mocking. She had hated it when he'd begun to come home with Margaret. Lillian had hinted that her daughter should visit alone when Jim was at work or playing base ball in the evening, but Margaret didn't understand. She had always been a foolish girl, never seeing Jim or any man for what he really was. Lillian snipped a twig so hard it flew into her face. She swiped at it angrily. She heard the trout splash in the tank behind her, mocking her, too.

Laughing, teasing, his gray eyes shining, making himself at home in her house as if he owned it. Putting his cup on the table without a coaster. Leaving his shoes on in the house, telling her what plants to put in the garden, what she should cook for supper, what shows were best on television.

The man had been thoughtless, rude, loud and irresponsible right from the start, but Margaret hadn't noticed, even when Lillian had pointed it out, even when she had finally asked Margaret not to bring him around the house any more. Lillian had thought that, for once, Margaret would argue or sulk, but she had simply shrugged and begun staying out late at night. And then she had married him. How like her father, Lillian thought savagely as she wrenched off a stubborn branch. Lillian's ex-husband had been just like that—nothing could influence him, words ran off him like rain off a roof. Shrug and smile, listen and do nothing.

But he was gone, now, she thought with satisfaction, and so was Jim. Two weeks ago she had found a three-pronged carrot and put it in a bucket to wash. It wasn't exactly a mandrake root, but it would have to do. She'd left it there all morning, even when they'd gone out to shop. So he was nearly gone; regretfully, she'd overlooked something. There was still the fish, but she would soon take care of it, too. She glanced at her watch. It was nearly 11:15.

She and Margaret had been shopping for groceries at Safeway when the police had found them. Lillian remembered her joy at seeing the constable. Not only joy at his news, which she knew already, but joy that he could stop Margaret. Lillian had been unable to. Not twenty minutes before, Margaret had cried out and stumbled over to the live fish tank beside the poultry counter. She had been frantically peering inside the tank, making moaning, beseeching noises. The whole thing had been very embarrassing, not to mention unplanned-for.

In the manager's office, the constable had told them that Jim was dead; his truck had rolled into the river, he hadn't gotten out. The constable had offered to drive them home, but Lillian took over. She'd take care of her daughter, she could handle it. There had been no way of getting Margaret to leave the store without more fuss. She had insisted on buying a trout, one particular trout, a trout that had stared back at her with large gray eyes. The same eyes that now watched Lillian from the porch.

Lillian glanced over her shoulder as she climbed

down the ladder. It was 11:30. The trout was swimming back and forth with agitated twists.

She leaned the ladder against the plum tree. She still had time to put in a flat of petunias before noon. She deliberately turned her back on the porch and strode down the flagstone garden path next to the garage. There were sweet peas along the fence and gray Dusty Miller and Red Salvia in regimented rows framing the grass, but it lacked something. There was too much lawn, not enough ornamentation. Still dissatisfied, she found a paper bag in the garage and knelt on it by a flower bed to pull out a few stray bits of stinkweed. One Dusty Miller was leaning too far into the aisle, so she uprooted it and replanted it. She heard a splash from the porch.

Margaret had barely spoken to her since the news of Jim's death, but she had hovered over that miserable fish tank, whispering to the trout, smiling at it. Lillian hadn't counted on Margaret's bringing the fish when she came to stay. The slimy thing had watched her constantly, even when she was asleep. Lillian had slipped into her room one night and the fish had been there, motionless, watching Margaret from the tank. It had turned its great gray eyes to Lillian indifferently, then returned to watching the sleeping form on the bed.

The phone shrilled from the house. She jumped and trotted quickly up the neat stone path. The trout anxiously broke the surface of the water as she passed it. Her watch said 11:55.

It was the nurse from the hospital. Margaret was fine, the head was showing, the baby seemed fine, and she had to get back to the delivery room, she'd ring Lillian later, goodbye.

Lillian strode out onto the porch. The aquarium was empty. The trout lay on the doormat, gasping. It looked as if it had been trying to flop its way into the house. Lillian poked at it distastefully with her foot. It arced violently into the air, trying to fling itself at her. She dodged, and it struck the screen door. Falling back to the mat, it lay motionless. After a moment, she poked it again, more cautiously. It quivered, but seemed too weak to move otherwise.

Squatting down near the fish, Lillian saw that it was still breathing, though painfully, drawing air through gills meant for cool, thick water.

She sat back thoughtfully, her gaze never leaving the trout. It couldn't die, it seemed. Not until she killed it would Jim's soul be free to enter the body of his newborn son. Suddenly Lillian realized the baby was a boy, had to be a boy.

Gingerly she picked the trout up by its stiffening tail. Its mouth gaped open, then closed, but it remained motionless. A small, ugly smile crossed Lillian's face.

She dropped the trout back into the aquarium, where it gulped water and fled into a corner. Lillian wiped her hand on the seat of her jeans. A trout pond would be nice, she decided. In the back section there, by the Dusty Miller. And maybe some cress and lilies along the edges. She smiled at the fish, baring her teeth.

The phone rang shrilly inside the house. That would be the nurse, Lillian knew, announcing the stillbirth of Margaret's baby. She stood to go inside, taking her time.

Illustrated by Charles Rosenthal

Illustrated by Art Thibert

Redmond
by
Kenneth Schulze

About the Author

In part, for winning Second Place in the second quarter of the Writers of The Future contest, Kenneth Schulze was recently named one of the "86 Most Interesting People" in Cleveland, Ohio. Schulze, 34, is also an actor, and the winner of an intramural basketball free-throw contest at the University of Michigan.

He has taught freshman composition at the University of Illinois and has published some stories in small-press journals. "Redmond" is his first try at popular fiction. It comes after years of attending academic writers' conferences, and of entering contests. (Before his W.O.T.F success, Schulze won honorable mentions for a short story and a novel in two other contests; neither work has been published as yet.) Serious about writing in general, and his own writing in particular, he takes an academic approach. That hardly means he's solemn, or even reverent, as a reading of "Redmond" will demonstrate. It may be, however, that it took a devotedly analytical reconsideration of vampirism to unearth some of the hitherto unremarked aspects of vampiric behavior which are incorporated in the following pages. On the other hand, it may simply be that Schulze is a madman.

***Werewolf, vampire, ghoul, unnameable creature from the wastes. The monster never dies. —Cujo,* by Stephen King**

That spring, we learned one of the most promising young bionicists had conceived a secret plan to annex the Soviet Union. After years of research, he apparently possessed the means to do so. Whatever his motives—patriotism, xenophobia, greed, lust for fame, compulsion to ascend the dilatory ranks of his federal agency quickly, to improve his family's standard of living—the Central Intelligence Agency had kept his scheme assiduously under wraps.

It was news to most junior members of the National Security Council, including myself and my gorgeous colleague and occasional mistress, Viv Mitchell. That evening, before our special meeting in Washington, Viv more than counterbalanced my annoyance at having been kept in the dark so long, with her radiant health and good cheer beside me at the huge round table in the main conference room.

"A.Z. who? Never heard of him," I told Viv, enviously, over our surprise agenda. "Another pet of Doctor Friedrich's, I suppose. He's always looking for new blood."

Viv raised her carefully penciled eyebrows. "Tooshert? Sure. He's a gene whiz. His parents were bionicists from Transylvania. They cloned the first Rumanian supergymnasts. Nobody knew until they tricked the KGB and defected in coffins. They settled into an obscure and apparently happy retirement out West. Their son grew up, studied at Southern Cal, did grad work on the Moon. Tooshert's the fellow who developed that Lunar garlic bulb with eighty-six medicinal properties. Remember? Astronauts go wild over it."

"Ah, yes. Wish I had your photographic memory, darling. You've no idea how many newspapers a man in my position has to skim. To say nothing of bulletins and memos, journals——"

Our moderator, Friedrich, interrupted me and others with a remarkably brisk entrance. The fleshy face atop his tall physique was florid with excitement.

"Ladies and gentlemen, I believe we've found the object of our deepest desires at last!"

Our applause was general, polite, politic. And encouraging. Too encouraging, in retrospect. I wish I'd brought my vaporizers. Had I guessed what was soon to transpire I'd have quite possibly tried to blow Tooshert and Friedrich away on the spot.

But of course our guards were forbidden to admit anyone with guns. And it's questionable whether a single brace of vaporizers would have stopped the involved undertakings that had been set in motion long ago by our mutual rationale and the complex machinery of one intelligence agency and another.

At Friedrich's signal, a grinning Tooshert rolled a full-length mirror into the room. "Straight from Westin Hotels," Viv observed to me in a sexy murmur. "Just like the three at my place."

"One for each lover?" I said, hoping she'd deny it,

that she'd profess love for me and me alone. "Or for each couple?"

"Pay attention," Viv admonished me sternly but fondly as she picked at a loose thread on her expensive dress. "They may teach you to turn invisible, or something."

I smiled. "The operative in you will out."

Like others, Viv supposed Friedrich meant to show off the latest in undercover optics—for example, laser derringers or lapels, a pocket door-destroyer, instant camouflage for cameras and personnel—for our next assignment, as in my case, or, in Viv's, her next class. In its faithful reflection, Viv primped a bit, having been too busy, she said, for her wonted powder. For some reason, the diamond necklace I'd given her held my attention. Maybe it was the untimely yet welcome surge of libido I felt. I wanted to rip it off her lovely neck. I'd have given Mercury itself just then to be kissing her. Tickling the insides of her eager ears with my tutored tongue. Licking her creamy throat. Tasting her nepenthe nipples. . . .

And yet, surprisingly, I lacked the erection I got often at thought of screwing Viv. I put it down to age, preoccupation with departmental budgets, and too much vintage burgundy imbibed with another mistress of mine the previous night.

Then again, I can't stand meetings. Official meetings. Maybe that's why they kicked me upstairs. I always want to get away to enjoy the good life. I felt supremely unsuited to be a yes-man. A function, I regret to say, I expected to fulfill that evening. As if it were business as usual.

There was a brief disturbance out in the hall. Something banged around, but muffled, in a small space, as if an animal were trying to escape in a cage. "Tooshert?"

Friedrich said alarmedly.

Tooshert barked—at a third party, it seemed. "Is this how you guard brass? Put your cross back in your uniform! He'll calm down in a minute."

The flurry subsided to a raspy groan. Soon that petered out.

"Recidivists," Tooshert muttered. "Christ Almighty, when will they get with it? A cross in this day and age! Here, of all places."

Friedrich and Tooshert conferred in low voices. You can't foresee everything in Defense.

Lester Lafontant, portly executive of the National Reconnaissance Office, sat drinking-in Viv's shapely profile with his good eye. He'd confessed to me in our cups frequently he was a womanizer who often worried less about his work than the effect his eyepatch had in public. To help finance his engineer's degree he'd sold his right eye to science, and as a result he had a terrible inferiority complex. Much as I sympathized with him (I'd sold my colon for a bachelor's degree), I found myself unnerved by his lecherous fixation on the beautifully vivacious object of my most comforting dreams.

"Think Weapons has come up with another aphrodisiac?" I leaned over my full ashtray to ask. Lester answered in an undertone: "I don't know. Something's sure making me thirsty."

I poured him a glass of water. He shook his head. He reached in front of me, grabbed the pitcher, and guzzled. Such rudeness was most unlike my normally considerate friend, who'd refused my offer of a fifth Manhattan but a short time earlier on the grounds that he was full. For a while there, I wondered whether the mirror wasn't the prototype of an installation calculated to drive troops to water—a tactic maybe key to ambush—or a building material designed to remedy alcoholism or induce some craving for a new product only certain contractors could supply at profit. I resented feeling a bit like a guinea pig, in view of the many years I'd sacrificed already for the Service, even as I washed down an aftertaste of liver.

Friedrich cleared his throat and raised his hands for order, very much the up-and-coming committeeman with a sense of mission to impart as he set out to prove his foresight in having held Tooshert, his favorite protégé, back in privileged obscurity until now.

"I'd like everyone to get a good look at this mirror just in from Westin. Assure yourselves that this is a standard mirror without gimmick or distortion and in no way unusual."

One by one we all inspected the mirror. All except Cassandra, our necromancer from Venus Six. Cassandra hurried to put another finishing touch on her long-awaited memoirs during spare moments before her turn. Tooshert rolled the mirror solemnly around the table for us. He was a small, dark-eyed fellow, with an air of sang-froïd in contrast to the nervousness of his boss. Friedrich always feared seeming overly ambitious.

"Cassandra?"

When the mirror reached her, Cassandra looked up from her memoirs as from a great distance. Her orange eyes widened as if in fright. She pleaded a full bladder and fled.

Alas, it was the last we ever heard of her. Maybe she flew back to Venus Six while there was still time.

"Okay, okay," I said. "It's a normal mirror. So? Will you tell us what this is all about, Mister Chairman?"

"You'll see." Just like a magician, Friedrich was setting us up. Except Friedrich was the assistant, Tooshert the ostensibly ingenious one. Tooshert kept a low profile, however. Possibly so his mentor could take maximum credit for success, at least at first. And to protect his own budding reputation if anything fizzled.

"This had better be good," Lester muttered to Viv. "I have a tennis match tomorrow morning."

"Skeptic." Viv smiled prettily at him between sips of water from her glass. "Where would we be without you?"

So we amused ourselves with banter. Yet, underneath it all, frustrated by the repeated failure of our best spies, we hoped to succeed in some sensational way before voters decided the fate of our President. Impatient for a final solution to the common imperative of physical and moral conquest of our expansionist adversary, we all were willing to consider anything of substantial promise then. Anything.

"Proceed," Friedrich told Tooshert. The hall was silent. Tooshert signaled the guards. The stronger guard rolled in a Plexiglass booth that contained a tall, still, cadaverous figure of indeterminate age in the neatly pressed tuxedo popular behind the Iron Curtain. Its eyes were shut, and for a moment, I thought it a waxwork. It exerted a strange fascination on everybody. The longer I stared at it, the more it reminded me uncomfortably of a monstrous beetle mounted in a cabinet in a local museum—some mutant from our nuclear blasts on Mars that explorers had captured alive and kicking at great loss of human life.

"Great Caesar's ghost," I heard Viv whisper to me. "I've seen him in a movie somewhere. A golden oldie, maybe."

"Yes. I can't put my finger on it, either."

Lester asked, "Another android?" Others echoed his disdain. "Come, come! We all know the pitfalls of android circuitry. Suppose they reprogram him? Remember the Peacekeeper Rebellion!"

"Now, now. No call for alarm, I assure you." Friedrich motioned to the guard, who lowered his vaporizer—rather reluctantly, it seemed—and stepped out into the hall, where a faint crunch-crunch of peanuts, perhaps, perhaps jawbreakers, had replaced the more distracting chatter of the other guard's teeth. Friedrich regarded a sheaf of computer printouts from his own jacket pocket. "This . . . man . . . is flesh and blood."

For a moment I thought I saw the statue's ashen eyelids flicker, as if in a dream, or as if Friedrich had just uttered a magical word. Friedrich nodded at Tooshert and then, with a sigh of relief at having done his duty by us, poured himself a glass of water several bodies'-lengths from the mobile exhibit. Tooshert explained with a hint of pride:

"This, ladies and gentlemen, this is our ultimate weapon."

By now, tobacco smoke had thickened so it bothered even some of the addicted among us. I rose to turn on fans. "Don't bother." Friedrich motioned me back to my seat. "We've sealed the vents expressly for this demonstration."

"Ultimate weapon in what sense?" logistics expert Leland Yamamura asked, his wrist computer ready to calculate optimal damage. "Don't tell me this one contains warheads, too. Somehow, the Kremlin's metal detectors always trip us up."

"Oh, no," Tooshert said. "Only a tiny but powerful destruct mechanism implanted in his skull. Thanks to my engineers and neurosurgeons, I control Redmond with this handy device." Tooshert held up a metallic wafer with several buttons.

"One false move, and—*poof!* He knows that. Now." Tooshert rolled the mirror behind Redmond. "Notice anything out of the ordinary?"

Rob Jones, from the State Department, was the first to gasp.

"He casts no reflection!"

"Impossible," said Pete Montgomery, chief of the Defense Mapping Agency. "Isn't he matter?"

On inspection, Montgomery confirmed the astonishing fact that Redmond cast a shadow but had no reflection.

"What did you do, immerse him in molten mirror, then?"

"They're working on it," Tooshert said in answer to Viv's question. "But with androids. No, this fellow'd rather be dipped in something else entirely."

"Formaldehyde?" I quipped. Friedrich and Tooshert gave me withering looks.

"Very funny. Check your superstition banks."

I meditated a moment. But my cranial computer had nothing pertinent on matter visible and invisible to the same person at the same time, or anything else that seemed appropriate to the situation. My neonatal clinic had frowned on superstition.

"Doesn't Redmond ring bells with anyone?" Friedrich asked. We sat there stumped. Friedrich turned, smiling triumphantly, to Tooshert.

"Bravo, my friend. Bravo! A century of forgetfulness is on our side. Perhaps even Transylvanians will have forgotten. . . ."

"It's coming to me," Viv said.

"Think hard," I said.

Viv said, "It's on the tip of my tongue."

"If this is the 'invisible man' you've been crowing about to us for so long now," Lester said, "I'm not impressed in the least. Is he bionic?"

"Better than bionic," Tooshert said. "Redmond's a vampire."

"A what?" some asked in perplexity. Their nurses might well have omitted "vampire" from their vocabulary implants after birth, on the assumption they'd rarely if ever see one gathering intelligence. Hence they probably would have considered that information superfluous for future agents. But almost instantaneously one of us made the proper connection. Connie Furmorton, Rhodes Scholar and director of the Federal Research Division of the Library of Congress, exclaimed, "Brilliant! I see now why they call you creative intelligence personified." Was it her blush that intensified my thirst? I helped myself to another pitcher of water. Tooshert shook his head. But I drank anyway, under a strange compulsion, and, momentarily, I felt my blood pressure rise. Some of the others, I noticed, looked popeyed, full of fluid, the way I felt. Furmorton concluded with enthusiasm:

"You plan to resurrect superstition and spread it abroad to subvert the Reds at the very source!"

"I'm flattered," Tooshert said. And Friedrich: "Thank you. It was one of my more fruitful suggestions, if I say so myself."

He smiled expansively, and a bit cockily, at Tooshert. Tooshert shot him a murderous glance. Friedrich had a habit of appropriating whatever important proposals he felt he could get away with for his own advancement. Someone stood to get a raise and promotion, maybe even a Medal of Honor, if this project panned out to the satisfaction of our Commander-in-Chief. After thought, Friedrich added, to my initial puzzlement:

"But I'd hate to steal my friend's fire." He turned once again to Tooshert. "Do the honors, pal."

"Of course." Tooshert recited to us a definition from the *American Heritage Dictionary of the English Language:* " 'Vampire: In folklore, a reanimated corpse that rises from the grave at night to suck the blood of sleeping persons.' "

Tooshert left a pregnant silence. "Naturally, we had a hell of a time finding Redmond. Ours was the first official search for a vampire in many decades. But with persistence and a little luck—"

"Omigod," Viv interjected.

"What?" Montgomery asked her. Viv looked at him in consternation.

"Are we gonna bleed Soviet teams during Olympics? That'd be so unsportsmanlike."

"That's one potential application," Friedrich said with a mixture of approval and forgiveness. "I'm sure we all can come up with many, many others. Hands on this one."

I raised my hand. Friedrich nodded. I said: "We could prolly assassinate virtually every homosexual agent they've got."

"Good," said Tooshert. "Fortunately, Redmond is no respecter of gender. Male or female's fine with him. Race? Likewise. He'll even drink Martian, if our laboratory reports are correct. Another benefit: You needn't be asleep for him to bite you. In fact, I rather think he'd prefer you awake. The sense of achievement and all."

I could have sworn I saw the ghost of a smile cross Redmond's anemic face. What succulent delights did he see on the screens of his lids? Russians, I hoped. Could he hear us? Through a speaker perhaps, like a subject about to receive final briefing before waking to start an experiment outside its incubator. Or like a star witness shielded from hit men in a state case against the Cosa Nostra, what with the brutal cast to what some might have seemed aristocratic features in the lowest range of charm. As if any contemporaries of his were still around to dispatch him. Has Tooshert had a grave robbed? I wondered. Or, Tooshert's assurances aside, was this Redmond actually some top-secret experimental model from InfoAndroid?

It turned my stomach to envision what must have been a whole network of Earth satellites probing necropoli and the odd field, cabbage patch, backyard and penthouse garden for how long to detect a hypothetical anomalous rate of decay without the least assurance of locating a corpse like the decidedly ghoulish Lazarus in our midst. What an expenditure of resources! And yet necessity's necessity . . . and it had worked!

"Where does he bite?" Viv asked.

Friedrich said, "Why don't you ask him yourself? Go ahead. Redmond can hear you. We've put speakers in his cabinet. Then he can show his stuff."

"Wait," I said. "Let me go get a gun."

"That won't be necessary." Friedrich evidenced contempt for my precautionary request. "We control him, remember."

One of the guards handed Tooshert a box, then shut the door to the conference room. Tooshert opened the box. "Douay Bibles," he said, "from museums." He handed one to each of us.

"What are Bibles for?" Montgomery asked.

Friedrich said, "Ask the forcefield expert."

"I've never seen one," I said, examining the moldering artifact before me with a curiosity shared by other advisors. "I do remember my grandparents saying there were Bibles before the Frost Wars."

"The ancients used Bibles," Friedrich said. "To ward off evil."

"Evil?"

"Bad influence. It's irrelevant. Just hold it up," Tooshert said, "if Redmond happens to come at you. I doubt he will. We've exposed him repeatedly to plenty of lab assistants without incident."

"If you say so."

Tooshert stuffed the crack between carpet and door with a garlic-scented strip of insulation. "Just to be on the safe side. Redmond can transform himself to a certain extent. That's why we sealed the vents."

"Don't forget the top," Viv said. "Sides, too. If he's that protean."

"Don't worry. He isn't," Tooshert said, "but just in case. . . ."

Tooshert stuffed the crack between the doorframe and top of the door. "Satisfied?" he asked. Viv nodded in compromise. Tooshert went and unlocked the cage. He left the door wide open, as a coroner might an upright coffin for inquest. Until the vampire came out of his trance, Redmond himself evoked some humongous antediluvian bird with one thin wing out of shell. The inner surface of the cage door mirrored the far wall, but according to Tooshert it had prevented Redmond from seeing himself standing there on display. In his shoes, that would have tormented me to no end. No wonder Tooshert had nearly blown his top at the guard. A lowly guard with his crucifix had jeopardized Tooshert's research and career with a potent fetish.

After hesitation, Viv let me pen crosses surreptitiously on her palms and then penned crosses on mine. They'd all come off soon with sweat. . . .

Presently, Redmond took a breath. And smiled to himself, as if relieved to see we hadn't condemned him to a painful adjustment, for example, to an otherworldly atmosphere of methane, or a torture chamber and test sites in orbit. The sight of his two fangs caused Viv and others to gasp.

"Can he retract them?" Montgomery and Yamamura asked.

"I'm afraid not," Friedrich said. "We tried cosmetic substitutes, of course. But Redmond rejected them. He'll just have to keep a straight face in public."

"Whose fangs are those, then?"

"His own," Tooshert said. "Our dental surgeons claim he can grow fangs as easily as hydras can heads.— "Redmond?" Tooshert pressed a button on his control wafer. "We moved your mirror. You can come out now."

Redmond opened his eyes and stepped abruptly from his hell into ours.

"Ah! Free at last!"

Redmond seemed so voracious for sensation as he stood there, between Friedrich and Tooshert, sizing up his interrogators with briefly crazed eyes, that I nearly pitied him. Redmond probably hadn't a friend in the world. Who would, with fangs dripping saliva (or is it venom, as many contend for current lack of specimens? Or, as descendants of his maintain, moving in conversationally for the kill, is it rather nectar from a fountain of youth?) while he stared at you as if you were his first square meal in centuries? His dark eyes glittered—was it menacingly?—with the almost lunatic avidity for company that assails many cosmonauts on return to Earth after a seeming eternity in space. His attitude seemed more assertive by far than one would expect of a rejuvenated corpse conditioned to cooperate with his saviors. It was as if he'd hopped off a slab in a morgue, delighted someone had pronounced him dead by mistake, and rushed to us to deliver a speech on resurrection, with gusto.

"Welcome to your briefing," Friedrich said. "These

folks all have missions to give you in coming days. For every mission completed, remember, you get a whole death row in the state of your choice. We'll throw in a fatso for every current formula or blueprint that's eluded our top operatives. Who else would offer you such a deal?"

Redmond spoke with a cold smile that gave me shivers. "Why, the other side. But of course, I *am* looking forward to a feast of Russians. Very much indeed."

For all her documented resistance to hypnosis, Viv sat nearly mesmerized, like a mouse before a snake. Several other women sat that way, too. More so, it seemed to me, when finally I tore my gaze from him, than we men did.

But the possibility he could ever supplant me in Viv's affections came to seem ludicrous when he got his drip under control. By an effort, maybe, of will. Because neither Friedrich nor Tooshert had done anything to stop it.

"We'll forget about those custodians you mistook for supper," Tooshert was saying. "Stick with Russian agents. And remember, every Russian agent less on Pennsylvania Avenue is one step closer to a truly glorious fulfillment on Nevsky Prospekt."

"Fine," Redmond said. "Fine!"

He watched Montgomery drain the last pitcher of water with much the same sort of fascination with which we watched him breath. Maybe it was Montgomery's sanguine features, shiny with perspiration, that caused Redmond to laugh, hollowly, for a moment.

"How well you've provided for me!"

Redmond licked his thin, bloodless lips in anticipation.

Furmorton glanced at an evaluation screen before

her, then fixed Friedrich with her green eyes, while Viv, acting as our secretary, monitored a recording computer. Someone might take us to task for this, success or no success. The president supported our initiative secretly, without Congressional approval. Of course, we could always bury inquiries in red tape. For decades, if necessary. But once the media got hold of Redmond, so would our enemies. Secrecy, we all agreed, was of the essence.

"I assume he has a language converter, cranial transponder, and self-destruct mechanism designed for this project."

"There's no point implanting self-destruct when I can explode him myself by satellite," Tooshert said. "He does have the transponder built in and can send over whatever information he gathers."

"Suppose he gets caught."

"Then we explode his head and they have one hell of a mess to clean up."

"Redmond has everything he needs," Friedrich interjected. "Show us what you can do with your foreign tongues."

"Restate!"

Tooshert impaled Friedrich with a sharp glance, then he said to Redmond, "What he means is, speak Chinese."

Redmond spoke ten dialects of Chinese. Then, without prompting, Russian. Polish. Czech. German. Swedish. Norwegian. Japanese. Burmese. Thai. Korean. Various dialects of Hindi and Arabic. Swahili. Portuguese. Spanish. Basque. French. Colonial Titanese. He also had a considerable number of jargons—medical, military, bureaucratic, psychological, and others—at his command. And he could speak each orally, albeit with a slight Rumanian accent, as well as via cranial transponder, in case of jamming or electrical malfunction. It was a most impressive, if ghoulish, demonstration of InfoBiotechnology, not to mention collaborative perseverance. Some applauded. Others, including Viv and me, withheld judgment.

Friedrich smiled at me.

"You look doubtful, Conrad."

"A vaporizer is far more efficient."

"True. But woefully limited. Can a handgun discredit an entire government? Once word gets out that the top Soviet brass is all vampiric, and the populace feels threatened as never before, Ivan Ivanovich will be ripe for revolt. And revolution is your forté."

"You see, his bite is contagious," Tooshert explained to everyone. "The more Redmond bites, the more we have on our side. Neat and sweet."

"Suppose he bites one of our own."

"We dispose of accidents. As in any operation. Redmond may be dead—and our monitors all agree that he is—" Here Friedrich smiled graciously at Redmond, who bared his fangs with a facile expression part leer, part snarl, in ugly imitation of Friedrich. "—but we could always incinerate him. Drown him in acid. Deprive him of his native soil, which restores his functions during daylight. Or send him to another galaxy. The possibilities are infinite."

"Yes," said Tooshert. "Or we could simply drive a stake through his heart."

Viv shuddered. Tooshert nodded. "It was an awfully crude way to go. The ancients were into saving souls, if you remember. Our friends in the black market say someone drove a stake through Redmond's heart. But apparently medical students removed it to study him. Hence we've given him a Jarvik AC-XIV with antistake radar. And a homing device for good measure."

"In any event," Friedrich followed up, "the Russian

people will dispose of their own living dead as they see fit. Meantime, we replace their leaders with our trainees. On the most attractive terms, of course. Eventually, we may all be one big, happy family. Although I don't see that happening for several centuries, at least." He left a pause. "Are we agreed, then, we ought to request six trillion from Appropriations? The Redmonds of this world are certainly cheaper than any battlestation over Moscow."

"That goes beyond saying," Yamamura spoke up politely. "But first, I think we'd all like to see your brain-child in action."

"I'm glad you ask." Friedrich addressed the inter-com: "Bring in the prisoner and the nets now."

We expected an assistant. The woman failed to show. She was maybe scared. For all we knew, she'd been getting drunk on vodka with the prisoner.

"His last request was for a case of Smirnoff's," Friedrich remarked in a matter-of-fact voice. "Believe me, this is more humane than electrocution or canning."

Viv was about to speak up when Friedrich put up his hands. "Relax. This man Nash went apeshit. Killed over three hundred civilian spectators at a soccer match. Hand grenades and laser."

"I didn't think you'd choose just anyone."

Part of one wall swung open, silently trundling in a young man with a ruddy complexion. He wore a prisoner's uniform stained with vomit. Nash stood, bound to a post, beside a stack of butterfly nets, which Tooshert distributed promptly to each of us. Friedrich and Tooshert each took one, too. I watched Redmond. Redmond's head swiveled like a roof beacon atop a patrol car. Scanning, maybe, for stakes. He took a step toward the door and halted. Maybe the garlic was too much for him. He noticed the mirroring cabinet door and recoiled as if stung. Tooshert seemed to enjoy his reaction and ensuing decision. Redmond stared, his eyes somehow hardened before us, at the vent nearest Viv. A long moment later, his gaze slid away again, to my immense relief, to thick curtains drawn across the window, beyond which you could hear the faint roar of a distant jet.

Maybe Redmond was homesick. I didn't ask.

Friedrich ripped Nash's shirt open to the waist and then stepped away. "Will the vodka affect Redmond at all?" Jones asked. Tooshert clucked. "Of course not. He's dead. He'll pass it naturally.—Redmond?"

Redmond said, "My pleasure." And turned into a bat. Just like that. In a flash. One man cried out in fright. Redmond's tuxedo collapsed instantly into a heap on the floor. Redmond himself circled overhead. We had to duck.

"Go to it!" Friedrich said. Redmond hovered over and shat on Friedrich. Friedrich yelped in surprise and indignation. And pain. Tooshert, who'd been laughing at Friedrich, exclaimed: "That's enough of that!"

Friedrich's hair was singed.

Momentarily, Redmond flapped over the table toward Nash. Nash gaped drunkenly at his now hideous executioner. Redmond's transformation into what we all considered a repulsive creature had reduced his mesmerism so that, when Redmond hovered over him, Nash fought as best as he could. He strained at his tight bindings, and, failing to escape, hit Redmond with gobs of spit. Redmond retreated, like a jet pilot startled by fire from a reportedly harmless target. He went into a holding pattern over Lester.

Lester cringed. "Not me!"

Tooshert exclaimed, "Your Bible!" Lester seized his Bible and held it high. Redmond veered away toward Viv and me. We warded him off with our own Bibles. His guano burned holes, in both, from cover to cover.

"Indoor napalm!" Tooshert said in amazement. "That's great!"

I thought otherwise. There was an ugly burn now on Viv's palm. Viv bit her lip, but her eyes watered. I felt like giving Tooshert and Friedrich each a good solid roundhouse to the kisser.

"Did he ever do this in your lab?" Friedrich asked.

Tooshert said, "Hell, no! He was gentle as a lamb!"

Redmond headed toward Tooshert. Tooshert crossed himself quickly, as he'd shown us how to do, but it didn't seem to faze Redmond in the least. Tooshert dropped his net and crawled beneath the table in alarm.

"Remember, I can blow you up!"

I volunteered to catch Redmond, but Friedrich and Tooshert talked me out of it. "He's just working out the kinks," Tooshert hoped.

"Somebody zap that bugger!" Nash cried. Redmond buzzed him once. Nash spat a hocker that missed. Redmond dropped instantly and fastened onto his bare throat. Nash screamed. It paralyzed us all. We watched Redmond draw in his wings a bit at either side of Nash's neck so that Nash seemed to be wearing a magnetic bow tie. A giant black bow tie that slurped.

Nash jerked his head violently. "Help!"

Still Redmond clung on, riding a crimson wave. "That's more like it," Friedrich said. "Good, my friend! Good."

Nash gave blood-curdling cry after cry. The guards knocked loudly on the door. Friedrich assured them everything was going according to plan. Nash's cries subsided to gurgles. And soon ceased.

"Ah, well," Tooshert said. "Guess he was just hungry, eh?" Tooshert ventured soon into the open.

Redmond continued to feast.

Tooshert remembered to time him by a wrist watch. "We need to know what his capacity is in real life."

At length, however, Friedrich sought a halt to the demonstration. "You're getting our carpet filthy," Friedrich said. Blood continued to run down the front of poor Nash. Viv, Montgomery, Yamamura, and others turned away in disgust. "He's dead. Why don't you call it a day?"

"You can take human form again," Tooshert said. "We're satisfied."

But Redmond was not.

"We've got a nice, fat orangutan for you," Friedrich said, coaxingly, with growing impatience. "Back at the lab."

But Redmond remained a bat. On a sudden he disengaged himself from the slumped-over corpse, squealing an eerie squeal that gave me gooseflesh. It haunts me even in sleep. It was a penetrating, sinister execration such as might well be flung by a prisoner of centuries whose hatred had remained as intense as ever—a harbinger of havoc and ruination such as I'd never heard, not even in battle. It was as if whole ages of famished animosity had found voice, found release at last, through the red, dripping rictus of a ghastly face that was no longer the face of a bat but of Redmond's corpse. His leering head was now the size of a quarter as he flapped, mothlike, with what grotesque mockery of his makers, over us. He flew much faster than before, refueled. His wingspan inches wider. His ejecta hotter yet, in his stinking breeze.

"What the devil! Shape up, or we deactivate you." Friedrich aimed at sternness, but stood trembling at this turn of events. "Fine way to start your career!"

Redmond made another bombing run. His guano

blinded Jones for life. Montgomery lunged a net at Redmond, but Redmond dodged easily. Tooshert yelled in anger: "What, are you crazy? You might kill him! Think of our project, Monty! Our nets are only for emergency use."

Heedless, Montgomery and others swung their nets in a frenzy. They drove Redmond back across the room. Redmond perched, on the curtain rod, the size suddenly of a mouse, wings tight against his panting little furry abomination, explosive vermin.

"What do you say we hook you up regularly to an IV bottle?" Furmonton cried up to him in a futile attempt to negotiate, while Lester and Montgomery stalked Redmond from either flank. Redmond dripped fire on the curtains. Flames started to lick upward. Viv screamed. I spun around. To my horror, the dead Nash stepped grinning, fanged now, from the post. Nash passed through his bindings like mist, and then stopped short, corpse intact, as if awaiting orders.

"My sincerest congratulations!" Friedrich said to Tooshert. "You had me worried there, old buddy. Now get our friend here to behave. . . ."

Redmond flapped through smoke, then settled, grinning, upon another section of curtain rod near Lester. Lester pushed abandoned chairs aside for a clear shot at Redmond. He was about to lunge netfirst when Friedrich tackled him from behind. They wrestled. Tooshert tried to tackle Montgomery. Montgomery flung Tooshert aside.

"Idiot!" Tooshert hissed above the control wafer, still in his clutches. "I could have accidentally wrecked him! Guards!" he yelled. And Montgomery:

"Guards!"

The guards pushed the door in with difficulty and rushed in over fallen garlic rags, vaporizers drawn, while

Tooshert pointed excitedly at Montgomery. "Arrest that traitor!"

"Bring an extinguisher!" Montgomery ordered. One guard ran out the door with a shriek. The other froze. Room temperature seemed to plunge the moment Nash strode to Viv. Viv cried out, then gazed in sudden fascination into now deadly eyes. So did I.

"I'll make it all better for you," Nash said, in a croak like Redmond's, as he embraced her. "Your every conquest will be delicious."

Cries of "Stop him!" and a sharp shove from Jones broke my brief trance. I threw myself at Nash and tried to cut off his wind with my bionic grip. Nash laughed. In a flash he escaped me by changing into a bat.

Now there were two of them.

"Why in hell doesn't Redmond answer our transponders?" Montgomery demanded. Tooshert denied any responsibility whatsoever for our plight. "He's on your frequency now!"

It was mayhem. Jones, Yamamura, and others beat a hasty retreat out the open door, through which a draft fed the curtain flames. It seemed many minutes before we heard alarms sound in the hall.

It was many more before police and firemen arrived. By then it was too late.

Redmond and Nash flapped overhead, now near each other and now far apart, like two balls in a video breakout game, adding to the smoke with an amazing amount of incendiary excreta that burned clothing and scalp, shoulders and hands, foreheads, as well as furniture and carpeting, while we struck out with nets. Lester had knocked Friedrich cold with an uppercut to the jaw. Now Redmond and Nash harried Lester. Lester guarded Friedrich with more than dutiful swings of his net, while

Redmond and Nash bobbed in mid air just beyond its swell, as if daring him to go after them. His lunge at them nearly put out my right eye as I started to drag Friedrich toward the door. I managed to duck the darting Nash. But Redmond landed smack on my back. Instantly, Lester and Furmonton and Viv rained blows on Redmond and me with their net handles. Redmond squealed. I rolled over, unbitten, to see him spiral overhead, a bomber pilot getting bearings, and suddenly I felt my left cheekbone burn. I bear scars of his scattershot to this day.

"Got him!" Montgomery cried exultantly and swung his net to the floor. Nash flapped entangled in mesh. "Don't!" Tooshert screamed. "That's science you're destroying!" But Furmorton raised her boot anyway.

Nash turned into a mouse. In a flash he nosed through netting and scurried beneath the table.

"Listen," Tooshert instantly tried to wheedle him in a fit of let's-be-reasonable-about-this-little-snafu. "You can have all the cheese you like. Just cooperate with us."

Furmorton gave chase. Tooshert shoved her against a chair by the table and she sprawled. I got a glimpse of bare thighs. Nash must have, too. Before anyone could catch him, Nash ran up her dress. It startled her so she banged her head against the tabletop. She crumpled. At once Viv went and ripped Furmorton's skirt open to get at Nash. She clapped a hand over her mouth in horror. "Hell, we'll never get him out of there!"

Furmorton screamed bloody murder.

"Shoot me! Strangle me! Hurry up! Electrocute me or something!"

Viv stood over her, ready to bash Nash if he should appear. But Nash remained hidden.

Our distress calls brought an Army helicopter. We

heard it, over crackle of flame, over the smashing of the glasses and pitchers and evaluation screens we threw to bring Redmond down, over our frantic oaths, before we spotted it. The first guard returned with an extinguisher and got the second to help him put out the fire. The blackened ceiling may have been fireproof, but the curtains were half gone, and one wall was partly charred, by the time Lester and others and I ripped the rod out from paneling above the window and stamped out embers.

Redmond harassed others of us, impervious maybe to fumes that made us mortals cough, our eyes to water, while he dodged Bibles and nets and shards of mirror from his erstwhile cage, which someone had smashed. Redmond could have flown the coop if he could no longer smell garlic in the burning stink, but remained maybe to protect Nash and enjoy our panic.

And suck our blood.

The overhead lights went out all of a sudden. Left in faint moonlight, I thought the fire had shorted a wire until I saw Tooshert by the light-switch. Tooshert called the helicopter by transponder in a code I wasn't privy to, and got a terse reply. Maybe the crew realized that he'd gone mad. Because when I requested help, the pilot assured me he had vaporizers trained on us all.

"Fire!" I yelled a command.

But he didn't vaporize us. Instead he switched on a powerful searchlight that threw us all into stark relief. That made Redmond squeal—although it didn't seem to harm him—and made Tooshert swear. Tooshert kicked me in the groin. I doubled over on the floor. Montgomery fetched Tooshert a blow that knocked the control wafer from his hands and sent him staggering backward. Tooshert groaned, fell on his knees, and groped wildly for the wafer. He didn't see it. I crawled painfully toward it.

Montgomery ignored my plea for help and instead stalked Redmond in anger again.

Viv screamed. I turned to see her standing still above Furmorton, who lay undergoing a metamorphosis that chilled me to the marrow.

"Fire!" Lester repeated while he tried to corner Redmond. But the pilot told the gunner to hold fire till orders came from headquarters.

For Furmorton lay growing. Her waistline was suddenly a bulge and then rose steadily like so much dough in a hot oven, as in a movie of a human pregnancy run fast forward. It ballooned through her torn dress. Simultaneously her hair turned white, and the rest of her body shriveled up. Her legs shriveled up. Her shoulders. Arms. Hands. Neck. Face. Her teeth fell out, her hair. Within moments, she turned sixty, eighty, one hundred. A hag. Her screams ceased only when she sprouted fangs and lay inert, skeletal but enormously pregnant. Nearby, Redmond circled overhead, like a hawk above its nest.

"What are you waiting for?" Viv cried. "Fire!"

And the pilot: "We can't! We have orders now to record. We're filming you all for Research and Defense."

Several more advisors fled.

Friedrich was coming to. Several bodies'-lengths from Friedrich, meanwhile, Lester sought to drive Redmond into Montgomery's net. Why doesn't Redmond change back into human form to hypnotize us? I remember wondering. Maybe he wanted his god-children to see him a bat when first they all saw light . . . so they wouldn't mistake him for one of us . . . and maybe he feared that a man-sized target would get zapped.

Tooshert used a net to trip up the first guard, who fell on his vaporizer and disappeared. Plaster dust and soundproofing fell from the hole shot in the ceiling and

A. Thibert 85

briefly blinded me. I heard Viv yell above me: "Guard!" When my sight returned, through tears, I saw Tooshert kick her, snatch up the vaporizer and turn it on the second guard. The two of them vaporized each other.

Friedrich got up and lurched toward Redmond. Redmond swooped toward him. Montgomery's net missed Redmond by inches. A fatal miss, for Redmond went straight for the jugular—and connected. Friedrich screeched; his hands fled to his throat to dislodge Redmond. Redmond proved faster.

"Jesus," Lester said. "Break his wings!"

Montgomery and Lester started toward Redmond. "Stand back!" Viv yelled. "Conrad found the controls."

I had the destruct wafer. I waved it. They tipped the table over together with a mighty oomph and dove behind it. "Wait," she cried, pointing. I looked. Friedrich staggered with his last mortal strength to the window, Redmond wedded to his neck. I jumped up to pull him away.

But at that moment Furmorton's corpse exploded bats. A cloud of bats the size of small moths settled almost instantly on Friedrich. Another came at us.

I hit the destruct button. Blood, bone, bits of Redmond's and Friedrich's flesh splattered the wall behind us. We waited.

It was weird. The window had blown out in the explosion, but no bats attacked us.

We peeped over the table. What was left of Friedrich's body—legs, fingers, viscera—lay on the floor, among dozens of bats, some twitching, others inert. And many, many parts of bats.

We looked in vain for an identifiable trace of Redmond.

"God," Viv said. "We've done it now."

To our mutual horror, one bat flew up and around

and out the blasted window frame. Another followed suit. Another. And another. And another. Wings grew heads. Heads grew wings. Body bits regenerated within moments and took wings. Until we had the room to ourselves.

That was last spring.

It's a different world now. By far. You daren't go anywhere without a plexiglass collar on. That's if you can afford one. Even then, you're at constant risk. People report vampire bites on all parts of the human body, although the jugular seems the prime target in 89.55% of verified vampire attacks here and abroad. When you meet somebody now, outdoors or indoors, the first thing you remember to check is their throat. A blemish the size of a pinprick there shuts door after door . . . can endanger your career, family, friends, neighbors, and you.

Since Redmond, of whom researchers say our only trace is his innumerable descendants, people have killed at the drop of a hat over a tracheotomy. Hickey. Bee-sting. Smudge. Refusal to remove a bandage or scarf on request. Heaven help you if you're Rumanian, you own a cemetery, often visit cemeteries or other places where vampires may congregate during daylight, avoid mirrors, or don't surround yourself with garlic, Bibles, biblical bookmarks and other religious incunabula. And heaven help you if you have long teeth. . . .

People have paid fortunes this past year to have scars or beauty marks removed from their throats or permanently concealed. Lots of people wear turtlenecks around the clock, even in muggy weather. Hence it's become customary to expose your plexiglass for at least a moment before you say hello, shake hands, take tea.

At times, as after a particularly vivid account of a witnessed vampirization, or after a nightmare, I sleep with one hand taped to my throat under my plexiglass. That's regardless of whether I'm naked—for example to console Viv and others on the loss of loved ones—or, more often, dressed in reflective clothing, all the rage the world over. Of course, like so many of the affluent, Viv and I wear garlic blessed by one cleric or another.

You can't be too careful. Even with bodyguards, with dogs, early-warning devices, charms, incantations, blood offerings. Most attacks seem to occur after sundown. But people report attacks with alarming frequency in underground garages, missile silos, mines, wine cellars, bank vaults, tunnels at all hours.

Everyone wants a submarine. Ship companies offer vampire-free submarine cruises now to Antarctica and the Arctic. At present, I'm on twenty waiting lists. So's Viv. Even with our clout as government employees, however, years may pass before our names top any of them.

Vampires are everywhere. Even, some say, in space stations, on the Moon and Mars, and elsewhere in our Solar System. I shudder to think some may be bound to other parts of the Milky Way without our knowing it. Already, the federal government, foreign governments and various international agencies are radioing messages to the effect that if aliens happen to discover vampires aboard our probes and ships it isn't our fault and can anyone help?

With or without intervention by aliens, however, mankind will probably survive, if often on the threshold of mass hysteria. Vampires require fresh human blood to thrive. My constant fear is that one of these nights they may round up everyone like cattle somehow to control our population. On the other hand, they all may leave on ships we supply this month, when Washington and Moscow start to carry out our joint promise to cede them a planet of prisoners, freaks, and other human misfits thousands of light-years from Earth.

In the meantime, I always keep at least one vaporizer within reach.

Mudpuppies
by
Robert Touzalin

About the Author

Robert Touzalin is not his real name; his real name, he says, is "too plain and common to be memorable." Who are we to argue? One of an artist's privileges is to invent himself, especially if he is as good as the author of "Mudpuppies," which won First Place in the second quarter of the contest.

Touzalin is 29, and some years ago took a writing course under William Kloefkorn, the Nebraska state poet; other than that, he has simply practiced writing for ten years while working toward a teaching certificate in Natural Sciences. He is also properly proud of being able to drive a forklift, fix a glue gun, and of his being a pretty good runner "in spite of short legs and wide hips." Manual dexterity, persistence, and pride are valuable attributes in the arts.

Since winning his quarter, Touzalin has sold his first novel to a publisher, at the recommendation of contest judge Robert Silverberg. He has also sold "a small story" to an SF anthology.

If attitude counts—and sometimes it does—Touzalin's sort of modest confidence and well-organized unpretentiousness augur for a long and successful career, or at least one in which quiet satisfactions prevail over dramatic traumas. To quote Silverberg on reading "Mudpuppies," "I knew from the first moment that I was in the hands of someone who knew what he was doing." We think you will agree; we rather think that Touzalin is already beginning to make a name for himself.

I hear them. I feel them coming, their bare feet on the smooth bleached planks of the dock, and I stand and lay my book on the chair and then turn. They are a gaudy pair, I think—lean enough to be brittle. Their scalps are shaved slick and tatooed with 3-D scarlet snakes, and all they wear are Army-green shorts and necklaces of Ganymede ice and small diamond rings on every toe. I can see the diamonds glitter. I spot a familiar something in one of their faces. "Yes?" I say, my voice glancing friendly. "What can I do for you gentlemen?" My manners are crisp, as always, and thoroughly dressed for dinner.

"We have a boat," says one, handing me a crumpled ticket damp with sweat. "We're early but thought you'd take us as we are."

I open the ticket and read. "Okay," I tell them, "you'll need life jackets," pointing at the rack where dozens hang. "Read the rules of the lake, please, and then I'll sure take you out."

"Fine." He spies my book and pauses, reading the title, his expression cool and passive. His friend—the one with the familiar face—begins fiddling with the jackets. I turn and watch him, noticing how glassy his eyes seem. He is moving as though in a dream, pulling straps through buckles, and he is smiling altogether too much.

I stroll closer, studying him.

His friend sees me and comes to help him, pulling the jacket snug and turning him and reading with him the list of Do's and Don'ts.

So I decide to wait and watch and hope that something will happen to make up my mind for me. I leave the boathouse and squint at the water, out at the slow August day. There is a gusty wind and a peaceful heat, and with summer old the lake is empty. Paddleboats creak and rattle beneath the dock. A rubbery mudpuppy, black and gruesome, swirls from the bottom just to snap at the air. All the sailboats, bright and ready, are clinging to foam-metal buoys by lengths of soggy rope. Theirs has a red-and-white sail on which the emblem of the Enclave is pressed: a simple tree growing on a simple mountain, the sun a lightless circle behind both.

I wander down to the end of the dock. They follow. I step down onto the boat I use for patrols and shuttling, slipping into my own jacket; then I steady the scow for them and wait, the foggy familiar one suddenly full of grace and precision.

They settle in, side by side and facing me. "It's a nice day," remarks the talking one.

"Very."

"I'd like some more wind, though," he claims, telling me, "I love sailing. The more the better."

"Too much wind kills the fun."

"Do you think?"

"Too much wind and you'll have to come in."

"Fair. Fair." He elbows his friend. "Isn't that fair?"

The foggy one nods, smiling broadly, and the snakes on his head seem to squirm a little closer. I'd fear being bitten if I didn't know better. "Ready?" I start the outboard and putter us out, thinking. Suddenly I recognize the foggy one's face, remembering that nose and those cold blue eyes on the news the other night—absent the pharmaceuticals and plus a dense carpet of white, white hair. The Nobel Prize winner who belonged to that face, now deep in his nineties, had told me to vote for an increased fusion program. He had assured me that my billions would be wisely invested, pooh-poohing the technical problems that had plagued all efforts before.

This version of him, maybe eighteen, is hawking a different product. Reaching into the bulky pockets of his shorts, he finds a piece of hard candy wrapped in household cellophane. This he hands to me, grinning. I quickly slip the gift into my own pocket, telling him, "Great. Thanks," without enthusiasm.

The talking one is watchful, gauging me with clear brown eyes.

I think, "I'll watch them. I'll keep with them. If they're sloppy, I'll drag them in."

I pull alongside their sailboat and hold us to it, and they clamber over and get themselves set. The talking one tells me, "Thank you." The foggy one gives me a small sideways look, another smile, then makes a pill-popping motion with his wrist and hand.

I push away.

They manage to unclip themselves from the buoy and sail away, not with skill exactly but with workable techniques. I move out onto the lake with them, the outboard softly purring. I can hear their triangular sail shudder with the gusts, and they turn and tack, growing smaller on the water. I keep watching and moving. Feeling the "candy" hard against my thigh, I take it out and unwrap it, sniffing and smelling an odd sweetness. "Children," I say aloud to no one, throwing the candy into the glittering water. Then I rev the outboard, the boat's nose rising, and make a hard turn, a tight fishhook, managing a brief leap over my own frothy wake.

Most of the dock is set high over the water. The big pilings show stains from a fuller lake. Behind the dock and boathouse is a parking lot. To one side are the clubhouse and swimming pool and tennis courts, parents and their charges scattered here and there.

Spread through the wooded hills beyond is the rest of the Enclave—homes and schools and the small modern hospital where cloning was done until last year. Every morning I drive through the Enclave on my way to here. The homes seem neat, small and cared for, and the streets are like any streets, but for the names: Newton and Freud and Crick.

In spite of what the first critics said, this is no enclave for the rich and the privileged.

The disrepair of the dock and boathouse prove as much—a carefully cultured shabbiness brought on by an absence of paint and a raw face pointed into the prevailing winds.

A couple are standing on the dock. I swing in beside the dock's low end and climb out and tie up, all in a single practiced motion. They pay no attention to me. They are watching the red-and-white sailboat, pointing and talking. She is a handsome woman, overdressed in a tasteful way, with enormous sunglasses riding on a carefully tanned nose. He is a soft man of medium height and build, his suit of one hard color, a realtor's patch shaped like a shield sewn to the breast pocket.

"Can I help?" I wonder.

She looks at him and he looks at me, assuring me, "Yes, you can." He points. "That boat . . . could you tell us who's on it?"

I give them the name on the ticket.

She says, "That's Sarah's and John's boy."

He nods.

"We told him to stay away from that addict."

He nods and says, "I thought we did."

She lights a small cigar. "Maybe we should have him"— meaning me— "bring James in?"

"James?" I ask.

"Our son," the husband explains.

"It looks like James," she says, confidently staring at two spots beneath a tiny striped sail. She makes her husband describe their son, and when I concede that he is out there, the mother says, "He knows he's to meet us here. Now."

"Maybe that's not him, dear."

"Hah!" she laughs.

"Maybe he's lost track of time."

"Sam," she snaps. "We have to be in court. He knows. And look at him! He can't appear before a judge dressed like that."

Sam fidgets. The condition seems wholly natural to him.

"Let's give him a minute," he offers.

"Why?"

"Just try. Please?"

"Shit." She curses in an educated way, as though she pulled the word from a textbook and practiced its use while alone, watching herself in a vanity mirror.

A truce is declared. They stand and wait together, without patience or talk, and I back away and sit and read. After a time, poor Sam comes into the boathouse, chastened, and asks something he cares nothing about. "What's the book?"

"Essays in Exobiology," I tell him.

"You're a student?"

"Most of the year, yes." I press a corner of the book,

the liquid crystals within changing and changing—forming page after page.

He tells me, "We've a younger son interested in exobiology."

"Is that so?"

"He's hoping to spend a summer in Houston, working with the experts."

"Is that so? How old is he?"

"Eleven."

"Well," I say, "good luck to him."

"Thanks." Sam nearly turns to leave. He comes close. But then he seems to remember something, and he gives me soft eyes and says, "I was wondering. Could you tell James his folks are waiting? There's an appointment he has to make." For an instant he pauses. Then he's talking again, seemingly to himself, telling himself, "It's not so bad, really. Kids. You know kids." He looks above and to one side of me, saying, "We just are a little anxious for him. That's all."

"Sure," I say. "You want him brought in?"

"Just tell him. If you would."

"Sure." I walk to the boat and strap on the life jacket again, my hands knowing how without involving my mind. Then I roar away, the wind slapping my face, and I begin thinking about the same matters that have shuffled through my head all summer long.

I am a wanderer. A survivor. After years of this and that, I've gone back to school; and I work where I can to get by.

The Enclave hired me because I know boats, and because I seem to be balanced. To have a deep keel. Then, having hired me, they warned that I shouldn't be too impressed with the clones. I couldn't let myself be taken in by all the famous faces.

"Treat them like ordinary children," they said. "To you they are anyone's kids, subject to the same rules and respect all of us are due."

Of course, by then it was obvious how badly the Enclave had failed. The suicides of two clones and the trial of a third for murder and rape had finished the reputation it had once enjoyed. Friends of mine, and family, were of two minds when it came to my working here. The pay and experience might be well and good, but they wondered what sort of madness I would find.

As did I.

The Enclave was built some thirty years ago—when I was a wad of potential myself. A chubby pink drool machine. It was planned and paid for by that most peculiar of American phenomena—the rich Texan. As I remember it, this Texan was the last of the oil barons. He was old and knew it and knew for certain that the world was going to hell. So, with the boldness of the breed he set up a trust fund and a foundation and hired the best people. Never was there any secret about the Enclave's intentions or means. And while cloning had never been ordinary or widely accepted, the Enclave managed to show a saintly face. Few could fault its goals or methods, and even my family, soaked in twentieth-century values, felt the experiment was in some small way good.

"If a few Einsteins can be brought back to help the world," went the reasoning, "then maybe it will be worth the blasphemy involved."

Chosen for cloning were people of proven worth—quality humans judged by several measures. Chosen for parents were childless couples, principled and bright, who satisfied batteries of tests and battalions of interviewers. All good things were to flow to the clones. This was assured by many means. They were to be cared for but not spoiled, educated but not programmed, and from time to time they were to be reminded what was moral and fine in a world sorely needing such distinctions. And finally, with all of this understood, they were actually planted in the wombs of their foster mothers, carried full term and born.

Several dozen to the year.

One or two to a couple.

A host of perfect little drool machines destined to be hoisted high very carefully, then scrutinized without end.

The grown drool machines pause in their sailing when they see me. The talking one, James, turns into the wind so that they coast, the graphite cloth of the sail hanging limp.

"Your folks are waiting," I tell him.

"Are they?" The clean white main sheet lies limp in his hands. The foggy one is sitting peacefully beside him, smiling blandly and giving me a little wave.

After a moment I wonder, "Are you coming in?"

"In a minute." He is lying. He wants me to know this.

"I'll tell them you're coming."

"Please. Do."

He shoves the tiller, and the sailboat turns and slides away. The frictionless fiberhull tilts with a gust. The two wiry bodies lean automatically, bringing it down, and I blow air through my teeth and come around and twist the throttle hard.

Vapors of methanol are lingering about me, the wind is so strong.

When I look over my shoulder, squinting, I can just see the tiny sail tip and rise again, nodding in and out of the foam-flecked waves.

"They said they're coming," I tell the parents.

"You could have brought James," the mother informs me. "That would have saved time."

I think for an instant, then claim, "I wanted him to stay with the boat. He's the sailor of the two."

"He's a fine sailor," says the father, affecting a certain pride.

The mother is tensely quiet, smoking and smoking.

Sam tells her, "Be patient, dear."

"Shut up, dear," she responds; and Sam does, nodding and rolling his eyes as though he deserves that barb.

I go about my reading. Sitting on the folding chair deep in the boathouse's shadowy heat, I study an article about Jupiter. For several minutes I manage to concentrate, blotting out my surroundings. Then I look up and see the mother pacing about, examining everything without interest: her face the picture of worry and haggard dignity; her cigar being smoked loudly enough to be heard.

The scent is sharp, sure to linger. She is still wearing the dark, dark sunglasses, and I can't imagine how she can see through them. For a moment she pauses beside the tall table where the boathouse com-system had been, and gingerly she touches the glass fibers and copper wiring that remain now, dead and coated with grime.

I volunteer an answer to the question she might ask: "Kids broke in last winter, I'm told. They made a real mess and took that."

She says nothing.

"Last for repairs. Last for replacements. That's me." I tell her, "Here I sit, without so much as a phone."

She walks on, circling me. I try to ignore her, to return to my book, but I find myself listening for the dull clicking of her heels on the wood. She is passing the berths where old boats, lake-stained and perhaps broken, lie awaiting refurbishment or resale. My mind's eye sees her stroll beside the rack of life jackets, the listed laws of the lake, and finally the chicken wire cage where I store methanol and spare outboards and the assorted odd ends one needs in any boathouse. And now she is close and suddenly pauses, saying, "You seem engrossed," to me.

I look up. "Pardon?"

"You seem engrossed." She is beside me, looking at my book, and with her I read the lofty title:

DNA Synthesis Upon Airborne Silicates Suspended in Reducing Atmospheres.

She says nothing in a certain way, and I think she means it as a question. "It's about something they found last year, during the Jupiter expedition," I explain. "That automated balloon they dropped in? That spent months on the wind?" I look up. Her face is close, and I can see twin reflections of myself on the mirrored lenses of her glasses. I look fit and tanned. "Anyway," I say, "it found DNA, the basis of all life, being formed on dust particles. Millions of metric tons to the year."

"Is that so?" There is a second folding chair, and she sits heavily and remarks, "Have you ever been tired before?" She seems tired. "No, I wasn't aware they found life up there."

"Not on Jupiter, no. No." I tell her, "The Jovian atmosphere is too unstable. The DNA is always pulled into the lower reaches, the hot reaches, and degraded. Which is ironic, of course."

"Is it?"

"There's a planet with all the ingredients for life. The chemicals and energy and so on. Yet Jupiter insists on cooking the lot of it, and life never quite gets started." I am animated, discussing what I know, and rather happy. "It's a sad waste," I swear to her, smiling. "A tragedy if ever there was."

Her expression changes, suddenly and mysteriously. "I'd rather not hear the words 'waste' and 'tragedy,' if you don't mind," she says, her tone cool and easy.

I say nothing.

She says, "Personally, I don't believe in those words. To me they don't exist." She pauses, then claims, "To me, what happens to a world, or to a person, is simply destined to happen. Just because things don't turn out for the best . . . well, you can see what I mean. You're bright and you understand."

I say nothing.

She begins picking at lint on the front of her shirt. Her shirt is a soft yellow pullover, made from one of the new summery fabrics with tiny tubes woven through and through. Chilled water flows in the tubes, keeping her comfortable. A pump and tiny refrigerator are likely hidden somewhere behind, near the small of the back. The coolness of the fabric is what brings the lint; it catches in that ever-present layer of condensation.

For some time she picks and picks, thoroughly determined; then suddenly she stops and looks up and informs me, "I've lost my patience."

"Pardon?"

"Please," she says, "if you would, go get my son."

The wind is stiffer now. The waves have height and foaming crests. My kidneys take a pounding as the spray comes chilled and fine over the bow—my own crude form of air conditioning—and I look about for a boat that seems to have vanished somehow.

"I'm not in the mood," I warn the wind. "Don't test me."

I watch the shoreline for the red-and-white sail. Here and there are thick pipes made of clear plastic. The pipes run out of the lake and into the fields beyond. I can just see the crops in those fields—corn stalks bowing under eight or ten ears; wheat too stout to obey the wind; and alfalfa so very green that it looks black and waxy. I wonder. When I was a boy, I remember, farmers wore jeans and drove tractors and smelled of their trade. Now they sit in offices far from the land, pushing buttons, and robots tend lands as manicured as their own soft hands.

What does it mean, I wonder, when you're thirty and feel like a traveler through time?

There is a back bay on the lake. I round a point and look in and spot the sailboat beached beside a small grove of trees. I can see the orange of the life jackets heaped on the bow, and the sail being pushed this way and that by the wind. I cross the little bay. No one is in sight. I beach my boat and climb out and prepare to be angry in a calculated way, telling them in my head to get the hell back to the dock.

Winding into the grove is a narrow trail.

I walk in quietly, watching and listening.

Where the trees end they are sitting, side by side, in the sun. The foggy one is laughing. Neither is speaking. When I am close, James looks up at me in a certain way, and I forget my speech. Instead I sit opposite them, on a stump, and summon a frown.

The look goes out of James' eyes. He says, "We're found," to his friend. "We're caught."

His friend giggles.

"You must think we're bandits," says James. "Thugs."

"No."

"My folks think I'm the shit of the world."

I say nothing.

He is sober. His eyes are clear and sharp. As if for the

first time, I am looking at him, ignoring the red snakes and the jewelry and seeing instead a boy who is never quite with me, who is always distracted, that look coming into his face every so often . . . an expression of despair or anger or sheer exhaustion—I am never entirely sure which.

"So," he says. "Tell me. Why'd the Enclave fail? Hmm?"

"How do you mean?"

"Why'd the clones turn out so bad? You've worked the summer. You've seen."

I tell him, "They aren't all that bad. Considering."

James seems amused.

"Considering?"

"Considering."

"I know a cloned poet who makes her money giving head."

I say, "Is that so?" I say, "So. Read history. That's a minor crime for poets."

The friend has found another piece of candy in a pocket. He gives it to James, and James holds onto it, and in a little while he unwraps it and hands it back.

"I wrote symphonies," says James. "In my former life. By the time I was twenty I was famous around the world."

I am still and quiet.

"Fuck music," he says.

I rise and tell them, "We've got to go in." I ask James, "Can you handle the boat by yourself?"

That look is welling up inside of him. He seems distant, even when he answers, saying, "No."

"Your friend's in no shape," I say. "I want him with me."

"The candy cuts higher functions," he claims. "His motor functions are fine. Believe me."

They stand and we walk. I watch the foggy one step carefully over downed limbs and such. At one point an irrigation pipe crosses the trail, and he straddles the pipe and sits, smiling in his easy drugged way, gazing at the lake water being pumped through.

"Come on," I say. I look at James. "Get him up, please. I'm in no mood."

"Shh!" Foggy raises a hand and points with the other. "Look," he says softly. "Look."

The water is unfiltered, greenish and flecked with bits of twirling sediment. Being carried along with the water is a mudpuppy, thick and ugly and utterly helpless, twisting aimlessly as it tries to swim.

"Goofy critters," snaps James.

"I like them," I confess.

He snorts, disgusted with me.

I explain myself. "There's a creature on Europa that looks like that." I pause and say, "Europa's a moon of Jupiter."

"I know."

"The creature lives under the ice, swimming," I tell him. "Its environment is constant, cold and dark and poor." James is purposefully ignoring me, staring up at the wind in the treetops. "But sometimes there's a meteor strike. Or a volcanic eruption. Sometimes the ice melts and the weak sunlight causes a plankton bloom. A short-lived spring."

"So?"

"So during the boom times it breeds. It lays eggs in thick rafts and millions are born, and if there's time they'll grow and breed too, as do their children and their children's children and so on." I pause, then say, "It gets dark again. Cold. The plankton mostly dies." I tell him, "In those times the mudpuppy reproduces itself rarely. Just a few eggs. And mostly by cloning itself. There's no breeding on any scale, you see."

"No," James swears.

"Nature knows what Nature needs," I explain. "Cloning only makes sense when the environment is unchanging. Successful forms make successful forms. But when things are in transition . . . well, then you want new models. New types. You want sex and the mixing of genes."

"Okay."

I assure him, "It's like that everywhere."

"I believe you. I do."

"You asked before . . . about what went wrong."

"Thanks," he says, staring at me. Then he reaches into a baggy pocket and pulls out another piece of candy, and after showing the candy to Foggy he throws it towards the shore.

Foggy is up and running, tearing through the trees.

"He's an idiot," says James. "I like him just fine."

Eventually they climbed aboard the sailboat and put on their jackets. I wish Foggy was with me, I tell James, and he claims, "You don't want him. Chances are he'd jump out of the boat in the middle of the lake."

"If you say so."

Grabbing the lower boom, James tries to turn the sail into the wind."We're stuck," he says finally. "Our keel."

The keel is mired in mud. I have to tow them free. Then I remind James to head straight in, if he please would, and that look comes over him again.

"They'll be there?"

"Your folks?"

"Will they?"

"Sure."

I leave him. I hurry in and find them where I left

them. Quiet and tense, they look like a delegation of citizens sent to greet the Huns. I pull up against the dock with a crunch, tie up and climb up and join them, shielding my eyes from the glare with my hands. After a time the red-and-white sail comes into view, and the mother says, "You know, we're late as it is. We'll never make court."

Sam sighs.

"What would you do with a son like that?" she wants to know, glancing at me.

I shrug.

"I'd appreciate an opinion."

"He's not hopeless," I hear myself say.

"You don't know," she claims. "You can't."

I'm in no mood. "I've seen worse this summer," I say. "Believe me. I've seen some real pricks down here."

"You have?"

"I could tell stories."

"You could?"

She wants a contest . . . whose child is the most demented.

Sam interrupts. "The man's right, dear. There's a difference between shoplifting and murder."

"He's more than a thief and you know it!"

He looks at me. "She exaggerates," he wants me to know. "Really." He seems to doubt that I'll believe him.

She drops her cigar and crushes it, then immediately lights another. The smoke she exhales is blown behind her. I can scarcely smell it over the rich stink of the water.

"You're bright," says Sam. "What sort of lessons have you garnered from us?"

Something about this place, it seems, makes people accept scrutiny and second-guessing. To them it is as natural as the air.

"Do you mind telling?" he asks. "I think we'd both

like to hear what you have to say."

"Sure," says his wife. "Tell me why my boy's gone bad."

"It's a tough situation he's in," I admit.

"Oh?"

"Sure is." I say, "He's given a second chance at life, and deep down he doesn't feel worthy. So much is expected of him, and he knows that no matter how well he does he'll always fail. That the James before him will be the James remembered."

"That's stupid," she informs me. "How can he *know* that?"

"He is," I remind her, "an intuitive genius. They all are." I ask, "That's why they're here, aren't they?"

She is steaming. Looking at Sam, she seems to expect him to defend some sort of family honor. But instead all he does is shrug once and remark, "Maybe he's got something."

"Oh, dear God!"

"Well, look around," he says. "Look at the children born to wealthy families. Or to talented ones. They have troubles, don't they?" He regards me with earnest eyes. "Are they crippled by their promise? Is that it?"

"Maybe." I nod. "Maybe they are."

The sailboat is close, criss-crossing the water. Watching it, I wonder what James stole. Something trivial, likely. Maybe absurd. Then I am full of charity, wondering how it is to be these two—dedicating their lives and self-esteem to raise boys of proven worth, and then seeing one of them do anything less than shine.

"I know what it is," says the mother finally, firmly. "I think something went wrong at the hospital."

"Maybe," echoes Sam with conviction. "Maybe that's it."

"I don't understand," I say. "What?"

She's not looking at me, telling me, "There was no way for the doctors to know if the cell they cloned was healthy."

"Well, there are tests. . . ."

"Oh, no! After a point, no!" She maintains, "It could have been mutated. Or damaged somehow during implanting."

Says Sam, "It's an idea of ours," with a curious pride. "Mutations," he says, as if naming the infliction can somehow lessen it. Somehow make it manageable. "It has a certain logic, doesn't it?"

"I suppose."

"What do you think," he wants to know. "Speaking as a student of biology."

I tell him honestly, "I'm not qualified to say."

Sam nods, satisfied with my non-answer.

"Fate is Fate," says his wife softly. "There's no escaping it." And with that she gives the slightest of smiles—as if in some mysterious way victorious.

The boat is coming now. I walk to the low end of the dock, trying to put distance between them and me. I am thinking, imagining myself as a parent to a clone. I feed my vanity with mental pictures of normalcy. Of sanitized scenes of domestic bliss.

The sail has been let out. The graphite cloth is taut and filled with twisting air and summer sun. I can see James pulling himself past the mast, sliding on his belly, keeping his head low below the boom. He seems tense, sluggish. When he reaches the bow he fishes the rope and hook out from the rushing water, preparing to latch onto the buoy.

There's no life jacket on him, I realize.

He must have taken it off so that he could move more easily, I think, and I grimace.

The boat is making straight for the open buoy. Instead of turning up wind and gliding to touch it gently, the other clone simply clings to the tiller and lets the wind decide. There comes a gust. James reaches sideways and grips the big eyehook on top of the buoy, and somehow, somehow, he manages to hold on and is swept off the bow. Gone in an instant. Pulled under.

I hear a little shout, from Sam. Foggy does nothing. He seems unaware that he's alone, his face empty and his eyes focused on infinity—the boat piloted, for all intents and purposes, by an upright and rigid cadaver.

The boat brakes. I can see it slow, the keel biting into some solid thing. I stand on the balls of my feet, thinking, trying to will myself into motion, considering fast and hard what to do.

I turn finally, then run up to the boathouse, to the chicken wire cage, and grab the first pair of goggles I see.

Coming back into the sun, still running, I see the boat driving into the soft muddy shore.

"Get help!" I shout.

The parents are side by side, watching the empty buoy and the empty water around it.

I tell them, "The clubhouse! A phone!"

They turn. They have been talking, I somehow realize. Not weeping and not moaning, but talking. And now Sam puts up his hand in a gesture meant to mean "Just a moment."

I slide, stop and stare.

His hand remains up, as though he has forgotten it. His face is brave and uncertain. He says to me, "Give it a chance," in a whisper. Almost desperately he says, "Please."

"What?"

He cannot say.

And I know what he means. What they want. Good God!

"A phone!" I scream. "Find one!" I turn.

His wife cries out, "You don't understand!" She claims, "This might be a blessing. Please!"

I am running. I drop into the boat and untie myself and touch the starter and go. No one else is moving. I pull along the dock, shouting. They are staring at me. I might be miles away.

She seems to be saying, "Fate," over and over, without sound. Her sunglasses are off now, folded in her folded hands. One of her eyes is blackened, the flesh puffy and glistening where tears run.

I curse. I turn and roar towards the buoy, killing the motor and holding my breath and hoping no shaved head strikes from below.

Now every simple motion is agonizingly slow.

I tie onto the buoy.

I spit on the goggles.

With both thumbs, I spread the saliva.

Then the goggles are on and I leap off the bow, my curled toes leading the way.

The water comes dark and warm over me, for an instant blinding me. I pull myself deeper until cold silt grips my feet. Then I turn and turn, looking, kicking up a cloud of silt. Beside me is a bed of weeds, green and tangled, and when I move close the bland, ugly face of a mudpuppy rushes at me, startling me, causing me to blow my air and scramble to the surface.

I breath, then dive again.

This time I search downwind from the buoy, looking through the weeds, and when I see something shiny I reach and grab toes and diamond rings. "Lord," I think, pulling, wondering if half a corpse is going to pop out. But the scrawny legs yield a scrawny trunk, limp but whole, and I grip James under the chin and kick to the surface and hold him there somehow, his face in the air and the red snakes on his scalp snapping at me.

I begin to swim, on my back, aiming for the dock. Over the sound of wind and water I can hear the distant wailing of a siren, the sound gaining strength. Someone must have called, I realize. Help is frantically coming, and I feel relieved. The swimming is exhausting. James insists on sinking. The waves throw us up and down, and my legs grow leadened; and at one point, just when I know I am about to cramp up and die, my right heel clips the soft bottom and I can stand, the lake not even reaching my chest.

There are people on the dock—from the clubhouse and swimming pool—boys and girls with famous faces and the adults who hold them back. The siren is blaring, blotting out every other noise. Sam is at the edge, reaching out, and I ignore him and lift myself up and then hoist James up onto the bleached wood by my lonesome.

He seems to weigh nothing, he is so thin.

When his father offers to help once more I use my elbow on him.

The siren quits. The crowd scatters. A man and a woman in white come running, kneel and set to work on James. I slowly step away, letting my breath and nerves return to normal.

To me, now, he seems so small. More starved than drowned. The parents are close, sharing one of his hands, muttering the things good and concerned parents should say.

I watch them.

Illustrated by Greg Petan

After a moment the mother looks up, her sunglasses on again, and for an instant I can see my reflections on them, sliding without friction and leaving no trace.

I walk away. Two little girls are in the cage, and I chase them out and put the goggles away and then recall the sailboat.

It is against the shore, empty, and I have a feeling. Looking through the small crowd, I don't find Foggy. So I walk around the boathouse, out into the parking lot, and spot the ambulance waiting, its back end open and its motor clicking as it cools.

There are feet sticking out of the back, pale pink soles and socks of black mud. I come around and see the Army-green shorts on a slender torso. The clone is rifling a drawer. I watch. The cloudy baubles of his necklace sway, and I softly clear my throat.

He turns. As if he expects me, he nods and smiles. Then he turns back and crawls in further and opens a second drawer.

On the windows of the doors I can see myself. My hair is darker than my folks' hair, and my nose seems a touch Arabian; and when I was a boy I secretly wished that I could be a clone. I use to pretend that I was a despot reborn—and my hope of hopes was to live my life so well that it wouldn't matter.

"Hey," I say. "Professor." I tickle a bare foot and tell him, "It's time to go."

He turns. Out come his hands. Suddenly he gives me a mess of vials—each filled with a pretty colored liquid—and I hold them until he looks at me and does a ludicrous doubletake, declaring, "It's not you!" and deftly takes back every last one of his treasures.

The Single Most Important Piece of Advice
by
Frank Herbert

About the Author

Frank Herbert was born in 1920 and died of a lingering illness in early 1986. He was a reporter and editor on a number of newspapers before becoming a full-time writer.

Although he had been publishing short fiction in various SF magazines since 1952, he became an "overnight" success in 1956 with his first novel, which was serialized in John Campbell's Astounding Science Fiction *magazine as* Under Pressure. *(In book form, it's known either as* Twenty-First Century Sub *or* The Dragon in the Sea.*)*

His career took a major turn with the 1963 ASF *publication of the first* Dune *story. After that, of course, Herbert and the* Dune *stories have become world famous. It can be fairly said that Herbert was the last of the* ASF *"Golden Age" writers. Although those fabulous days had drawn to a close, the sweep and grandeur of Herbert's work during the last years of Campbell's editorship compellingly recall the very best of the* ASF *spirit.*

In bringing classical science fiction to worldwide prominence, Herbert ranks among this field's major contributors. An uncompromising stickler for the kind of storytelling principles that are a vigorous SF tradition, Herbert was both popular and respected.

Here is, to our knowledge, the last essay Frank Herbert ever wrote. He gave it to us while in pain, but with the clear purpose of fulfilling what he saw as a paramount obligation to his art and craft.

Proud of his contributions to the Writers of the Future project, as a judge, we had asked him for the single most important piece of advice he would give a beginning writer. Here it is:

The single most important piece of advice I ever got was to concentrate on story. What is "story"? It's the quality that keeps the reader following the narrative. A good story makes interesting things happen to a character with whom the reader can identify. And it keeps them happening, so that the character progresses and grows in stature.

A writer's job is to do whatever is necessary to make the reader want to read the next line. That's what you're supposed to be thinking about when you're writing a story. Don't think about money, don't think about success; concentrate on the story—don't waste your energy on anything else. That all takes care of itself, if you've done your job as a writer. If you haven't done that, nothing helps.

I first heard this from literary agent Lurton Blassingame, a highly respected expert on successful storytellers and storytelling. He's a man who's been watching writers' careers and building writers' careers for decades. And I have heard essentially the same thing from many other successful figures in writing; some of the top writers in the world have said it. It is the best advice I can give beginners.

I'd also like to say something about older hands helping newcomers. Like many other established writers, I teach students on frequent occasions and lecture to many other audiences anxious for advice on writing. I'm very happy to be able to lend my help to the Writers of the Future program. From time to time, though, people have come up to me and asked why I want to "create competition" by helping newcomers.

Talking about "competition" in that way is nonsense! The more good writers there are, the more good readers there will be. We'll all benefit—writers and readers alike!

So the other piece of advice I have for newcomers is: "Remember how you learned, and when your turn comes, teach."

Dream in a Bottle

by Jerry Meredith & D. E. Smirl

About the Author

"Dream In a Bottle" is our first collaborative winner, taking Third Place in the first quarter of this year's contest. (In case you didn't know it was possible to submit collaborations, please take it as given that anything not expressly forbidden by the contest rules is permitted.)

"Dream In a Bottle" is also this year's winning entry from the same writers' group that last year brought us A. J. Mayhew's "In The Garden," which appeared in Writers of The Future Volume I. *Judging by the record of such groups vis-à-vis success in the contest, it would seem useful for young writers to find the very best one they can, and join it.*

As is almost mandatory in collaborations, the left hand didn't always know what the right was doing. Jerry T. Meredith, a bookstore manager in Charlotte, N. C., had written a solo story to use as a contest entry, and happened to call his friend, Dennis Smirl, the computer expert. He just wanted to satisfy Smirl that Dennis's constant prodding had paid off, and Jerry was indeed submitting a story. "Oh," said Smirl, reminding Meredith they had collaborated on an earlier work. "I just sent 'Dream In a Bottle' to the contest," thus breaking the news that he had finished the final draft. However, when we later spoke to Smirl and asked him which of them had actually completed the story, he honestly couldn't remember. This may seem as if our two authors are a little at loose ends; actually, the best collaborations seem to work that way.

In any case, it seems quite fitting that "Dream In a Bottle" should be a story of identity . . . a very good, powerful story of the crises that may well await us as we venture into the deeps of space, bearing with us the gulfs within ourselves.

The sleepcase lid purred back. I sat up, pulled the plug from the back of my skull, stretched, and noted Buster's pale frightened eyes as he lowered himself into his own cocoon.

"Bad dreams?" I asked, grinning.

"I can't stand flying with the Ancient Mariner," he complained. "I always feel like I'm on the edge of losing it."

"What happened this time?" I clambered out of my cocoon and did a few knee bends to banish the cold from my joints.

"He won't stay in his bottle," Buster grumbled as he snapped in his plug in preparation for debriefing. "He keeps bleeding into the other dreams. I had a bad time keeping the other jinn clean. I thought they screened those brains before putting them in our ships."

"Good brains aren't necessary to run a ship," I said. "Just brains that run good."

"Then you'd better hope these run like your sweetest fantasy. The Sheik found a cloud straight ahead. We'll be hitting it in just three hours."

"What's its density?"

"About three and a half per cubic meter. Dessert time for the engines."

"Good," I yawned, feeling the chill finally burn from my bones. "We can use the kick."

"Keep your eye on the Mariner," Buster warned as he wiggled into his restraint harness. "That jinn just doesn't know his limits."

"But we needed someone who could trim the sails," I answered innocently.

Buster snorted, then jabbed the lid control. Through muffled plastic, just before the white cloud of cold sleep enveloped him, he growled, "Good luck. You know the Commander. Some people have to have a problem or they go crazy."

I headed for the bridge. The muscles in my legs unkinked, and the nightmares—those formless memories that haunted even my cold sleep—faded. So the Mariner was bleeding into the other bottles. That was one jinn we didn't want loose. It was bad enough keeping track of eight separate fantasies without worrying about contamination. But then, it was my job to worry about it. During my tour of the bridge I monitored the jinn to make sure the Ancient Mariner, the Sheik of Araby, Sweet Alice, Bullwinkle, Naugahyde, Sigmund, Thoreau and Escoffier stayed happy as they dreamed us through space. They tuned the ramscoops, trimmed the sails, searched out food for the engines, and kept all the pretty lights on the life support modules blinking merrily. And people like Buster and Sonya and me tried to keep them from catching on to what had been done to them.

Because they weren't really jinn and they weren't kept in bottles. They were brains who labored as living computers, working in concert with the ship to control systems far too important for any machine to handle. And their bottles were merely psychological restraints locking them into fantasies related to their part in running the ship—a kind of Boölean Psychology that let them go so far and no further.

At least, that's how it was supposed to work.

And a ship with jinn who learned the truth—that they had been ripped from dying bodies, placed in nutrient tanks and fooled into believing they were living perfectly normal lives, complete with friends, lovers, occupations, pleasures . . . well, such a ship died an ugly death. It had happened before. It could happen again. That's why we were careful.

Halfway to the bridge, I heard a rumble speed through the ship. The sails must have slammed through a rich field of hydrogen. Delighted, the engines gulped it down, belched it out the back, and gave us a touch more acceleration toward our rendezvous with Zeta Reticuli IV.

On the bridge, I plugged into my womb and checked the monitors. The Mariner was back where he belonged, for the time being. Good thing, too. I didn't want him shutting down the sails or leaving them spread out over five hundred kilometers of space. The magnetic fields might rip to shreds like the canvas for which they were metaphors—and a ship without sails . . .

The Ancient Mariner and Sweet Alice and all the others were nicknames invented by a shadowy figure back on Triton Base, a J. R. Mayhew, whom I'd never met but knew by virtue of the original—and perceptive—labels he'd given the jinn. I, too, had pet names for the separate systems. But as the voyage continued, I found myself thinking of them in J. R.'s terms rather than my own.

For example, the Ancient Mariner and his wife, a charming, tiny woman with wind-burned hair and nets of wrinkles fanning out from the corner of her eyes, sailed a twenty-foot ketch through the islands of the South Pacific. The seas were usually calm and the islands were always inhabited by primitive but friendly natives. Occasionally, the computer threw in a little storm just to enhance the illusion. Winds howled. Palm trees bent and hissed. The sea boiled over sand and reef. And the Mariner and his wife, safe in a hut provided by the island's chief, would make love and afterwards talk about how romantic their trip was, how much like paradise was the life they led.

But what was Sweet Alice to think when she came out of her forest, a world populated by dwarves, elves, sentient animals, and talking teapots, to find a seascape where fields had been, and a man walking on a beach who looked too real to be a part of her world?

No, that wouldn't do at all. I needed some way to strengthen the taboos keeping him in his fantasy. It wouldn't be easy. The Mariner, like most sailors, was naturally curious and too intelligent to believe in falling off the edge of the world.

I saw it was time to awaken my partner for the tour. "Good morning," I crooned perversely. "Bid your sweet dreams farewell and come back to the world of work. In short, haul your butt out of that case."

"Michael? Where are you?"

"Where else? On the bridge." I checked a screen. Alex had climbed out of her case and was pushing herself through a rigorous set of exercises. Small, wiry, with tiny breasts outlined against her jumpsuit, and black, curly hair that accentuated her boyish face, she reminded me of a child working too hard to pull her weight in a world of adults. She bobbed up and down on muscular dancer's legs, her face tight as she concentrated on getting every muscle in the right configuration. She always wanted everything just right. That's what made her such a pain in the ass.

"Any problems?" she asked.

"The Mariner again. I dispatched a couple of cretins to make sure there's no hardware malfunction."

"Any contamination?"

"Buster said an albatross showed up at the Queen of Hearts' banquet."

"Liar." She glared at me through the monitor, hands on hips breathing evenly. No sense of humor.

Then I told her about the cloud. *That* brought a smile to her face. "It's about time we had some good luck," she said. "I'll be right up."

The monitor blinked. "Take your time," I muttered. Alone, I stretched out my senses along the circuits of the ship. I felt what the sensors sensed, saw what few men could ever imagine. Our sails glowed a deep purple, ultraviolet batwings beating against an eternal vacuum. My eyes filled with stars, my fingers throbbed with each molecular annihilation. I could have remained there forever. The Company didn't need jinn, just men like me. Let them argue with their board members about applications of space technology. I didn't care. I wanted to see what was out there. I wanted to know what moved in the darkness. Maybe there was chronite in the atmosphere of Zeta Reticuli IV, maybe not. But to see it for myself, a dozen years down the line, that was my ambition.

Six-tenths Cee. One hundred and eighty thousand kilometers per second, or four and a half times around the world in the space between the ticks of a Grandfather clock. And in less than an hour, we were going to crash through a gas cloud at that velocity. Probably, it would hurt. We were trading our margin of safety for time, for a hundred kilotons of raw hydrogen snared by our sails, funneled into magnetic confinement, then fused into a second spear of thrust. We would gain a three percent increase in acceleration, and a corresponding reduction in time-until-turnover. It would hasten deceleration for the stately pass through the Zeta Reticuli system, give us time for a leisurely look at Reticuli IV and to launch the jinn called

Snow White, sleeping now, into orbit over that tantalizing blue-white planet, while her seven drones went down to the surface and beamed data which she would pass on to us as we accelerated away. If we lived. If the collision with the cloud off our bow didn't smash us into stardust.

"Come down from the mountain, Michael. You can't have the stars all to yourself."

"Huh?"

"I like tasting the stars as much as you do, but why hasn't the Mariner reconfigured our sails?"

Alex, settling into her womb, was staring at me. "I asked you. . . ."

"I know what you asked. Reconfiguration isn't scheduled for another two and a half minutes."

"That's cutting it too close."

"Don't tell me about it. Argue with the manual." I sent the lines of text to her monitor, then turned back to study the words flashing across mine. The steady cadence of flickering letters seemed hypnotic, and I had to shake my head to clear my thinking.

"Where've you been?" Alexandria asked once she'd scanned the entry. "For a while, your face was as slack as your gut."

"I was thinking," I snapped. "And any time you want to go a couple of rounds with this slack gut. . . ."

"You were philosophizing again. And as to going a couple rounds, any time you think you're good enough for one. . . ." She stopped, looked away. Our bickering had taken a sudden nasty turn in a direction neither of us wanted to pursue. "I'm sorry, Michael. I didn't mean anything by it."

"The Mariner's trimming the sails now," I said. Then I watched as the sails retreated toward the ship.

Their color faded, shifting from the normal deep purple through a dusky pink to mottled orange, then regained intensity to settle into a cloudy russet—a smaller, angry funnel poised to slash its narrow way through the cloud in our path.

FIVE MINUTES TO CONTACT.

The words crawled across my monitor, then were replaced by a microsecond countdown displayed in the lower right-hand corner of the screen. I tried to imagine what contact would be like, but gave up. My imagination runs too easily to scenes of Armageddon.

"Thruster termination in ninety seconds, Michael. Check your restraints."

As I fumbled with the stickystrips, I asked, "Why do we do this, Alex?"

"So we won't float around the bridge, Michael." Her hands were stabbing at her controls. Running Naugahyde was her job in this situation.

"Very funny, Alex. And you know that wasn't what I meant. I was asking why we snap at each other. Every time we have a watch together we try to rip each other to pieces."

"Don't do this to me," she gritted. "Not now. Do you have any idea how difficult it is to turn the main thruster off?"

"Of course I do. I modify Sweet Alice's fantasy, or the Mariner's, or Bullwinkle's when I have to." *And I could handle Naugahyde's too, if the computer would just let me,* I told myself.

"I know what you're thinking, Michael, but you don't ever change the core of anyone's fantasy. For years, Naugahyde has been driving down the highway in his sports car, picking up pretty female hitchhikers. That fantasy is the core of his autonomic operation of the main thruster, and when it shuts down, he's going to experience that as an interruption of his journey. It's going to take all my concentration to keep him from trying to start his car before we're through that cloud. So will you please leave me alone?"

"I'm sorry I bothered you," I answered. She was right, of course, so I turned my attention outside once more and ignored the heat in my face. Some day, I'd be over her. Some day. I stared at the stars, blue-shifted ahead, hard points of diamond brilliance converging in our path. Their apparent dislocation only hinted at the starbow that waited for the crew who could coax another twenty-five percent from the all-too-primitive hydrogen rams we flew. And somewhere, millions of kilometers ahead, a star waited to be born from a cloud of gas. But we'd mine that cloud first.

It came so quickly, I'm not sure I ever really saw it. One moment, stars and emptiness. The next, a shimmering translucence pierced by the angry protuberance our sails had become. Then blindness, agony, a scream so profound I shall be haunted by its sound forever. They say there is only silence in the vacuum of space, but at the leading edges of our sails, at those points where they slammed into the heart of that cloud, the molecules of hydrogen accumulated into an incandescent plasma that shrieked and howled and moaned into the darkness like a chorus of mistuned violins.

On impact, the ship draped me with restraint webbing, an indestructible gossamer of molecule-chain. Startled by its sudden touch, blinded by the flash of collision, deafened by the echoes still pounding through the hull, I fought the clinging web for a brief eternity. Then, training took over and I relaxed. The engine rumbled, roared, crescendoed—a perfect restart, thanks to Alexandria's brilliant touch.

The web dissolved. I fell back into my womb, exhausted. One by one, the bridge consoles flickered back to life. Waiting for my vision to clear, I called, "Alex? Alexandria? Are you okay?"

In a peculiar, quavering voice, she answered, "I'm not sure, Michael."

Muscles complaining, nerves still shaken, I turned to look her way. A figure dripped water between us. Tall, craggily masculine, with a deep tan and white hair, he wore sun-bleached pants and a soggy cotton shirt that clung to broad shoulders and thick biceps. Silver hair billowed from the opening of the shirt. Astonishment widened his blue eyes, and as he glanced from Alex to me, he seemed breathless.

"What's happened?" he blurted. "Where's my Marcia?"

Alexandria's mouth had dropped open, and I suppose mine had, too. The Ancient Mariner was loose on the bridge; and if we did anything to make him suspect that the seas he sailed were not of Earth, then looking foolish would be the least of our worries.

I steadied my voice. "This is a dream," I said. "A nightmare. In a moment you'll wake up and everything will be fine."

"What kind of place is this?" He turned his gaze from us to the monitors. The lights dripped red, green, blue over his features. I think that's when I really began to get scared. He was so solid—so real! I'd heard of bizarre superimpositions creeping into experiments, ghost-like images occurring for a few seconds in labs. But not in real life. Not on a ramship dependent on sane jinn to keep its heart and organs running.

I'd never been in this kind of situation. No one had. Then Alex, her voice edging toward hysteria, asked,

"What are we going to do, Michael?"

"Find out what happened."

I took a deep breath and dove into the Mariner's fantasy. Nothing. Just darkness. Then, a dance of stars above, rising, falling. Water, water everywhere. Wavelets slapped against a capsized hull. Debris bobbed in lazy swells. The collision with the cloud had blown a hole in his bottle. Frantically, I searched for the Mariner or his wife . . . and found nothing. He had broken free from the dream completely.

So where was he? He couldn't have an existence separate from his fantasy. Jinn weren't supposed to get out, no matter how hard you rubbed the bottle.

Unless I was dreaming, and he had slipped into my dream.

DON'T THINK ABOUT IT! I screamed to myself. *DON'T GET LOST DOWN THE RABBIT HOLE!*

The Sheik of Araby didn't give me any time to worry about rabbit holes. His sensors found something new and he told us about it. Warning bells, lights, and buzzers went off all at once. Alex scanned the information first. "Sweet Mother," she breathed. "There was another cloud hiding behind the first one. Not as thick, but thick enough. We'll be colliding in eight minutes."

The Mariner took a step forward, bunched his hands into fists. "This is some kind of a ship, isn't it? You rammed my boat. You murdered my wife."

"It's a dream," I insisted. "Nothing more." Somehow, I had to get the Mariner back in his bottle so he could trim the sails. "Alex—"

"Don't bother me now. I have to get us ready for the second cloud. Naugahyde isn't going to believe it—engine trouble twice in one day." Her fingers brushed connodes. "Six minutes."

The ship shuddered, plowing through a fringe of the cloud ahead. Like a moan from high in the throat, the engines hummed and whined and threw us forward, ever closer to Cee.

"Not bad," Alexandria said grimly. "It could be a lot worse. It's thin, maybe two million kilometers through. Just a wisp of smoke. It's probably a shred off the main cloud."

Mesmerized by the data surging across my monitor, I almost forgot the Mariner. Then he moved. At the edge of my vision something shifted; a flash of color changed shape. When I snapped my head around, he was standing next to Alexandria, muscles bunched tight in his neck, rage purpling his face.

"Tell me what happened to my wife!" he demanded. Then he reached down and tore the filament from the back of Alexandria's head.

Alex disappeared.

The Mariner froze. The filament fell from his hand. Blood decorated its socket. "Where is she?" he asked.

"Gone to Hell," I answered. "And she's taking us with her."

I felt cold. A quick glance at the monitors revealed some of the life support systems were already deteriorating. There was no telling what damage had been done to the cerebral centers. But that wasn't the worst of it—I was no longer in control of the ship. Alex, my link with control, was gone, dead or catatonic, her fantasy shattered by the rage of the Mariner.

FOUR MINUTES flashed on the monitor. Thank you.

"She's dead," said the Mariner. He coughed, wiped the back of his hand across his mouth, then rubbed at his temples. "The seas were high. She was not a strong swimmer."

He mourned his fantasy wife. I mourned the woman I loved. Who is to say who felt the sharpest pang? My woman's name rolled from my memory with an easy rhythm. Alexandria Lightfoot N'komo, whose ancestors had maneuvered dugouts down the Niger, crept through Appalachian forests, fired on Confederates from Cemetery Ridge, marched in Selma, mined asteroids, walked the high steel as they built the cities of Titan. Alexandria, who might have wanted the stars more than I did. Against all rules we had fallen in love and considered ourselves fortunate that, together, we would see wonders beyond belief.

Until her accident.

Her flitter stalled as she attempted an unpowered landing on a strip near LookLookie on Titan. A sudden thermal crumpled one wing and all she could do was hang on. Unavoidable, the board of inquiry ruled. Structural failure due to catastrophic stress.

They pulled her out, more dead than alive. No way to repair the damage, another board ruled. They invoked the clause written into our contracts, removed her brain, and set her up in a bottle. She was part of my ship when we launched for Zeta Reticuli IV. I was there to reinforce her fantasy.

She had what she always wanted. All I had was dross.

The command console yanked me out of my regrets. I had an incoming message. I just couldn't think of anyone who would be calling me.

"What do you want?" I growled.

"Michael?" a weak voice answered. "Is that you?"

"Alex? Where are you? Are you all right?"

"I don't know. I'm in a telephone booth. I think it's in

Bullwinkle's bottle. I'm frightened. Michael, how can I be here?"

"Systems malfunction. Don't worry. You're right here on the bridge. The Mariner must have caused a line surge that blew you right into the most available dream." It was gobbledygook, but she was frightened, and there was a chance she'd believe it.

"Michael, I don't like this place."

"Look around. Tell me what you see. Try to help me see where you are."

She hesitated a moment, then began. "I'm in a large city. Tall buildings. Paved streets filled with cars. And crowds. Everywhere I look, people pushing, shoving, hurrying. I understand some of what they say, but I can't read anything. I think the signs are written in English."

"Is there a large, red lighted sign high up on one of the nearby buildings?"

"I can't see one like that."

"Please, Alex," I urged. "You have to help me."

I suffered for long seconds before she spoke again. "Yes. I see the sign. Almost straight overhead."

"Good! Hold tight. I'll be there in a minute."

THREE MINUTES TO CONTACT. Damn it to hell! Not enough time . . . Alex was trapped in Bullwinkle's bottle, which meant she was standing on a street-corner in Manhattan some time during the latter half of the twentieth century—a Manhattan, however, formed from a Peter Max poster, in which war, murder and television blended with caped crusaders, the Fab Four, and a flying squirrel who doubled as an existential prophet. I spent as little time as possible in that dream. Unlike the other jinn who endured with pleasure a structured, almost ritualized fantasy, Bullwinkle reveled in a world in which everything was constantly in flux; forming, reforming, painting fantastic shapes on a bizarre canvas. Alex couldn't stay there long and remain sane. No one could, except Bullwinkle.

As I collected my thoughts, the Mariner moved so close I smelled the salt spray trapped in his clothes. "Are you real?" he asked, choking back a sob.

With that, I knew how to get him back in his bottle—if I had enough time. "I'm not real," I explained. "None of this is." Then I jabbed my finger at one of the monitors. "That's what's real."

In the screen, it was dawn. A rising sun gleamed off the sluggishly heaving swells with a slick light. Off to one side, a capsized hull drifted, losing its struggle with the elements to stay afloat. Beside me, the Mariner sucked in his breath.

"There it is," I said. "A raft."

"There was no raft."

"Of course there was." I made a raft, and a swell lifted it, tilting it for a split second. There was no one inside.

"She's gone," he said. "She didn't make it to the raft."

"Wait. Watch."

The light spread across the water like oil. The raft rose, fell. A hand broke the surface. Fingers scrabbled at the gunwales, clutched at the yielding rubber. A face popped out of the water and gasped.

"Marcia," the Mariner said. "My Marcia."

The woman struggled to pull herself into the raft, but she was near the end of her endurance. Her grasp on the gunwale loosened and she fell back into the sea.

"*You're* in the raft," I said. "If you don't wake from this nightmare and take her hand, your wife is going to drown. *You* have to save her. No one else can."

I turned my head from the monitor to check his

reaction. He wasn't there. Back on the screen I saw him scramble out of the bottom of the raft and hoist his Marcia in. It was going to work, but I had no time to gloat. There was a sail to trim, and as yet, none on the raft.

I made oars for him, telescoping metal tubes that formed a crude mast when fit together and clamped upright in a socket on the floor of the raft. A small canvas bag contained a lightweight sail and rigging. I watched the Mariner assemble his sail, but before he could raise it, a squall moved in. He tied everything securely and waited for conditions to improve. His wife, clutched in his arms, looked into his uncertain face and smiled. I disengaged from their bottle.

Next problem. "Alex?" I shouted. No answer. A read-out marched across the monitor, telling me I was running out of time. I stretched out my senses. From my previous excursions in Bullwinkle's Manhattan, I knew exactly where to find Alex. That is, if she hadn't moved, or if Bullwinkle hadn't redesigned the city. I uncapped the bottle and jumped in. Light boiled up, and sound, and smell. Crowds surged forward. Vehicles raced by, filling the air with the stench of burned petroleum. And within this sea of harsh noise and bright color, Alex, tiny and vulnerable, cowered in a telephone booth while an irate fat man in a cowboy outfit beat on the glass doors and screamed at her to leave.

"Alex!" I screamed over the din.

Her chin popped up. "Michael? Where are you?"

"Right here." The wall of the booth shimmered. A hazy glow spread over the glass, and when it faded, only a doorway remained. I reached for her. "Come on! We've run out of time!"

A shudder rippled through her body. For an instant her knees buckled and I started through the doorway to

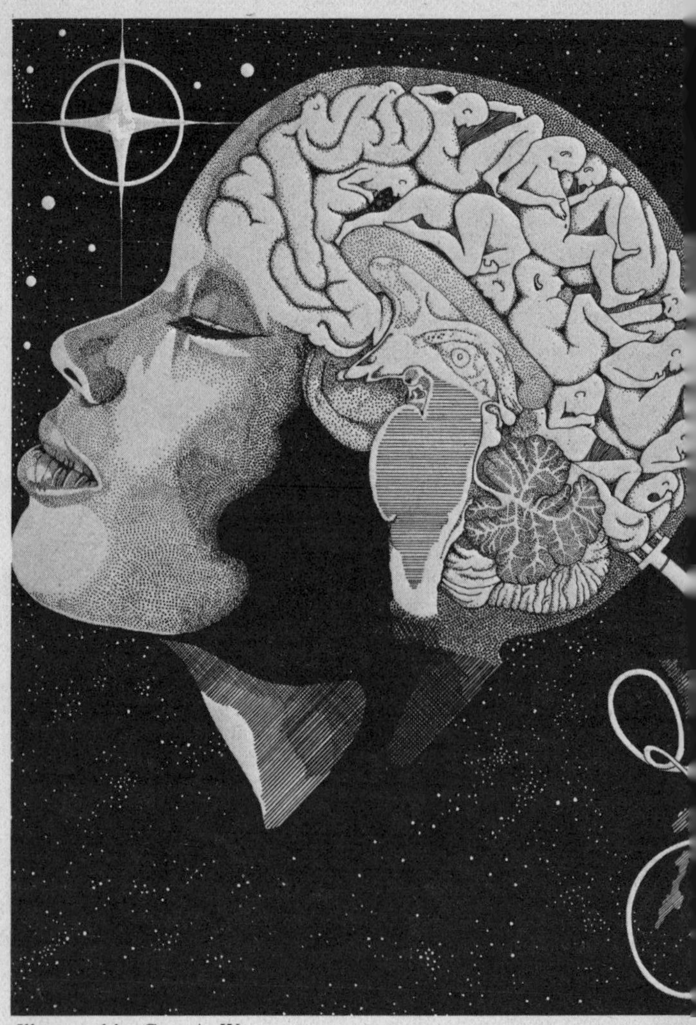

Illustrated by Greg A. West

g.a. West
© 1984

take her out. But she backed away, a piercing, cryptic look in her eyes. "I'm one of them, aren't I, Michael?"

"Don't be silly. Come on, Alex. You have to shut off the main engines."

She shook her head. "No, Michael. The Mariner pulled my plug, and now I'm not on the bridge. I'm here. That means one of us, maybe both of us, lives in a bottle. Tell me the truth, Michael. *Am I one of them?*"

She was right. She was always right. I couldn't lie to her. She knew my voice, my expressions. In the time we'd spent together, she'd unravelled all my secrets. And only my pain—knowing her truth—kept us bickering.

"Yes," I said. "You're a jinn. But, listen! You have to come back. If you don't work on Naugahyde's fantasy, Buster and Sonya and all the others are going to die. *I'm* going to die." I beckoned, I begged through the doorway. "Please. Come back."

The line outside the booth was growing nasty. Someone in the back said, "Watch me pull a rabbit out of my hat . . . ooops! Wrong hat!"

Tears wet her face. With a ragged sob, Alex took my hand, and I dragged her through.

Somewhere in the Nevada desert between Tonopah and Goldfield, the driver of a propane truck pulled out onto the highway without checking his rear-view mirror. Coming up from behind at 115 mph, a college student in a Porsche slammed into the back of the rig. The crash triggered an explosion that blew the truck a hundred feet into the air and vaporized the Porsche and a Greyhound bus that had the misfortune to be coming from the other direction at just the wrong time. The highway was completely blocked, so that when Naugahyde drove up a moment later, he had to pull to the side and wait for the wreckage to be cleared.

Two hitchhikers, a man and a woman he had picked up in Tonopah, clung together in the seat beside him. "I think we'll be here for a while," Naugahyde said. He gestured at the inferno raging in the twisted metal and glass. "And there, but for the grace of a long pit-stop, burn we."

The woman swallowed hard. "Perhaps you should turn off the engine," she suggested.

The man nodded in affirmation. "Yeah. Don't waste your gas."

"Humph." Naugahyde turned the key. The engine stopped. "Dyin' ain't something I like bein' near," he said, not looking at the couple but at the gray mountains in the distance. "But I don't mind hearin' about it on my radio." His tweed driver's cap had somehow turned into a straw ten-gallon hat. But the important thing was he'd killed his ignition.

The ship rammed the cloud, shuddered, tore through.

"It's all right, Michael," Alex said as she stepped into her sleepcase. "Of all the dreams I might have had, they picked the one I most wanted to see come true. That's why this is so easy to accept. I'm getting what I want—I'm going to the stars. Whether as human or part machine doesn't really matter. Not to me."

She lay down in the sleepcase. The socket clicked into the back of her head. "Poor Michael," she said. "Poor, poor Michael. Can you be sure you're not one of us? Can you really be sure?"

The lid closed. Fog poured over her face. I stared at my monitor and cried. The ship didn't need me now.

Not really. The Sheik of Araby, gazing at his thousand-member harem, would let me know when I was needed again. I hoped it would be a long time.

I eased the plug from the base of my skull, climbed down the shaft and found the lid of my sleepcase still open. I palmed a control pad. In the case next to mine, a face appeared behind plastic. The lid opened, mist escaped. With a sigh, dark-eyed Sonya sat up and shivered. "Already?" she asked. "Anything interesting happen?"

"Not a thing," I answered.

I climbed into my cocoon and fitted the plug to my head. "Sigmund?"

"Yes?"

"I'm frightened, Sigmund. I don't know what's real anymore."

"Don't worry, Michael," he whispered as the cold mist poured over me. "We'll take care of you."

The Cinderella Caper
by
Sansoucy Kathenor

About the Author

Sansoucy Kathenor now lives near Ottawa, Canada, and has sold two stories before entering the contest. Since winning Third Prize in the second quarter, she has sold two more.

She's been extremely active in pursuing her goals as a writer. She has published a collection of poetry, Temple Into Time, *and had several stories printed by small-press magazines. However, it wasn't until she formed a local club, the Lyngarde Writers' Group, that she was fully able to break out of a mind-set that has unfairly held back many a novice.*

"Everyone I knew in youth," she says, "believed that real stories were written by a vague mass of disembodied Professional Writers. Family and friends laughed at the idea that anyone from our small town might ever join those distant ranks. Teachers were alarmed at a student's writing anything beyond essays and reports, and were sternly repressive instead of giving advice. That kept me from believing I could ever sell stories."

It happens. Judging by what we hear from professional acquaintances, in about half the cases a would-be writer encounters scorn and opposition based not on an appraisal of the work but simply because of this sort of prejudice. Sansoucy's experience changed when she met some Ottawa SF fans. "Fans know that writers are real and that today's aspirant sometimes does become tomorrow's professional." As a result, she and some other writers formed their club, and several members have since been successful in the professional market.

It does happen. Take our word for it. Or, failing that, take Sansoucy's.

It started with a laundry robot which kept trying to ingest and wash the living-room rug in a household on Level A-9 of the city tower. The autorepair units were helpless, so the annoyed householder phoned a demand for a live worker to the coordination center in Level D. A succession of technicians adjusted the machine, but to no permanent avail. The phone calls became more demanding and more sarcastic, until the center promised to send its top appliance engineer.

She arrived promptly, with a cheerful, "Good morning, Mr. Banks; I'm here to fix the washer with the appetite."

"I hope you *can,*" said Banks. "I've put up with all I intend to take with that thing."

"You won't have to put up with any more," the technician assured him. "If I can't fix it, we'll shoot it."

"You'll *what?*"

"Shoot it off to the scrap pile," she smiled, "and put in a brand new one."

Banks suddenly observed her as a person instead of a mere worker, and matched her smile. "What's your name?"

"Verena." She did not bother giving the number that was the only surname a technician had.

Banks watched her as she opened the malfunctioning washer and ran extensive tests on its modules, replaced several, made adjustments, reclosed it and made even more exhaustive checks of its software, with further modulations. He asked a few tentative questions about the machine and Verena's work, getting the same sorts of cheerful, whimsical answers. When the machine had been tested out and had disdained the opportunity to clog itself again with a corner of the carpet, Banks delayed Verena's departure with an offer of refreshment—one of the sweet herbal teas only the wealthy could afford to import.

Verena was surprised, but accepted, and remained chatting with him, surprising him in turn by having some knowledge of subjects of interest to A and B-level citizens. When at last she left, Banks insisted that she return daily to check the washer.

She did so for a week, Banks each time treating her as a guest. He learned that her husband—Banks did not correct the term, though workers' marriages were not recognized as legal—was deceased. She told him she had an eighteen-year-old daughter who had already qualified as a robotics engineer. Since lower-class education did not bother with such non-practical refinements as literature, history, or other cultural subjects, it comprised very concentrated training. He also heard a little about the drabness of life in the D levels among the unpainted cinder-block walls, minimal furnishings, and the repetitious fed-in entertainment, and especially the pervading sense of unworthiness, balanced only by the enjoyment of work that required both physical and mental application.

Verena in turn learned that Banks had moved up from a middle B status by virtue of his money-making talent, and would have been yet higher had he not bought himself two expensive divorces when he tired of his partners. He also derived so much satisfaction from his financial maneuverings that he felt little need to participate in the artistic and social activities that charmed possible boredom away from the upper levels.

At the end of a week, Verena declared the machine fully cured, and Banks declared himself infatuated with Verena. He invited her to become his third wife.

"They'd break you down to a B-50 if you married someone who has soiled her hands with physical work."

"I can pay enough bribes to halt my descent at about B-10 or so. And I can work my way back up. I enjoy doing that."

"You wouldn't have me for long. I've been inhaling pollutants in my work for years; I'm told I haven't much longer to live."

"If I may be frank, my dear, that's an advantage; we won't have time to tire of one another."

"Well, I like you, and I certainly wouldn't mind having a taste of B-style life in my last days, though I'd miss my friends. . . ."

"If you're discreet, you could slip down and see them occasionally."

"Then I'll agree, on two conditions: that you legally adopt my daughter Ella, so she'll have your status, and that you train her for an upper-level career."

"Agreed," said Banks, and the arrangements were promptly carried out. The two women moved into the household, which was immediately moved down to B-14, and began a comfortable, if rather dull life, while Banks worked to recover some of his lost status.

Until Verena's death, half a year later, Banks made no progress, although he continued to increase his wealth; but once his unacceptable wife had ceased to exist, he began again to receive social notice from higher levels. It was not many more months before he married again, this time to a widow named Urbana Hill, from B-5, who had two daughters named Narcissa and Fossetta, slightly older than Verena's girl.

Banks' wealth now enabled the family to live on B-1, and all but Ella to participate fully in the social life of the upper-B and lower-A levels. Banks, however, did not have long to enjoy his return to grace: At a drunken party on A-7, some exuberant youths decided to hoist a grand piano up to a chandelier. Naturally, they knew nothing of such manual things as breaking-strengths. Neither did Banks, who wandered under the piano just as it obeyed the tug of gravity.

With Banks' demise, the situation in the household changed. Ella's re-training as a lady ceased, and her right to remain was cast into doubt by an astute lawyer hired by her step-relations, who also began a campaign of demoralization. They took to calling her "Cinderblock Ella"—in reference to the drab construction of her level of origin—eventually shortening it to "Cinderella."

Their intended victim did not in the least mind the nickname: she felt no shame over her origins, and thought the new name had a nice ring to it. However, she had no intention of being kicked out of what was now her rightful place, even though she felt it would be a much more fulfilling life to return to useful work. For her own amusement, Ella had kept all the household equipment running in top shape, in spite of the continual abuse it received from the Hills. In a subtle counter-campaign, she now ceased to do so.

Chaos was prompt in arriving. The Hills carried ignorance of the workings of machinery to the extreme of refusing to learn even how to operate it, and affected a pretense that the psychic aura of their gentility kept even robot machinery subdued and submissive. In reality, their clumsiness kept causing breakdowns. Cinderella's strike brought on a crisis: They would either have to placate her or call in a stream of repairers, to the laughter of their neighbors. And they had the wit to see that the problem would be a recurring one, so they offered Cinderella a deal.

The deal was presented to her by the younger sister, Fossetta, who had the Hill family's nearest approach to brains, though she wasted it by aping the empty-headed Narcissa. "What it amounts to," said Fossetta, handing Cinderella the lawyer's ramblings, "is that we'll drop the eviction attempt if you agree to be a sort of resident repair technician—secretly. You'll get room, food, and clothing, but you won't count as a member of the family socially."

"Social affairs bore me," shrugged Cinderella. "My mother and I attended the few we got invited to only out of a sense of duty. In fact, if it weren't so uncomfortable in the D levels, I'd be tempted to go back there."

"Does that mean you agree?"

"If you accept one other condition. I get to take whatever additional technical training I want, any time I feel like it, even continually."

Fossetta sighed. "The lawyer won't like having to rewrite this."

"The lawyer doesn't have to live with your malfunctioning robots. Besides, it's to your advantage that I keep abreast of recent developments, so I can cope with anything new you decide to get."

The deal was made, and the group settled back into routine. Cinderella repaired the secretary, which had been making hash of the family's appointments; ordered replacement parts for the gameplayer, which had made hash of one of its own modules; and reprogrammed the cook, which had literally been making hash of the family's food. She then enrolled in a couple of part-time courses, where she not only was able to keep her mind honed but also had the pleasure of talking again with fellow technicians. They quickly learned her history; but since she now went by the nickname commemorating her D-level origin, they accepted her, acknowledging that any reasonable person would prefer comfort to squalor.

The Hills, meanwhile, were being less successful. The two daughters had no talent for either business or professions, and therefore no hope of upward mobility by means of either money or prestige. With Cinderella's guidance they might manage to maintain their high B-level position, but this was not enough: It was their ambition to reach the A levels, for the A class had the privilege of doing nothing but socializing. The only remaining road to the upper levels was a suitable marriage, so the Hills concentrated all their efforts on social affairs attended by A-class families.

Cinderella endlessly programmed the sewing robot to produce the latest fashions for the three Hills to wear, selected hypnotapes for them to learn the latest criticisms of whatever drama or concert was the current fad, and repaired the reducing machines, make-up robots, chef, cleaners, and the ever-clogged disposal units.

Matters continued thus until shortly before the annual Mayor's Masquerade Ball, the grandest affair of the year. It was held on the very top floor of the city tower, with the most elaborate decorations, catering, and entertainment that could be invented each year by professional party organizers. Most important, the invitation list extended beyond the five hundred people of the ten A levels to include the hundred of B-1—which, in turn, included the Hills.

Mother and daughters were in a frenzy of excitement and anxiety over their chance to mingle with all the A's, right to the top. They obtained a great variety of designs for Cinderella to program into the sewing machine, so they could see the 3-D images of the garments before making a choice.

Urbana's only demand for her own clothes was fashionableness, so Cinderella had only to provide her with the latest fad, adapted to her stoutness. Fossetta was inclined to let Cinderella make the decision for her, trusting the younger girl's judgement, but Narcissa rejected all advice on her own and her sister's behalf. Cinderella allowed Narcissa to bedizen herself in a tasteless collection of opulence, but rewarded Fossetta by pretending to make equally bad choices for her and letting Narcissa sneer her way down to an attractive outfit for her sister.

At last Cinderella was able to punch in her stepsisters' measurements—which she knew by heart from frequency of use—and, after fending off the two over-eager women while the machine was working, delivered the garments. Leaving the sisters to their tryings-on and posturing, Cinderella thankfully escaped to her current class in advanced hyperspace theory and the enjoyment of using her mind again.

During break, she entertained several of her fellow students with the latest developments in the tale of the Great Outfitting Session; and after class two of these students, Fabron and Heber, detained her. "Cindy," said Fabron, "we want to ask a favor."

Cinderella said firmly, "If you want me to check that endless calculation you're doing on Bellinger helices——"

"No, no," Fabron assured her. "I conned someone else into that. This is quite different. We want you to infiltrate the Mayor's Ball."

Heber put in, "You've got sufficient knowlege of etiquette and fashionable talk; and you've got the facilities to dress yourself properly."

"All true," acknowledged Cinderella, "but why should I go? I expect it'll be excruciatingly boring, even if you add in the danger of being discovered as a gate-crasher."

"We're not suggesting you do it for kicks," retorted Fabron righteously. "It's part of a plan to improve the lot of the worker."

"Really?" said Cinderella. "I didn't even know there was a revolution going on."

"It's not a revolution," said Fabron. "None of us wants to trade our useful lives for the emptiness of upper-class life. We just want to acquire some of the privileges of the middle class. We can't see why technology isn't as good as commerce. After all, we're just as vital to the city. If we all stopped work, the whole tower would grind to a halt."

"So why don't you?"

"Because it would cause so much damage and discomfort for everyone. What do you think we are, anarchists? Technicians build; they don't destroy. Even if we just cut off one level in a demonstration, we'd disrupt the commerce and daily life of the city, and perhaps shatter our society. We don't want that. We've got complaints, but we know even the worst-off of us are living better than most people used to. Nobody freezes or starves or gets tortured."

"So what *do* you want to do?"

Fabron glanced around reflexively and lowered his voice. "We're going to grab Mayor Ulric's son, Royce, as a hostage. The mayor's got the authority to grant our demands."

"What's all this got to do with my proposed gate-crashing?"

"Our problem has been to find a way to get Royce

out of his usual haunts, where our chances of making the snatch are poor. . . ."

"And you figure I can do the snatch for you? No, thanks!"

"Don't run without load, Cindy. All you have to do is get near him carrying a bit of equipment we'll supply. It broadcasts a subliminal psychological lure, tuned to his brain pattern type; it'll fix his attention and emotions on the woman who's wearing the lure."

"And then I'm supposed to lead him out to you?"

"No. The only way we could get a lot of us into the top level all at once would be to sabotage some equipment *and* its alternative *and* its back-up *and* its emergency reserve. Even if we could manage all that without other techs fixing as fast as we damaged, it could hurt a lot of people. And Royce might get suspicious if you tried to get him to come down to a level where we could foregather easily. But we've worked out a way to make him come down on his own later looking for you."

"Great," said Cinderella sarcastically. "It's not enough that I have to barge in on him, now I also have to have *him* barging in on *me*."

"Oh, we'll get him before he gets to you," Heber assured her.

"I expect I'll be sorry I asked, but how are you going to work all this?"

"It's a masked ball, so he won't know who you are; but you'll leave him a clue to follow."

"Games, yet," said Cinderella. "What kind of a clue?"

"A shoe."

"A *shoe?*"

"The guy's a shoe fetishist; so we'll build the lure

circuitry into a special shoe for you to wear. The pair will be shaped exactly to your feet, down to the last toe-curve, and will be made of Glas-Clere plastic, so the fit can be seen—which his kink will make him notice. You 'lose' the shoe just as you leave him. With the lure continuing to work on him, and him fixated on you, he'll try to find the woman who fits the shoe. His hunt will cause confusion in the upper levels; and in the midst of it, we slip in and nab him. We've got everything else set up—hide-out, supplies—and from then on, you don't need to do anything. If anybody fingers you for your part earlier, you've done nothing but crash a party and try to catch a higher-level spouse."

"All neatly planned except for one thing. What if the mayor refuses to buy back his son with your privileges?"

"He won't. Royce is his only child; if he loses him, the mayoralty goes to a branch of the family he hates. And we could keep Royce in the lower levels indefinitely—certainly long enough for the other branch to insist on a legal appointment of a new heir apparent."

"All right," said Cinderella. "I've a hunch I'm going to regret this, but I'll help you."

The day of the ball was one of great excitement in the Hill household. The mayor's bachelor son was the head of a list of eligible young men who would all be at the party, all glittering potential passports to a life of pure socializing in the A levels. So, of course, would the most eligible rival young women, but Narcissa was vain enough and Fossetta romantically impractical enough to believe their own chances were good. However, the importance of establishing good contacts during this once-a-year opportunity made them nervous, an emotion augmented by the urgings and twittering of their mother, Urbana. All three of them, as usual, took out their feelings on Cinderella as she labored to get them ready, reproducing their chosen gowns, as they had already damaged the ones they had tried on.

"Cinderella," demanded Fossetta, "why did you have the jewel-synthesizer turn out blue sapphires for me when you've chosen me a pink dress?"

"Shh!" said Cinderella. "Because then Narcissa is sure to demand I re-order it in blue."

"Cinderella," demanded Urbana, "where is my mink cape?"

"Coming right up."

"Cinderella," demanded Narcissa, "why isn't this make-up robot working?"

"Because you haven't turned it on, Narcissa. This button. . . . "

"Cinderella," Fossetta prompted her, waving the pink dress now delivered by the sewing robot.

"Fossetta!" exclaimed Narcissa. "You're *not* wearing *that* wishy-washy color! Did you let Cinderella pick it out again? Have you no taste of your own? Get something like this!" She patted her purple-figured orange gown. "Electric blue is what you should wear! Cinderella, fix it!"

Cinderella re-cycled the pink gown, which soon returned in the chosen shade. Fossetta looked at it a bit hesitantly, but Cinderella assured her that the make-up machine could adjust her complexion and hair shade to suit the strong color.

"Cinderella! Perfume!" demanded Urbana.

"Do you three want to match or contrast tonight?"

"*I* shall have Endless Yearning," said Narcissa.

"That's you, all right," murmured Cinderella. "How about Lucky Dip for you, Fossetta?"

"She will have Misty Hope," decreed Narcissa.

"And I will have Midnight Surprise," said Urbana.

"So you will," smiled Cinderella. "Now, is everyone ready at last? . . . Have a good time. I'm sure you'll find it an interesting occasion." To herself she added that if many of the guests were as weird as the mayor's son, "interesting" might be an understatement, even without her own performance.

"Of course we will. And we'll tell you all about it tomorrow," promised Fossetta.

"I'll be looking forward to that," said Cinderella, and ushered them out. For once they seemed to have forgotten nothing, for they did not phone back for her to send a delivery robot after them. When she was sure they were out of the way, she phoned a signal to the conspirators and soon their agent arrived.

The agent turned out to be Monica, a middle-aged woman who had been a neighbor and friend of Cinderella's family in the lower-level days; she had traded child-care duties with Verena, and so was known to Cinderella by the vernacular term of goodmother.

Cinderella showed her in, with a warm greeting and proffered hospitality, but the goodmother declined the offers. "Let's get you off to that Ball, girl. Here's the program for your costume and make-up mask. And here are the shoes—the lure's in the right one, so make sure that's the one you lose." She fed the programs into the appropriate machines while Cinderella tried on the shoes. The conspirators had her computer-code personal specs, so the fit was perfect, as promised.

As they waited for the clothing and make-up processors to prepare their products, Monica told Cinderella of the background work done by the conspirators. They had made a hologram of an aircar which, with the connivance of a bribed landing-terrace guard, would be projected there during the evening. That would lend substance to the anticipated rumor that the beautifully, elegantly-costumed gate-crasher was a visitor from the ruling family of another city tower. At the midnight guard change, however, the hologram hoax would be allowed to be discovered. By this plan they hoped to have Cinderella received with honor during the evening, but to let the mayor's son know that his later search should be confined to his own tower.

"So be sure you're away by midnight," Monica cautioned, "before any furor starts over the false aircar."

The costume was now ready; a silver-threaded white gown trimmed in the deep magenta shade called royal purple. Under the touch of the make-up robot, Cinderella's face was reshaped to the acme of the current taste in beauty; her hair was made midnight black and long, and piled into an elaborate coiffure on which sparkled a tiara of diamonds and pearls so realistic-looking that even this synthetic-oriented generation would hesitate to doubt them.

Since the ball was a masquerade, all the guests would wear pseudonym-badges, and Monica remembered to form one. "What name?" she asked, fingers hovering over the keys.

Cinderella thought a moment, then said, "Why not Cindy? Only my tech friends call me that, so it won't give anything away to the Ball crowd. And it's a nice touch of irony, considering its derivation."

With the aid of the suborned guard, Cinderella was smuggled into the Ball at just the point of bustle and swing calculated by the conspirators to facilitate her acceptance by people already happy from the variety of intoxicants and drugs.

Cinderella switched on her shoe-lure and was promptly assured of its potency. Although it was tuned to Royce, other men of similar brain type were also affected, to a lesser degree, and a small crowd of them was soon flocking around her. It was not long before Royce himself drifted over to see what the great attraction was.

He was easy to identify, for, as one of the host family, he was wearing his own face and name. He promptly used the leverage of his identity to pry Cinderella loose from her admirers, and thereafter monopolized her, ignoring all other women, so Cinderella concluded that the lure was as good as the conspirators claimed.

Cinderella had a technician's pleasure in any device that worked well. She was also able to enjoy Royce's excellent dancing and punctillious manners, and she admitted to herself a certain pleasure in glimpsing, now and then, the furious jealousy on Narcissa's face and the more wistful envy on Fossetta's. In fact, she indulged an impulse for revenge on the arrogant older sister by maneuvering to have the younger one included for a time in the cluster of favored people around herself and Royce.

But aside from these minor pleasures, Cinderella found the evening the drag she had expected. Royce was a bore. He had asked her a few questions about herself, which she parried on the excuse of maintaining her anonymity during the Masked Ball; then he proceeded to hold forth on his favorite subject: himself. He told her about the minutiae of his days, of the various arts to which he aspired: his sporadic attempts to do portrait busts with the aid of a measuring laser or to write poems in the latest mode, wherein each word came from a different, archaic language and line lengths were determined by a table of random numbers; or to compose absolutely non-repetitive music; or to choose an unending variety of menus to taste and rate. Cinderella eventualy lost track of what he was saying—unlike the fads he followed, he was not non-repetitive.

As time passed, general inebriation increased and so did Royce's infatuation. He began speaking of Cinderella almost as often as of himself, praising her beauty and trying to persuade her to confess her identity. Well before midnight, he was declaring his intention to drink champagne from her slipper. Cinderella thought this a disgusting idea but, since it was an excuse to get the shoe into his possession, allowed herself to be slowly persuaded to permit the act, surreptitiously timing her conversion so that she was able to slip away just before midnight as Royce was performing the grandstand gesture.

The guard and Monica helped her leave the level unseen and she was home, back in her own face, and in bed, by the time her relatives returned.

Her part in the conspiracy was now over but she felt enough curiosity over the aftermath of her act to be impatient, next morning, for her relatives to wake and begin the promised account of the Ball. Her patience was then further strained by the inevitable preliminary boasting by Urbana and Narcissa, faithfully echoed by Fossetta, about the success of the Hill women. Urbana usually favored Narcissa, who most resembled her but this time she switched to the daughter who had achieved the most for her. "Fossetta was actually in Royce Ulric's own group——"

"Briefly," snapped Narcissa.

"—and talked to him," went on Urbana firmly.

"What did you think of him, Fossetta?" asked Cinderella curiously.

"Beautiful manners, and such self-confidence. How I enjoyed listening to him talk!"

"You did?" said Cinderella incredulously. "You actually thought him a good conversationalist?"

"Well—uh—not exactly," admitted Fossetta. "I just thought he spoke well; I sort of stopped listening to the words. . . ."

"There's hope for you yet," said Cinderella.

Narcissa cut in again. Since her account of the—largely imaginary—attentions that had been paid to her had been upstaged by Fossetta's little moment of glory, she seized attention again by the extreme method of ceasing to talk about herself, telling instead of the dramatic events of the evening: the arrival of the mysterious beauty, whose identity no one had been able to guess; Royce's gallantry toward her; her disappearance and the discovery that she was not visiting royalty but an inhabitant of their own city.

To her alarm, Cinderella realized that the conspirators' lure had proved even more potent than advertised, as she heard that Royce had startled the assembly by declaring that he intended to marry the mystery woman, imposter or no. All the eligible women at the Ball had thereupon refused to identify themselves, in the hope of later claiming to be the mystery woman, and they promptly left the Ball to avoid the chance of being recognized. This broke up the evening at an unprecedentedly early hour, and opinion was divided as to whether the Ball had been a flop or a smashing success.

Discussion of this last was interrupted by a news broadcast Urbana had turned on, which announced that Royce Ulric had instituted a search for the mystery woman. Her manners and self-assurance he declared, proved that she came from the upper levels, though guessably not from among the families invited to the Ball. This should reduce the search territory to the forty-nine B levels below B-l; but Royce was being thorough; he was personally visiting each unit on every A and B level, to find and identify the woman who had not come forward in response to the appeals made in earlier broadcasts.

"Why, that means he'll be coming here!" exclaimed Fossetta.

Cinderella got up hastily. "I've got some extra classes to attend. It'll take the rest of the——"

"Oh, no, you don't!" cried Narcissa. "You're going to make the sewing robot produce us some lovely lounge wear, right now!"

"I really——" tried Cinderella.

"No!" said Narcissa and Urbana in unison.

"Don't you want to see Royce Ulric?" exclaimed Fossetta incredulously.

"Frankly, no," said Cinderella, deciding on shock tactics. "I hear he's a creep."

"What?" yelled all three of the others.

"A neurotic, or worse."

"So what?" said Narcissa. "He's still the mayor's son, and a great catch."

"Well, I hope you catch him, then. You deserve him."

Fossetta, who trusted Cinderella's judgement, asked dubiously, "Is he really a creep? What have you heard about him?"

Cinderella told her what she had learned about the man, including her personal observations as reports. Since technicians picked up all the gossip and rumors, and Cinderella kept up contacts with them at classes, no one questioned her knowledge.

"Maybe you're right," whispered Fossetta, so that her mother and sister would not hear her agreeing with Cinderella's opinion. "And really, one of the other men in his group paid me more attention than he did. His name's Winslow, and he really seemed to like me."

"Oh, yes. That one's got the glimmerings of sense. A

good choice," approved Cinderella. "But you might as well stay in the competition during this search; the more women Royce has to check out, the better."

"Why?"

"It'll make his search, and therefore him, look more important. Everybody'll be happier," improvised Cinderella, whose real concern, of course, was to give Fabron and company a longer opportunity.

Fossetta looked a bit puzzled over that logic, but subsided, agreeable to any excuse for remaining part of the excitement.

Urbana said sharply, "Cinderella, you're not leaving here till you've got those clothes programmed. You're not to do *anything* else till they're ordered."

"Don't panic. It'll take him a long time to work his way through the A's, and I'll get the clothes started right away."

She hurried off, but went first to her own room to get into her technician's coveralls. She intended to take no slightest chance of being caught in the search, not only for her own sake, to avoid Royce, but also for the sake of the conspirators. If they had not managed to grab Royce by the time he got this far, she had to prevent the search from coming to an end. She could slip out while her relatives were engrossed in their new clothes and, in her technician's outfit, she would be beneath notice until she got safely out of the upper levels.

But she had not calculated on the aid of Royce's brainier friend, Winslow, who had taken Fossetta's eye. Winslow had crossed off the list all those women whom he or others had definitely identified at the Ball and whom they had seen there at the same time as Royce's fascinating mystery woman. If there were any error, these women could always be checked in a second round; meanwhile, the shorter list took the searchers more quickly through the likelier suspects. Royce's party arrived at the Hill household while Cinderella was still tapping figures into the clothing machine.

"Three qualifying females here," said Winslow, generously including Urbana, with an eye to winning her favor. "And one known personally to me who cannot be the one you want," he added firmly.

Fossetta alternately pouted and glowed over Winslow's determined exclusion of her from Royce's consideration, while Narcissa and a surprised Urbana frantically got into the best of their old clothes, refraining from yelling for Cinderella in order not to draw attention to her.

Cinderella thought furiously. She could still get out, but to leave after Royce's arrival would obviously be deliberate, not a mischance arising from ignorance, and would make her suspect. If she were identified but her location were unknown, Royce might give up his personal search and leave it to the Mayoral Guard to try to find her. Furthermore, the conspirators must be finding it too difficult to get near Royce after all; perhaps there were too many citizens everywhere, standing around gaping. It might be better to lure Royce down to the D levels, by leaving him a clue to her destination there and confirming her identity.

She quickly typed a note to herself, telling her to meet the writer at this time at a specific address in D, left the note paperweighted by the other party shoe on her dresser, and slipped out the back door while the Hills were still trying to prove they fitted the first shoe. She heard an impatient order from Royce to his companions to search the unit for the other female, so knew that her bait would be found. She trusted his impatience to make him follow

Illustrated by Greg Petan

the clue in person, as soon as he could gather some guards to hunt out and grab the fugitive gate-crasher.

Using a scramble code the conspirators had given her, Cinderella called Fabron on her pocket phone as she made her way down to D. He agreed with her new plan and promised to have reinforcements join her at the address she had given, a repair depot for mobile robots. Heber met her there with a pass key, and the others arrived soon after.

Cinderella's expertise quickly added a few instructions to the programs of some of the robots stored there. As Royce, with half a dozen of his aides and a like number of hastily-summoned guards, came hurrying along the street, the robots gently grabbed all of them and hustled them into the back room of the depot. There the conspirators took over. They drugged all the guards and aides, and whisked Royce away to the prepared hiding place. Cinderella, perforce, went along to hide out as well.

When all were comfortably settled, Fabron put the conspirators' demands to Royce. "We want an end to this rigid sorting out by work-type. Technology is no less honorable than commerce. Let the most productive people of *both* classes live in the A and B levels, and let the rest live in C. Put the machinery down in D. Having it in C is a way of making us live below the salt. It makes an artificial division that promotes class discrimination."

"*I* can't do anything about it," said Royce sulkily. "Go talk to my father."

"No, you're going to talk to him," said Fabron, pointing to the phone beside him. "Tell him if he wants you back, he's got to pass the decree switching us up to C immediately—and allowing us access to B and A as we earn it."

"Why should I? You can't hold me here forever," blustered Royce.

"We can hold you long enough to get you bypassed in the succession."

Royce shrugged. "I'm not all that keen on becoming mayor."

The conspirators began to look blankly at one another, and shuffle their feet. Then Heber suggested, "Get Cindy to work on him."

Cinderella was pulled forward, and reluctantly began to take a part again. "Look, Royce, it won't cause you any inconvenience. Why don't you——"

"Cindy!" Royce jumped up and reached for her. The conspirators grabbed him and shoved him back down by the phone.

Fabron tried to regain the initiative, but could only repeat himself. "You'll tell your father we want to live in C——"

"Oh, who cares where you live?" said Royce peevishly. "Give me my mystery woman, and you can have what you want."

All eyes turned to Cinderella, who looked alarmed. "No you don't! I never agreed to that! Turn off that blasted lure!"

This was hastily done as soon as they could pry the shoe away from Royce. But it was to no avail; he had become fixated on Cinderella. He declared wildly that he would sooner die himself than live without her, and would tell his father to reject the conspirators unless Cinderella were given to him.

Everyone again looked demandingly at Cinderella.

"Wait a minute," she said hastily, and drew Fabron aside. "Can you make an even stronger version of that lure?"

"Sure, but why? This one's working fine."

"Just get one made, fast, and show me to another

phone and a clothing robot."

She made her call and began feeding long-since memorized specs into the clother.

Twenty minutes later, she answered a hesitant signal at the hideout door and was greeting a perplexed Narcissa, who looked half-fearfully, half-disdainfully about at her surroundings, and said "I know you've never lied, but how can you possibly promise me Royce in return for coming here?"

"Never mind the questions; just put on these shoes and walk into that room."

Narcissa obeyed, and Cinderella held her breath until she heard cries of rapturous mutual admiration coming from Royce and her step-sister. Then she signalled the conspirators to re-enter with their demands, now enforcing them with the threat of removing Narcissa. Royce instantly agreed, and made the call to his father.

Between the threat to his son and the latter's news that he was now in a position to provide an heir in their line, to defend the mayoralty from take-over by the hated relations, the mayor cheerfully granted the conspirators' demands. Within a few minutes the signed decree was being churned out by the phone's facsimile printer, duly witnessed by the Council and registered in the Law and News banks.

The conspirators had remembered to make sure everyone involved was also granted a full pardon immediately; so everyone was able to return home and prepare for the upheaval of partial revolution.

And Cinderella, having escaped marrying the mayor's son, lived happily ever after.

The Helldivers
by
Parris ja Young

About the Author

Parris ja Young is 43 and lives in a cabin of his own building in the mountains near Missoula, Montana. He won Second Prize in the fourth quarter. (Finding him to tell him he was a contest winner proved to be a long drawn-out process.) He has a Master of Fine Arts degree in Creative Writing, and dreamed—literally, not figuratively—that he might do well if he entered the contest. His middle-name style, "ja," developed as the result of Army service, in which, as an Adjutant, he had to sign his name numerous times every day. So Parris Jon Arden Young became Parris ja Young. However, he points out, it is equally true that "ja" in Rastafarian dialect means "a spiritual man."

Make of that what you will. Young says he began writing at the age of 10, but, aside from a 1964 poem in the Northwest Poets Anthology, never submitted anything to publishers. After earning his MFA from the University of Montana in 1974, he felt that while his inspiration was boiling, he would not write until he was fully fevered. Hence, the cabin-building, and the decade or more of living without much reliance on modern technology. "The Helldivers" is his first work apart from some essays and poetry.

It also coincides with a return to dealing with the public. He is heavily involved with promulgating an "Olympics of The Mind" at the Alberton, Montana, public school. This is a prototype program designed to encourage creativity in children. Parris is also a member of two artists' co-operatives, and is doing local commercial art while also continuing his backwoods life as much as possible.

He describes "The Helldivers" as "cerebral." That it is; it is also adventurous, science-fictional, allegorical, technological and mystical. It is often humorous in dead earnest. And make of that *what you will.*

Illustrated by Brian Patrick Murray

I had exercised every delay I could imagine, but I arrived in Emergency Bay in time to see the incoming. Two of them: one on a roll- nurse, one ambulatory.

The woman horizontal was conscious and relaxed, although her lower face was covered with a liquid breathing bubble.

Bill Jennings, Traumatop, reported coolly as she was rolled by. "Chlorine damage; both lungs. Acid burns; right breast, ribcage, right hip. Tibia, right, broken." He looked at one of the attendants, "Change her fluid once again before you get her to Exam." He turned to me, "She'll be up in a cycle."

I heard this tangentially. My attention had been rivetted on the other casualty. He looked terrible.

Mason.

He was a large man. Big, warm and witty. I had first met him eight cycles ago . . . a casual contact in a mess hall. One of his admirers, seated beside me at a table, began to tell me of a Mason exploit. Mason had descended into a mining shaft to help a team balance a field generator that was wildly erratic and threatening to shake the asteroid apart. Before he got on the scene, the machine had shorted out for a moment—had created such an electromagnetic concussion that a portion of the asteroid had sheared and trapped Mason and his team. Mason had crawled for seventy-two hours through ventilation tubes before reaching the surface. Then he had crossed 300 meters of Extreme Low Pressure—a feat that most theorists will insist is impossible—before arriving at a functional cell.

"Hard vacuum," the starry-eyed young Tech had gone on to explain. "When Control had asked for my estimate of the damage to that pressurizing dome, I said, 'Sir, I'd bet my next R-and-R there's nothing in there but hard vacuum.' "

I looked across the table at Mason. "Lucky for you there was considerable gravity."

Mason smiled that winning smile and spoke in a gentle but powerful voice, "And a functional cell not too far."

I have run with some heavy company, so I pushed on him a little. "You climb out of there in fear? A man" (a real man, I implied) "would have hung around the location with his team 'til help arrived, just to encourage them."

Mason's eyes met mine levelly.

In the heartbeat of pause, the young Tech, seeking to avoid conflict, volunteered, "But help might not have arrived in time, because the locat——"

Mason replied with a quiet voice that somehow managed to interrupt the Tech in mid-word, "I've been known to be calm."

But the Mason now being helped across the bay was not the same man. I wanted to look away. He radiated fear and self-loathing. As he was led by me he looked up from the floor for a short second and reached for my arm. Irrationally I did not want to be contaminated, but I resisted the impulse to pull away.

"Thomas," he pleaded. I could tell it took effort even for this whimper. "Thomas, I'm afraid to go to sleep."

I stood cold as they led him by. If it could happen to him, it could happen to anyone. Fear, unfamiliar to me since my adolescence, froze me inert.

Jennings reported—was that a trace of awe in his voice?—"Mason's seen the ghost."

It's not easy, this job. Only job I know that pays Hazard even for the off-time.

We are the Helldivers.

The Dante-12 system is in the Milky Way, not far from Home, but still it had remained undetected for ages. Then unexplored. Then unappreciated. Then a Smithsonian Generalist integrated certain irregularities of visitor behavior at the Institute with proximity to the Dante-12 ore samples. Dantium, it was discovered, is a psycho-electromagnetic ore. The only one so far.

Now, you could sell twenty-five grams of that stuff on the black market and the rest of your life could be spent in luxury—if you could force yourself to part with the Dantium. It is hypnotic and a mood elevator. It is an aphrodisiac and a relaxant. It stimulates psi talent in some. A grain of it at twenty feet might yield you more charisma than John the Baptist. Closer, unless you were one of those who are very strong, you might drift into such a suggestive state that you were not legally responsible for your behavior. It has happened. And the stuff has many unsubstantiated and even more apochryphal qualities.

No wonder the stuff is strictly controlled and highly illegal, and that the Combined Government is busily mining it as fast as technology and manpower will permit.

Probably for weaponry.

I don't much care. I'm here for the money.

I'm already secure on my wages alone. Especially after this tour. That, plus the lodebonus I won in '72, and maybe another, and I'll be wealthy for life.

And, until this shift, I thought about danger, but not about consequences. Now, in my mind, I was rerunning mental videos of those who say that this place is Hell, and the souls from the universe-local gather here, attracted, chained, by Dantium.

Too abstract for this dog. I'm pretty much resistant to the effects, although I have a small ring with a tiny nugget of the stuff among my personal gear that I have a plan for smuggling back into Solsys.

Maybe I'll be smuggling back a soul or two back home. S'okay with me.

Outside Mason's door, I had another attack of anxiety. Mason was quitting.

"Going back to Denver. My brother has a farm there. I can learn to help."

"Mason, you're a legend! There's no better spotter than you in the fleet."

He hardly seemed to hear me. "Loping Boy is better. We're not far from the Mission in Denver. Maybe I'll start reading the Scriptures. . . ."

I looked at him carefully. His color was better, but his head hung low. He reminded me of a streeter among the wine bottles.

"You are recovering already, Mason. What could you have seen that would shake you?" I had been impatient to ask. It was not quite the right moment, but I felt that it was important to know.

He raised that great shaggy head and his eyes pierced me. "Maybe you'd better leave, O'Hara."

He seemed as if he was as big as a polar bear.

I left.

And standing there in the hall, I felt some ancient

wail in my nerves; some Celtic memory of talking winds and wraithlike spirits wrestling in the night.

My mother used to say, "And now, Thomas O'Hara, you be kind. You think before you kill that helpless creature. Remember, anything that moves has a soul."

I shrugged it off. I believe in hammers and nails. I believe in electricity. I believe in chemistry and in machines and in minichips with electricity flowing through them like water. I believe in bulkheads and gravity. And, although I could find no explanation for the odd goings-on at Dante-12, I did not, and most certainly would not, ascribe every coincidence, accident, oddity, anomaly, failure, vision, or misunderstanding to the interference of tormented souls.

"Ha!" I laughed aloud at myself. "My crazy mother even loved trees."

And now I've started dreaming.

I don't dare tell the Doc. He might hold me out for a cycle. I can't afford that. Six more cycles and I go home—a wealthy man.

Besides, it's just one dream. Not like I'm getting unstable.

Most of my dreams are the regular stuff, right?

I mean docking a fine specimen up the knife. Cutting it like a diamond. I'm a great laser/plasma man. I can get right down to indicated-ore with a minimum number of cuts and a minimum of waste. Cut. Blow the plasma. The tret drifts away without encumbering the operation. Next cut.

Or I dream of the women on Canton. Whew! Don't wake me! Or I dream of talking with the boys and drinking Earthwine naturelle. I can even smell in my dreams. Or I dream of betting and winning on the fights. Or of shooting my way out of prison.

But last night . . . I dreamed lucidly of deep stillness. The little storyteller in my dreams shut up. I was alone, standing at a door. I can't remember being so focused in a dream. The door opened. As it swung away, I remember reading "Dante-12" stenciled on it. I thought, "I was supposed to think something when I see that," but I waved the thought away when I saw the man waiting in the opened room. I can still see him clearly. I can still hear every word that he said. Just he and I standing face to face, although I had the feeling that he was very big. There was a nagging recognition that failed to interrupt my recall. He said, "I've been waiting for you."

Somehow I had entered the room.

Then I was startled awake by the sound of the door slamming shut behind me. It was the ring of heavy, high-carbon steel against steel. More than being startled, more than the feeling I had been manipulated and trapped, I was awakened by the sound of finality.

We are the Helldivers.

Descending.

Going into the matrix for the lodebonus. A payload of five hundred grams in one three-day-shift "dive," and each member of the team gets a five-thousand-credit bonus.

Russell Horton pilots the Miner-22. He follows the suggestions of our Spotter, Danny Loping Boy. Loping Boy has sensors and integrators, but often he closes his eyes, makes animal noises, then insists that we visit an exhausted or secondary sector where we find a rich vortex. Usually. He's not infallible. Even with his hocus-pocus routine, probably meant to create some respect among spotters, he will occasionally, but rarely, return with a mediocre load.

When he is "hunting," as he calls it, he walks with a strange gait: two steps, then a noticeable "pounce." His eyes are fiery with intensity. He carries his hands with a liquid motion and his fingers point forward, not down, at the ends of each swing of his arms. He makes me nervous with this witchy behavior—reminds me of my mother—but I don't care. He finds the ore. He never returns to the Bin with an empty poke. He finds the ore.

We are a crack team.

All of the teams are good. We are professionals. Sharp at our work and screened for resistance to psychic disturbance. "We've been known to be calm," Mason would have said.

There are eight teams. We run staggered dives. A dive encompasses a "day" of travel into the large matrix; three "days" of location, docking or juxtaposition, cutting, capture, poking, crude milling, insulation, stowage; then a day of return travel. With eight teams there are always two teams traveling, three teams resting.

Sounds simple, doesn't it? But rarely is there a dive without some emergency, damage or casualty, because the local laws are peculiar.

"Peculiar"? Ha! Bosons and beyond! There is no consistency in the law at Dante-12. Mass fluctuates. Particles accelerate or decelerate without cause. Baxter's team hit a floating mountain because, the trip-log recorded, they saw another team's Miner-22 coming straight at them. The survivor swore that it was ectoplasm. In this day and age? Particles that orbit like electrons around a meteoroid of too little mass to create such an effect; that I believe because I have seen it. A swarm of fist-sized meteoroids changing direction like a school of fish; that I can believe. But ectoplasm? I have seen what looked like a four-meter-long tubeworm writhing in hard space. Turned out to be a "cable" of rocks the shape and size of my finger. And everyone sees the little "misties" running around inside and outside of any craft. Some miners swear that the circuit problems plaguing us lately are Dantium-related. Maybe yes, maybe no. But ectoplasm? Some people will believe anything.

I wonder only a little about it all. Is it a tear in the fabric of space? Maybe it is a leak from another dimension.

And maybe it is really Hell.

The rest of the time I don't worry about it. I've got no argument with the Afterworld. I've been into Dante-12 pretty deep. Strange business. But here I am. Seen some weird misties, but I haven't seen the ghost.

I hit the cushion beside Horton. "We there yet?"

"Yeah. I just saw a mouse the size of my fist on the tower behind you a moment ago. Seemed to look me right in the eye."

As I was turning to look, I knew I would see nothing.

But there it was. Looking at me.

"Shee-it," I exploded, "I see it, too."

"We're both raving mad," Horton laughed.

Missey entered the bridge. Tough little gal from Felina. She saw the misty. "Oh . . . flowers."

She sat at her console and warmed up the zappers and shields. "Anything else?"

Horton responded, "I haven't detected much for solids."

"Yer a kid, Horton. I read all sorts of little bodies," she corrected. "Where's Loping Boy?"

"You're the one with the hot detectors," Horton sniveled slightly. I dislike the way he picks up Missey's jibes.

"Little bodies and hot detectors," I said in Missey's ear with a leer.

She turned and sparkled at me. "How're ya doin', Hi-gain?"

"Drunk on power. Loping Boy is trying to kill himself in the sauna again. So I decided to help him. As I went by I could hear him singing and banging on the water bucket. I cranked the thermostat up to 300 F. He should be on the bridge soon."

"Three hundred degrees? Wouldn't that kill him?" Horton asked.

"Not that ol' dog, if he is human." Missey spoke to me rather than to Horton. "Gets his detectors hot."

It was an hour before Loping Boy ambled in. We had pushed Horton into deviating course so Missey and I could zap meteoroids in a cloud moving roughly in our direction. She outpoints me in the long run, although I am a damn good shot.

"Hey-you, this team is playful. Where're we goin'?" Loping Boy asked as he sat.

"Hey-you, Indian Boy, you're hours late." Missey grinned.

Then Loping Boy withdrew from the play. I saw his demeanor change. "Good thing I showed up finally. These ones here are taking this billion-credit pickup up Death's left nostril." He was trying to remain playful, but I could see he was entering his hunting mode. "And speaking of God, anyone here try to kill me?"

He looked over us pleasantly enough, but there was no play in his eyes.

I met the gaze, "Three hundred degrees. I did it." I was ready for trouble.

A very slight smile creased the corners of his eyes, "You want to take a sweat with this Indian sometime?" Then he was serious again, "No. It was pegged all the way up." He looked at Missey and Horton. "None of you?

Well, my song saved my ass. Got hot quick."

I was considering who might have done it and what motive there might be, when Loping Boy turned to Horton. "Say, Russ, you head for G-sector, hey? I had a grandfather of a vision this time."

He turned again to Missey and me. I could smell sage and some other herb emanating from him. His eyelids hung low over his dark eyes. I could not see his pupils, and I knew for certain now that he was coming on to the fever.

"I saw God. He's just one of the guys, right? He said we could get a verrry big stone in G-sector. He said there was a 6.7 lodebonus in G-sector."

Missey exclaimed, "A 6.7! That's 33,500 credits apiece!"

Horton said, "G-sector's regulated."

Loping Boy didn't hear him. "I don't know if it was God, but it sure was one of the grandfathers. He told me how to get it: program a fly-through, pick it up on the wing." He turned suddenly on Horton. "Let's do it!"

Horton jumped to it, although it could mean his license. Still, he said, "I don't think we should. Isn't that where Mason——"

Loping Boy leaped to his feet so quickly that we all started. "You gotta be clean. Get clean! You're the only one I worry about on this can, Horton. Be a man, Horton!"

He stalked to the door, then turned on us. "You, you, you," he pointed at each of us in turn, "You know this is the storm, eh? This time we count coup. This time we count coup. You know this is so." He left.

"Shall I contact Mother?" Horton asked.

"He's nuts," Missey said. "But we could all get filthy rich."

"Maybe. And maybe I'll be the one without a license and the rest of you . . ."

"No one's ever seen a nugget that size," I said. "I remember that big one that Fulton poked in. . . ."

"Yeah, so do I. Nearly a kilo," Missey mused.

"Imagine one that's more than three times that size."

"Might drive everyone on the 22 insane," Horton suggested. "Not that it'd be much different."

Loping Boy burst back in. His face was radiant and his smile contagious. He was leading Julie from Refining. "See? This Horton. He will do it."

Julie looked at Missey. "I'm scared." She glanced aside at Loping Boy suspiciously.

Loping Boy put his arm around her shoulders to impart confidence and led her toward the door, "Oh, no, your conscience, is it good? Then what do you have to fear? Coup. We will count——" The door closed on his voice.

"I've never seen him so crazy this far from hot ore," Missey observed.

"Look," Horton said, "I'm going to program a sine through G. We'll go in right here, through the densest area, it's not too many klicks, then out here."

Horton was pointing out his program on his screen. He was actually a pretty hot pilot, once past his defensiveness. "We can say it was a fenestration error if we pick up a little in D-sector, duck an, ah, apparition, and break toward the core instead of the perimeter. We correct our error in seconds, but lo!, right through G-sector." Sighing at the genius of his flightplan, he turned and regarded us. "I like none of this."

Missey drew a breath to begin to needle him, but a misty drifted in through the bulkhead at the rear of the bridge, crossed slowly, and disappeared into the videos at the front. It looked to me like a huge jellyfish trailing tendrils of jungle lianas. It passed close to Missey.

Missey looked slightly shocked. She reached up and

touched her right cheek. "I felt that! Like cat-hair."

Horton snorted. "Smelled like the beach at Atlantic City."

My stomach felt like it was losing its substance. We were not that far in.

I was just going off-watch when Loping Boy came in. He looked other-worldly. He had the hunting lope and an odd serenity on his face.

"O'Hara goes to rest," he said to me. "You pray this time. You pray hard. You pray thorough. This time you count coup. We are the best damn team in this territory. Hell, we'll buy our own Catch, a souped-up Miner-22, and sell Dantium on the black market."

Missey, arising from her position, spoke up. "We'll have neon lights on the corners of our Credcards."

He put his arms around both of us. "We will not need Credcards, ha!, we count this coup." He spoke conspiratorily, but with a deadly earnest that gave me shivers.

I realized that "coup" might not mean lodebonus.

After eating and some attempt at carving, I lay down to sleep. Underwater dreams. No harm. Woke with a start. The ship had lurched.

Ships don't lurch.

Saal Jad was at shift piloting, but the entire team was on the bridge. Saal's eyes were wide. "No dreck I give you. These thing, it was come from Nord Pole. . . ."

Ben Tool, Deflection and Destruction, said, "I zapped it directly. Twice at five hundred parlum. Once at two thousand. Didn't faze it. I thought it was a king-sized misty."

"I did the evasion of it," Saal went on, "but collide we."

Collided? I looked around the room. We were deep in B-sector. The room was full of ripples, like sipping liqueur. Misties drifted in the cabin like cigarette smoke and hung on the instruments. It looked like the bridge of some ship after fifty years on the floor of some Earth sea. Cobwebs and seaweed. Moss and sea spiders. Julie stood hip deep in a rippling bank of moss. I ran my hand through a small drifting jellyfish.

Collided?

Impossible. I am sure misties are projections from our own minds. You can't bump into a dream.

"No damage, Sir," Denim of Communications reported.

"What's our course now?" Horton, always the pilot, asked.

"The Mother send autocorrect. But it is to reverse polarity, or . . ." Saal frowned, "we move toward Core. I cut Auto. Reprogram. We curve out, but first, G-sector."

I looked at Horton, then Missey, then I looked at Loping Boy. Loping Boy smiled and said, "It is so."

What? Circumstances conspired to send us directly through G-sector? Horton is blameless; his doctored program could be garbaged. Mother was as much responsible as anyone.

I shivered. Everything considered, this dive was spinning out like a weaving. Mason. My anxiety. Loping Boy's madness. This began to feel like fate. Fate? My eye caught Loping Boy's.

"It is so," he repeated.

We were into G-sector.

Both strings were on post. Missey and Ben Tool work tandem beautifully. What cannot be deflected must be destroyed, or cut—I sometimes help there—and then the pieces deflected or destroyed. They work like orchestration. They had just finished a beautiful chain of cuts and zaps, all done as the target twisted at us at high speed. I turned to compliment her and my eyes fell on her right cheek.

She had a series of red scratches, like cat scratches.

My nerves tightened.

"I don't care," I said aloud, "if those pustule misties collapse into their own evacuoles."

The air repeated, "Pusty mustules, pusty misties, pusty mistie. . . ."

I turned to look for the source of the warble.

Missey and Horton were laughing. At what? I wondered.

I moved my attention back to my own scanner. I could see only roughly, but it permitted me to move my attention out of the chaotic cabin.

"Hot stone at 14-8," Horton reported.

"Pass it by," Loping Boy ordered.

We passed it. We curved deeper into G-sector.

It began so gently that I hardly noticed it. A tender motion in my crotch. It was nice and I was responding, but it was a distraction and I assumed I would turn and see Missey. I wondered what could be on her mind at such a time. . . . I turned . . .

. . . and yelped. "Mason!"

It was him. It was not him. It was a nearly opaque misty.

"Oh, shit, I've just seen the ghost," I decided aloud with laudable presence of mind.

The misty laughed and thinned slowly. Misties with a sense of humor?

When I could see through it, I was looking at Missey. She was wide-eyed, looking into the same space, muttering, "Daddy, Daddy, oh, Daddy," like a little girl.

But her face did not register love.

It registered some complex tangle of feeling I could not unravel.

"Snap to it, kid. This is business," I said sharply.

She shook awake, tried to smile, and turned back to her screen.

"Ignore personal problems," I tried to advise sagely, "Remember that this is business. Don't let movies from your insides throw you off." I turned to my board, wondering momentarily if maybe I had a personal problem. Mason? What a mess. "Just misties. Hell," I concluded.

"Soon, through a vortex, then out," Saal reported.

Horton was at the spotter's console, "Wow! Look at that!"

His 'wow' sounded like how-ow-el, due to some anomalies in the air. The misties *were* impinging on the physical.

"I see it! It's beautiful!" Missey announced.

I went over to her long-range vid and looked.

It was beautiful. There was a large meteoroid the shape of a long capsule and the size of a Model-T or Chemofac, slowly rolling end over end. One end of it was positively gold. There was a fountain of colored tracers, glowing gold meteoroids the size of maybe marbles, shooting out from each end, falling back, circling the middle, then shooting out again.

Ben Tool looked up from his screen. "It's in color. Is that possible? I mean, the tracers?"

Loping Boy had gotten up from the Spotter's seat and stood looking over Horton's shoulder. "Figures. That is the one. Where there is the greatest activity, there is where we find . . ."

The lights went out. Many of the screens went out. Emergency lane strips lit up on the floor.

". . . the heavy spirit," Loping Boy concluded.

"You mean the big stone," Missey ventured, her face strangely lit by screenlight.

"No," I said. "He means 'the powerful soul.' He wants to count coup on something big."

I looked at Loping Boy, defying him to deny it.

He nodded approval to me.

Instead of the glee of catching out the schemer, I came away with the feeling that I had done my lesson well. I felt like a child for a moment. I did not like being humbled so off-handedly. But no one noticed.

I shook my head.

We were closing fast.

"Now you must tan the face of that rock. Push it with fire," Loping Boy instructed the other Cut-and-Catch and myself.

My screen does not detect at distance, but close-up my acutance is exceptional. At this distance I could see, but not acutely.

We fired at wide dispersion. Instead of cutting the meteoroid we vaporized surface rock. Between light-pressure and the exploding plasma, we began to push the meteoroid in our direction of travel.

The fountains broke up. The stone clad itself in a nimbus of green flame. A number of the small pebbles parted from it and fell toward us with increasing speed.

Zap. Zap. Zapzap. Missey and Ben fired faster than I could identify targets.

Still, we were hit. Air began to whistle. The air was so thick with misties I wondered that it could leak out. I wondered why the patching veins had not sealed the holes. I wondered why my hair was growing over my shoulders.

When I realized that my interface with physical

reality was slipping, I felt panic moving up out of the empty place in my stomach.

Then I heard what I thought was Loping Boy's calm voice, "Can you throw a spear? You harpooner, O'Hara? Can you cut her in half on the short axis?"

I couldn't answer. Sound doesn't travel in a vacuum.

I was in a sitting position shooting through the void. Frozen. By now I was surely frozen too solid to move. I was relieved that it had not hurt. But why hadn't my lungs burst? Shouldn't I have thrown up blood?

I reached for my lower lip. No blood.

"Locate your hands. . . ."

A voice I recognized. It didn't seem like Loping Boy's. I know where my hands are, right here.

"I am not frozen," I said aloud.

"No. You are fine," Loping Boy chanted, "You must cut the diamond. Cut. Now. Short axis. Cut now. Feel your tools. Cast your light. You are the Cut-and-Catch. You are the Cut-and-Net."

He was right. I could feel the panel.

I could see the stone and firefly fountain of little admirers. I cut her right across the middle.

The ship grew around me. I was back aboard.

Missey was rolling on the floor, wrestling violently with a dark shape-changer. I started to rise from my bucket to help her, but a strong hand pushed me back down.

"The time will come when you can help."

Missey was yelling, "Go away! Get! I'll tell Momma. I'll kill you. No. No. Oh, God, no. Yes. . . ." Something in my mind said snidely, "Most unbecoming behavior for an adult."

I thought about my own internals, shuddering. I

glanced helplessly around the cabin. It was chaos. I swallowed something bitter. And who would help me if I were to meet the same? "I think I'm going to throw up," I mumbled.

"Why?" a calm voice asked.

Huh? And the feeling was gone.

I looked for Loping Boy. He was not in the cabin. Perhaps hidden by one of the wraiths wreathing the air. Colored ribbons wide as a cot. One draped across my head and shoulders—wet wool on my face. It was hard to breath. "Shee-it, we're gonna miss it! Everyone incapacitated. Time too short."

"No. There's time enough," interrupted the calm voice. Where from? Whose voice?

I knew I had to vaporize the waste half of the stone. How did I know that? This time it must have been the tiny storyteller from my dreams.

I fired both lasers at full. The screen filled with plasma.

The halves of the tumbling stone were still rotating around their common center of gravity, when the dark half came around again, I hit it full power. This time as I burnt it, it broke free of the bright half and began to drift away. I persisted. The billowing plasma accelerated it. Then the golden half spun into my vision and I laid off the toggles.

Hot plasma cooled on the truncated golden capsule.

Then I left my body. My mouth dropped open. My soul came out of my mouth. I watched my body slump back against the back of the bucket.

Who was screaming?

I rose slowly out of my body. I penetrated the shell of the Miner-22. I could see everything. All my pain was at an end. She materialized in the night-without-bottom in my eyes. Tears were running down her cheeks, and I was torn to the depths of my being.

"I am sorry," I spoke more quickly than I could form the thought.

She raised her head slowly. So lovely. Like my mother when she was young. My wife. My lover. All-Woman. I knew: *Your lifetime. Forty thousand lifetimes. Kindred spirits. Separation insurmountable. Unsatisfied need. Eden unattainable. Fate aching.*

My heart burst and melted. Red swam in my eyes. My sorrow had killed me.

I knew further: *Now what? What now? Endless fire? Need unmet?*

Oh, Mother of Mercy, a wash of guilt and remorse cascaded over me. Because I had failed; because I had not been clear of mind enough to conceive of, to execute, some Herculean task; because I had not achieved some ineffable attitude, wisdom, and maturity: I was doomed forever to this incompleteness, this painful slow destruction by grief. I knew: *Now die. Release yourself. Graceful defeat. Gently rise. Gently sink. Come closer. Passivity permits. Union possible.*

I heard, from afar, the tide of sorrow worn gentle by aeons. A sea of aching hearts.

And I also heard a voice, calm and strong, "You are the caster of nets. You are the soulkeeper." It was the voice of the big man from my dream. "You are the son of the Iris. Gently and surely cast your net. She is your Death. She is your prize. Take your prize."

And I heard from my own mouth, "I am the soul-keeper."

And—Oh Lord, from where does this will arise?—I moved to take the prize.

"By the spirits of my forefathers, by the spirit of

Pwyll, by the spirit of Bran, by the spirit of Mother Erin, and by the spirit of the One, I will my net cast."

I opened the catbay port, deflectors and waldoes at the ready.

The angel raised her head. Her eyes changed subtly to reveal deep fires. Her hair stood on end and writhed. Each of my nerves died of agony in a symphony of increasing harmonics. I was paralyzed by pain.

Her mouth framed words, but her voice arose where conviction is nurtured in my mind. *You stir. You upset. You break. Bonds and waves. Promises and possibilities. Laws and words. Judgment: no peace.*

Beyond my credulity, the pain increased.

I shattered. I shook. Why did I not die? Why did I not pass out? How long must I endure?

She mouthed and I knew: *Hell's domain.*

No. No. NO. Oh, Lord, no!

Desist or die. Stop or suffer. Eternal suffering.

Impossibility upon impossibility. At this point the calm voice broke in, "That breaks it, doesn't it?"

I had nearly forgotten my will.

I moved in utter pain. Nearly insurmountable resistance.

But I rolled that nugget into the belly of Miner-22.

My hands were wrist deep in smoldering sulfur as I thumbed the hatch closed and sealed it.

Clang! High-carbon steel against steel. That's it.

I wondered if I had committed the unforgivable sin.

After agony, my shaky physical state, battered and exhausted, felt like one of those mornings when I was overjoyed to leap out of bed. I felt new. I felt light as a child. It was a joy to struggle against the heavy current to reach Julie at Milling.

She looked dead.

"Julie."

She opened her eyes instantly. But she undertook no flicker of awareness.

"Insulate the catch," I instructed her.

She arose and was active at the console for a moment. I could see she fired every foam tube on the vessel into the bay. Then she returned to her place on the floor and closed her eyes.

I did not try to understand.

I knew, somehow, that it was not my place to free her.

This time the current rushed me back to the bridge.

A hand grenade had gone off in the bunker. My friends were scattered about me. I was losing blood from several wounds. Shards of acid smoke hung on the air.

I knelt by Missey. I picked up her head and shoulders. "Missey," I said.

Her eyes opened instantly.

"Thank God you're still alive."

"Thank You that I'm still alive," she obeyed.

"Missey, what's wrong?"

"I am separated from the Oneness."

"Can I help?"

"Yes."

"Tell me how."

"Tell me how to forgive my father."

"Why?"

"He molested me as a child. He screwed me as a teenager. I learned to like it. I hate him. I hate myself."

"Forgive your father."

"Okay." She shuddered and began to moan. Then she began to shake. It was no seizure; every limb jumped and bent and straightened. Her spine, I thought, might break.

"What's happening? Missey. Tell me what's happening to you."

Out of her mouth I saw an ugly worm escape. It hung in the air between us. I brushed it with the back of my hand and it dissipated like a smoke ring.

"Tension. My muscles free of poison. But I am still separated. Oh . . . Arenolbdleindleronreprogonefibah. . . ."

She twisted on the floor.

I had an insight. "Missey," I commanded, "forgive yourself."

And she did.

Instead of her eyes looking limply into space, she focused on inner space. I watched her change. I saw more blood come into her skin. I heard her breathing deepen. I saw the tight lines around her eyes and mouth fall away . . . they left the scars that time had eroded, but now they were thin and supple. She sat up and continued her internal rejuvenation.

I knew she was mending.

Never has anything I have done given me such pleasure.

"Now do the rest yourself," I told her. Then to be sure, I added, "You will remember all of this."

I stood up and looked about the cabin. Heavy misties still drifted randomly. We would be in G-sector a while yet.

The air was clear about me but it glowed with a golden light. Around each of my teammates ghosts wrestled or hung limply.

I felt lucid.

I answered an inner urging and approached Horton. I could hear the sounds of the little misties. I suspected I was beginning to understand their nature. I smelled the beach of Atlantic City and I saw ghosts of children.

I helped Horton come back from his personal hell—because I am concerned about them all.

O, miracle of miracles, I care!

When we finally cleared the matrix, most of the crew was up. I searched for Loping Boy.

At the door of the sauna, I noticed the thermostat at three hundred. I knew he was in there. I cautiously opened the seal, afraid of what I might find.

He was sitting bone still, his wet wool blanket over his head.

I lifted it oh so slowly.

He peered out with a smile in his eyes. "You counted coup."

He stood up slowly and put his arm around me, "You, brother, tell this redskin where we are."

"Headed for Mother. The rock we netted is so strong that we are taking some misties across interstitial space with us."

"They don't bother you now." Statement.

"No. I can command them, somewhat."

"You shall mine no more." Statement.

"No. I am a healer now."

"New waters." He smiled and said, "You will go where healing takes you, O'Hara. I, too, go where I am asked to go." He looked at his hands, then he looked back at me, "But I have some words for you."

I waited.

"There are deeper waters than these. There are greater distances than these. To cross these distances, that is a gift. To swim in the deeper waters, that is a gift. You must never forget to pray; that is your talisman. And when you are victorious, you must never be defiant, for you do not win victory by yourself."

"That voice," I asked, "Is that the voice of God?"

He shrugged, "Beats me. But you, victory by victory, and by defeat when it comes, you are crossing to the presence of the One. A step down is Hell. A step up, Heaven. Many steps. The rainbow bridge is long."

He was silent and I looked at the wet blanket and the wet cedar. Cedar this deep in space is worth more than gold, but my prosperity only now begins to grow and it accompanies me wherever I go.

"Yes, you, O'Hara, you counted coup on the Devil. To go back now is, at best, pointless; at worst, it is defiance. You do not want to know," he smiled and held up thumb and forefinger to indicate small. "The Dantium Devil is only a so-so devil."

Tell Me a Story
by
Larry Niven

About the Author

Larry Niven broke into professional SF writing in 1964 and immediately marked himself out as an uncommonly talented and energetic individual possessed of a startlingly fresh creativity. Or, as he puts it in the following compendium of advice to the would-be writer, he found a vacant ecological niche. In the opinion of many, he has been brilliantly filling it ever since, and even expanding it.

When approached for advice, Niven tends toward the short answer and the epigram that makes perfect sense if you're smart enough. This can be a shock. Many writers more or less fit the naive popular image of the slow-speaking, contemplative thinker. (In quite a few cases, this is because they process ideas so fast that they have to slow themselves down to translate into conversation.) Some writers, however, are like Niven—straight-ahead chargers who bear no malice toward anyone until proven guilty, and who are perfectly willing to help, but are not willing to retard the pace of their thinking. The actual difference is not necessarily in the speed of thought; it is far more in the need to count the opinions of others. Niven, like a few others in every generation of top-flight talents, appears to have none of this need.

Consequently, there is much to be learned from studying his *opinions, and we recommend the exercise. Be smart about it. You will note, for instance, that he seems to be contradicting Anne McCaffrey's earlier advice on the advisability of showing your stories to admiring friends and relatives. We think, in fact, there's no contradiction at all, but you might see it one way if you're more like McCaffrey and another if you're more like Niven.*

Writers do differ, you know. We never said it was easy. Certainly, Niven doesn't say it's easy; he does say it's rational.

I can't help you sell your early work in the 1980's. To enter the field my way you'll need a time machine set for 1964. That's when every novice was trying to write New Wave, except me, and an ecological niche was left wide open.

I can't tell you how to write, not in a thousand words. I've been telling what I know as fast as I learned it for twenty-two years. My collaborators now know everything I do. I've spoken on panels and published articles on writing. Is there anything left to say?

Maybe.

I

If you want to *know* that the story you're working on is saleable, try this: I tell it at a cocktail party. I dreamed up "The Flight of the Horse" one morning, outlined it that afternoon, and by that night was telling the tale to a clutch of cousins. I held their attention. I didn't miss any points. I kept them laughing. The noise level didn't drown out anything subtle and crucial. Then, of course, I knew how to write it down so I could mail it and sell it.

I told the sequel the same way ("Leviathan!") and sold it to *Playboy* for what was then *fantastic* money.

This makes for good memories. It's also a useful technique.

Some of the best stories simply can't be told this way, and I can't help you write those. Nobody can. They are rule-breakers. Try some early Alfred Bester collections. But any story you can tell as a cocktail/dinner conversation, without getting confused and without losing your audience to distractions, is a successful story.

So. You want to write a story, and be paid for it, and know that it will be read? You want that *now*, no waiting? Tell me a story. Tell your brother/wife/cousin/uncle a story: tell anyone you can persuade to listen. *Persuading* is good practice: you need skill with narrative hooks. Watch for the moments where you lose your listener; watch for where you have to back up and explain a point. Your audience will tell you how to write it. Then you write it.

You won't need this forever. You'll learn how to tell the tale yourself.

(My normal audience in the beginning was my brother. Thanks, Mike.)

As for the untellable story, that one depends on subtleties of phrasing or typographical innovations . . . that one you can postpone. You won't have the skills to write it for a few years anyway.

II

We working writers, we're not *really* interested in reading your manuscripts. We can be talked into it, sometimes, via the plea of relatives, or sex appeal, or someone to vouch for you.

Do you know how difficult it is to persuade, say Ray Bradbury to read one of your stories? Have you tried yet? You'd be a fool not to, if you've got the nerve. An hour of a successful author's time could be worth a lot to you. What he says will apply to *most* of your stories.

Ray turned me down twenty-two years ago. He said he didn't have the time, and he was right.

But we *can* be persuaded. So here you are, a novice

who's sold a few stories or none, and somehow you've talked an established writer into reading one of your stories. What do you do then? Give him your worst story, the one that most needs improving?

A novice writer did that to me when I was also a novice. He told me so after I told him that if I could think of a way to make it saleable, I'd burn it.

Give him your *best* story! The best is the one most worthy of improvement. It's the one where your remaining flaws shine through without distractions, and you've picked the man who could spot them.

This shouldn't need saying, but it does. I've heard counterarguments. Look: even if you've sold one or two, they just barely passed; they could have been better. *You* know that. *He* knows *how.*

(But don't bother Ray. A thousand novices have broken their hearts trying to write like Ray Bradbury. He has a way of *implying* a story in insufficient words. It looks so easy, and it can't be done.)

III

If the story you're telling is a complex one—if the reader must understand the characters or the locale or some technical point to understand what's going on—then you must use the simplest language. Your reader has his rights. Tell him a story and make him understand it, or you're fired.

This is never more true than in hard science fiction, but it never stops being true.

If you don't have anything to say, you can say it any way you want to.

IV

Do your research. There are texts on how to write, and specialised texts on how to write speculative fiction.

Learn your tools. (For instance: the indefinite pronoun is *he.*) You can create imaginary languages, but it's risky.

Always do your research. One mistake in hard science fiction, in particular, will be remembered forever. Remember: you're on record.

V

Start with a story. Tell yourself a *story*. Are you in this to show off your stylistic skills? They'll show best if you use them to shape the story. Calling attention to the lurking author hurts the *story.* The best character you ever imagined can be of immense aid to the right *STORY*; but if he's getting in the way, drop him.

A good stylist really can turn a sow's ear into a silk purse; and he'll be forgotten in favor of the average yokel who had just brains enough to start with silk.

VI

Don't write answers to bad reviews. It wastes your time, you don't get paid, and you wind up supporting a publication you dislike. Granted it's tempting.

VII

Every rule of writing has exceptions, including these, and I've broken many.

You're not good enough to do that yet.

Welcome to Freedom
by
Jay A. Sullivan

About the Author

Jay Sullivan was a combat engineer, an illustrator for Army recruiting materials, and an administrative noncommissioned officer. For the post newspaper, he also wrote a column briefly reviewing new books in the Ft. Eustis library. Some of that—far from all of it—can be seen in his story, which was a strong runner-up in the contest.

He left the service in 1964 and was, over the next twenty-one years, a salesman, a warehouseman, a display designer, an art director and art studio proprietor, and sometimes an advertising copy writer. In 1970, however, he became a deputy sheriff, and shortly thereafter a municipal police officer, which he still is.

He has studied graphic design at the Cleveland Institute of Art and law enforcement at Cuyahoga Community College. Along the way he has taken courses in psychology, sociology, social science, philosophy and anthropology. He is just one of those people. A study of many SF writers' biographies will reveal that a high percentage of them are simply too interested in too many things to be categorized in any short description. Perhaps that's what eventually leads them to start exploring worlds other than the one we apparently live in.

Apparently. For who can be totally sure of who he is, where he lives, or why he acts as he does?

If you have an answer to that question, are you sure of it?

I didn't know who I was until I was twenty-nine years old. I don't mean I was unaware of myself or had no identity, but when I was twenty-nine, I learned the truth.

I, Mikhail Gregorevich Rostov, was a Senior Sergeant in Company 2, 17th Motorized Assault Regiment; a good soldier in a fine unit; sure of myself—proud of myself. We were training troops that cycle, conscripts from the Liberation of Mexico. They weren't eager to be soldiers; they would not or could not learn the language. We considered them rather stupid. It all started because of one of them, one day on the Grenade Training Range.

One of the Instructors, a young NCO, was trying to teach a particularly inept conscript how to remove the safety clip and throw a hand grenade. I saw he had a problem and started forward to help. Suddenly the conscript jerked at the clip, which yanked the now-armed grenade from the Instructor's grip and into the air toward me.

Instinctively I yelled, "Live grenade," and dropped —the grenade hit the ground in front of me and without thinking I slapped it away. I remember seeing it tumbling toward the frozen conscript, who watched it coming with a surprised look, while the Instructor dived away from the deadly object. I carried that picture with me into unconsciousness.

In case you wondered, the young Instructor was

wounded but recovered. The conscript died . . . but we had an unlimited supply of them.

I awakened in Infirmary, face heavily bandaged and skull echoing to a sledgehammer pounding. I checked my body and didn't seem to be hurt anywhere else. I steeled myself to bear the pain . . . I had been wounded before. I knew if I complained to the medical personnel they would think I was a bad patient. But good patients get extra food, and medication for pain.

I lay undisturbed for a time; perhaps I slept. When I opened my eyes again, a Captain Doctor stood at the foot of my bed looking at my record. He glanced up and saw me watching him.

"So, Mikhail Gregorevich, you are a real People's Hero." He held up a hand as I began to deny it. "No, no, you are. They say you saved at least six lives by diving for a live grenade and knocking it away from a group of soldiers. Good, good." He made a note on my record and checked my bandages. Then he patted my shoulder, smiled and left. Moments later, a Medical Corporal came in and gave me an injection. The pain was already beginning to lessen when I fell asleep.

I stayed in Infirmary for another week. My wounds turned out to be minor; a broken nose and some small shrapnel cuts. I was ready to return to my company but had to stay for the ceremony. Comrade Colonel Gorenchev himself, my Regimental Commander, presented me with the Military Order of Hero of the People, Second Class. I did not much mind staying. I was also enjoying the food, better than that served by the company field kitchen.

The day after the ceremony, the psychological officer, Major Doctor Kalnikov, sent for me—perhaps to be sure that I was prepared to return to duty. I talked to him of many things: my family, my years in the People's Army, my childhood in the suburbs of Komsomolgrad. He must have found me normal; two days later I was directed to report to the Office of Transportation to receive orders returning me to my unit.

I dressed in my field uniform, which I had convinced a conscript orderly to wash for me—actually I had to give him my dessert for two days. I wrapped up the razor and toothbrush Infirmary Supply issued to patients, turned them in and headed for the Office of Transportation.

When I reported, I found that my orders were not ready. I asked the orders clerk, a corporal with no combat ribbons and a face like a weasel, if there was a problem. He replied that I had not been cleared for release by the Department of Military Psychology, and he could not issue orders until I was cleared.

"Corporal," I said, "I was interviewed by Major Doctor Kalnikov himself, the Chief of the Department of Military Psychology. If you check carefully, I'm sure you will find an entry to that effect in my file."

"I have checked, Comrade Senior Sergeant, and I found nothing. I must have the proper clearance before I will issue you your orders."

Then I leaned forward, hands on his desk, and said, "Call Major Doctor Kalnikov at his office and ask him if I am cleared for orders."

Not yet afraid of me, the corporal showed yellowed teeth in what I took to be a smile and answered, "No, Comrade Senior Sergeant, I am——"

"That was an order, Comrade Corporal," I commanded in my parade-ground voice. "One more 'No' out of you and I'll see that you are transferred to *my company*—as a private."

He shrank back, paling, and reached for the telephone before he caught himself. "But, Comrade Senior Sergeant, you must have your annual psychological evaluation before you can—"

"Do it," I growled.

He began dialing with a shaking hand. Behind him, an inquisitive private peered at me, but retreated hastily between two rows of file cabinets when I glared at him. The corporal began muttering into the phone, so quietly I couldn't make out what he said . . . besides, I was feigning indifference.

Then he spoke a bit louder. "Yes, Sir. But Comrade Major, the regulations are very specific—"

A muffled roar came from the earpiece. ". . . waste my time . . . your name and rank . . . cleared . . . orders."

The corporal whispered, "Yes, sir" into the dead phone, wiped his forehead on his sleeve and hung up.

He rolled my clearance papers into his typewriter and made the appropriate notation, initialed them and attached them to my orders. He stood then, bracing to a sloppy attention, and handed the papers to me. "I apologize for the . . . inconvenience, Comrade Senior Sergeant, but you understand it was necessary that you have proper clearance." Still pale, he winced back as I leaned forward to read his nametag.

"Zelyetsin," I said slowly. "Comrade Corporal Zelyetsin . . . I'll remember that." I turned smartly and strode away, smiling to myself. These fussy little men were so easily handled if one went about it properly. Oh, he was right—my annual psychological evaluation had been scheduled for the day after the grenade incident.

The People's Army makes the annual evaluation mandatory for all troops from the Homeland, even to the point of canceling furloughs and sending Psychological

Units to combat areas. There was not much to the evaluation. You received an injection of a mild sedative to relax you, then you spoke for a time with the Lieutenant- or Captain-Doctor. When you finished, you returned to your duty. Only the conscript troops were not required to be evaluated: To me this showed the concern the People's Army had for its fighting men.

Although I had not been with my unit for my scheduled annual evaluation, I had been interviewed by the Head of the Department of Military Psychology at the Infirmary. Comrade Major Doctor Kalnikov had cleared me and filled the requirement of the annual evaluation, so the corporal's obstructiveness had been for no reason.

I caught a ride on a convoy headed in the right direction and was back with my company for the evening meal. There was some joking about my still greenish black eyes, respectful from the younger NCO's, sometimes less so from those of my own rank. But we were all comrades-in-arms and I took the jokes lightly. As my eyes healed, the bruising faded and so did the joking.

Refreshed by my week-long rest, I threw myself into my duties with a new zeal. By the end of the cycle, my conscript trainees were the hardest-worked and the best-trained in the regiment. We were rewarded by being chosen as one of the relief units for elements of the People's Army on garrison duty in southern Mexico, where foreign-supported insurgents were still resisting.

We spent three months on duty, relieving several units from the line for much-needed rest and troop replacement. We built an enviable combat record, crushing resistance in areas where it had been strong since the Liberation. As a reward, we were given ten days of furlough in the fleshpots of Novominsk before we returned to our permanent post.

After the furlough, we began another cycle of conscript training to fill the spots of those who had died. Some young sergeants were transferred-in as Instructors to fill vacancies left by comrades who hadn't made it back with us. As we came up once more to full strength, grenade training again was on our schedule. I resolved to keep a closer eye on the conscripts this time.

A day or two before we went into grenade training, I was jarred out of my sleep one night by a dream. In this dream, I recognized no one but myself. I wore the rank of Chief Sergeant, a rank which I had not yet attained but to which I hoped soon to be promoted. I led a patrol over a plowed field, through a wire fence which was cut for me by a faceless private, toward a small white farmhouse. As I reached the front yard, a man ran from the house onto the porch, looking over my head and calling to someone to run. I killed him. With a terrible scream a woman then ran from the door and fell beside him. I killed her also, and turned to see to whom he had called. A young boy, perhaps ten or eleven, stood at the edge of a grove of trees many meters away. I raised my rifle and fired, but knew I missed. Shredded leaves and pieces of shattered wood fell where he had been.

I sent my patrol to catch him. They surrounded the grove, searched till they found him and brought him to me. A dirty-faced little boy with tear-streaks down his cheeks, he faced me, trembling, fear and hatred mixed in his eyes. But he met my look and refused to drop his eyes. I was impressed by his courage and decided to save him. I told the patrol to take him to Headquarters and as they hurried him away, he looked back at me as though to say, "Beware—I will not forget."

I swung my legs over the edge of my cot and sat there

with my blanket pulled around me, trying to drive the memory of that little boy's face out of my mind. I finally gave up and went early to the showerhouse. I returned to the barracks and dressed, then headed for the field kitchen. I would have tea with the senior sergeant in charge and wait for the morning meal.

Several nights passed normally—and then I had the dream again. It was the same in all respects, but this time I thought I knew the boy. Again he looked back as he was taken away . . . and a tiny dart of fear stung me. I came awake with my heart pounding, and spent the rest of the night without sleep, smoking on my cot in the darkness.

The next night the dream, now a fear-spurred nightmare, struck again, and now I was sure I knew the boy, but could not remember from where or when. Again it frightened me into wakefulness and I slept no more, but lay curled on my cot wondering what I had done to be so tortured by my own mind. Was I sliding toward insanity? I knew I must force the memory of the dreams from my thoughts before it began to affect my performance of duty.

During the day, one of my assistants commented jokingly on the darkened circles under my eyes. I snapped at him, berated him . . . then, by way of apology, explained that I was concerned about the unit's combat readiness. We moved the troops into a difficult day of training—they needed the hard work almost as much as I needed the distraction.

That night I lay awake for long hours, smoking and trying not to sleep, but I was exhausted. My eyes closed, and I was in the dream again. Once more I killed the farmer and his wife, once more shot at the boy. Again my patrol searched and found him, again brought him to me—and now I knew his name.

"Mikhail, Mikhail . . . Why do you run from me? I am your friend."

Illustrated by Greg Petan

His blur eyes brimmed with tears and he answered through quivering lips, "I'm not Mikhail—I'm Mikey. *You're* Mikhail."

Suddenly I was that little boy, facing the cold-eyed sergeant while the soldiers clutched my arms—and then I *knew*.

"No! No!" I clawed my way up out of the dream, struggling against the grip on my arms, fighting to get free. . . .

"Sergeant." There was a pounding noise. "Sergeant Rostov . . . are you all right?"

Wildly I looked around, drenched with sweat. I was in my room in the barracks, blankets and sheet twisted loose and wrapped around me. "Wh-what?"

"Is something wrong, Sergeant?" It was Corporal Tchernov, one of the assistant Instructors. We sometimes drank a bit together.

"No, nothing wrong, Tchernov. Just a dream. . . ." I put him off with a shaky laugh and a bad joke about a tavern girl we both knew, and he chuckled as he padded away to his own room.

I rolled over and buried my face in the thin pillow. Torn fragments of memory fluttered through my thoughts; here I kicked a ball in the Sports Arena, there I climbed to my treehouse while my dog barked at me from below. I fished in the pond, caught a sparkling, flashing sunfish, and went on a class outing to the museum where I first saw the statues of the Heroes of the Revolution. . . .

Who was I? Was I Mikhail? Mikhail? No, I wasn't Mikhail—I was Mikey . . . Mikey . . . Michael. Michael who? Mikey . . . Michael . . . Michael Walters, yes, Michael Walters. Not Mikhail Gregorevich Rostov, but Michael Walters. Michael *John* Walters, after my father. I began to cry then, mourning the father and mother I hadn't remembered before. Racking sobs shook my body and I muffled the sound with my bedclothes.

Hours passed . . . how long I don't know. I had finally done with crying and was savoring the real memories. I had learned to differentiate between the real and the false. I had *not* played soccer in the Sports Arena, or seen statues of revolutionary heroes, but I *had* fished in our pond, and spent lazy afternoons in my treehouse. The false memories were like watching a play in which bad actors walk stiffly through the scenes, mouthing stilted prose and gesturing exaggeratedly for the audience. Now that I knew, I could recognize the false images, somehow implanted there for me to remember . . . implanted to cover the truth.

But the truth was that my parents had hidden me away in the grove of trees so that I would not be taken to the Labor Camps as the other children were being taken. Children of a conquered people, we were destined to spend our lives in forced-labor battalions, toiling for the People's Republic of North America. I hid in the trees for days, fed after dark by my parents. But after a time, I grew careless and unafraid, and I was playing outside the shelter when the soldiers came. I should have died there, murdered with my mother and father, but instead I was taken captive and sent to a Re-education Center where I was subjected to Training, a euphemism for that type of torture.

Frightened, alone, unable at first to speak or understand the Invaders' language, I suppose I was easily broken. Then I was rebuilt, given a language, a memory, taught skills and a craft—the art of war. And I learned it well.

But now a slow, cold anger began to grip me, growing stronger and stronger as I remembered. I resolved that there would be a paying of the debt for the murder of those good people, for the twisting of that young mind. I rose from my cot, dressed in field uniform. My weapons, unlike those of the conscript troops, were secured in my room and I brought them from the locked rack and loaded them. I would burst forth through my door and slaughter everyone in the barracks—they would pay for what they done, pay for my loss and humiliation and rage.

But an unexpected forbearance spoke to me. These conscript troops were innocents; they had no hand in my misfortune. Why should they die?

But if not they, then who would be my target? I sat down again, trying to think clearly, to reason. Were the noncommissioned officers at fault? No. In fact, I decided, some of them, perhaps most of them, were as I, manufactured into what the Invaders needed . . . men with false memories. I wondered if any others knew, as I did, how they had come to be this way, and toyed for a time with the thought of an underground of sergeants ready to revolt, to rebel and overthrow our masters. But perhaps I was the only one who was aware of what I had been. And I wanted my revenge now.

The line officers—the lieutenants and captains, platoon and company leaders—did they know? Possibly, but they had not caused it. Could I strike at the top—at the division and corps commanders? I decided not. I had no access to those headquarters and would waste my life foolishly. But the battalion and regimental commanders and their staffs, to whom Headquarters sent down orders, they were surely aware. And those I *could* attack.

I had my target—their dying would be a large downpayment on their debt. And they had forged the tool. They had made me a soldier . . . and a soldier's stock-in-trade is death.

The target chosen, I must now plan my attack

. . . and after the attack, my escape, for I did not mean to die just yet. Could I get away to join the insurgents fighting in the South of Mexico? Possibly . . .I knew the way, knew the country. Wait, better yet, stay here in *my* country and fight as a partisan.

Entrenched in the Northern Rocky Mountains, an unconquered enclave of resistance known as 'Freedom' still held out against the People's Army. Protected by nuclear armaments and a small air force, the remnants of the United States and Canadian forces had banded together there near the end of the war and lived free, if under siege.

The People's Republic described Freedom, called the Northwest Socialist State, as an autonomous province under the leadership and guidance of the Party; in actual fact, its defeat was reckoned more costly than it was worth. If Freedom unleashed its missiles, it would be totally destroyed in retaliation, but the heartland of the country would become uninhabitable and therefore unproductive. The Homeland dared not to provoke that attack, so Freedom was allowed to exist.

If I could make it to Freedom, I would be safe. I was a trained soldier and native . . . they would welcome me. Now I had a target and a strategy—it was time to plan my tactics.

I lifted a hand in response to the gate guard's nod as I drove out of the encampment that morning. I wanted to stay and watch the Regimental Headquarters explode in flames during the weekly commander's meeting, but I knew I must get away as far and fast as possible. The agents of the Committee for State Security would soon deduce what had happened and who had caused it. I had not had time to cover my actions well enough to stand up to an inquiry but, still goaded by anger, I'd had no inclination to wait any longer for revenge.

I needed to travel approximately 1600 kilometers northwest to reach the edge of Freedom-controlled territory. My vehicle carried enough petrol for perhaps 250 kilometers, but I dared not head directly toward Freedom. To misdirect pursuit, I had to appear to angle away. Also, my papers would not be good in the military district to the northwest; I would cover more ground in the long run by heading north. I would soon need papers for a new identity, civilian clothes, a way to drop out of sight . . . strange thoughts for a line soldier to have. They rattled in my head, but I clung to them. I had possibly eight hours to travel before the Regimental Headquarters exploded—and perhaps two or three additional hours before some bright young agent determined I was the outlaw they were seeking. That was the best I could hope for. As I headed north, I turned over alternatives in my mind.

I left the vehicle in a small gully close to a main highway late that evening. Covered with dirt and branches, its outline broken by a young sapling leaning over the hood, it was not likely to be found soon. It may sound foolish to have left it close to a main road, but patrols *travel* on main roads—they *patrol* back roads and countryside . . . I know.

I was now about 210 kilometers north and a bit east of the encampment. I shouldered my pack, slung my rifle and scrambled to the top of the gully. I found my direction from the stars and set off toward Freedom on foot, across 1400 kilometers or more.

The next nine months I learned many things. I learned that most farmers would feed a fugitive, that some would not. . . . Some were afraid if I were found on their farm that they would be held responsible. I usually traveled at night, on foot, but I stayed three days with a sick old man and when he died I took his truck. I drove 110 kilometers before I ran out of petrol that day. I dared not try to get more, so I abandoned the truck.

I lost a week or more, hidden in a cave in Colorado with a raging fever. My medical supplies were gone, as was my food. I made soup from moss and grass, and drank the icy snow-melt water. I left the cave just minutes ahead of a patrol with dogs. I escaped that patrol, but less than a day later I was trapped in a ravine by a corporal and four men. I suppose that since it was a grenade that caused me to start to remember, it was only right that a grenade should keep me from being captured. But I was sorry that they all died—the corporal was so young. I took all their ammunition before I left, and their medical packets and emergency rations.

I just kept going, heading for Freedom. Perhaps the most difficult part was when I reached the People's Army perimeter around Freedom—I had not let myself realize that it must be totally encircled. Finally, I stole a field uniform with a Senior Sergeant's insignia on the collar, and worked my way through the perimeter toward the lines. It took me two days to get to the Fire Zone. I might have gone faster, but I did not want to create suspicion about my movements.

Shortly after I reached the front line, there was a small outbreak of firing near me and I used the noise and confusion to crawl across the Fire Zone and inside Freedom's lines. I took off the uniform immediately and buried it, then crawled away. Later I thought perhaps I should have kept it on in case I was captured. I did not want to be shot as a spy after all I had been through to reach here.

When the troops captured me, I thought at first they were advance units of the People's Army that had crossed the perimeter in an attack, but then I saw the American and Canadian flags on their shoulders and I had tears in my eyes when I surrendered, for I knew I was finally among my countrymen. They brought me to a very young lieutenant and he asked me a few questions. Then he sent for this wheelchair for me . . . I must apologize for being so weak, but it must be some kind of an illness, perhaps the one that caused my fever before.

I reached for the glass of water and noticed that my hand shook slightly as I picked it up. I had lost more than eight kilograms, but I had always been healthy. A little rest and good food and I would be fine.

"Is there anything else which I can tell you, Sir?" I asked the captain.

"No, Michael, I think that's about everything," he answered, closing the folder on his desk. "We're glad you came over . . . we need good men. Now, the sergeant has a shot for you——"

"Excuse me, Sir," I asked, "What is a shot?"

"An injection," he replied as the white-jacketed sergeant swabbed off my arm.

"Oh, of course . . . for the illness." The injection was administered painlessly, not in the rough manner of the medical personnel of the People's Army. I nodded my thanks at the sergeant as he swabbed away a tiny drop of blood.

"You must excuse my English, Sir," I said to the captain. "I know I have an accent, and I am not yet familiar with many words." My eyelids began to close as I spoke.

"That shot'll make you a little sleepy, Mike. It's got a mild sedative in it to help you relax."

"Yes, Sir . . . I understand." I was fighting sleep by now and having trouble holding my head up.

"Mike? Can you hear me?"

"Yes. . . "

"The sergeant's going to take you away now, Mike."

"I . . . I go. . . " I concentrated and tried again. "I go to hospital?"

"Soon, Mike. First you go to psychconditioning and education."

I forced my head back and managed to open my eyes. He was blurry and I blinked, trying to focus on him.

"Don't worry, Mike. You'll be fine. We're just going to make a good American soldier out of you." He grinned and nodded at the sergeant. For a moment, he looked just like Major Doctor Kalnikov.

As the sergeant turned the wheelchair, I tried to move. I was trapped as securely as though I were encased in concrete. Almost unconscious, I heard the captain say, as the sergeant pushed me from the office,

"Good luck, Mike. And Welcome to Freedom!"

About the Artists

The artists appearing in the book are themselves newcomers to story illustration. All of them were enthusiastic about the stories, and about the concept of adding their own graphic dimension to the universe created by the writer. We feel they're outstandingly talented and that their contribution to this book is a vital one. Here they are:

David Dees illustrated two stories for us in *Writers of The Future Volume I*, and "A Sum of Moments" this time. He's a motion picture advertising-art creator with seven years' experience, and ours are the only three short stories he's ever illustrated.

Brian Patrick Murray's previous illustration experience is in comic books. Twenty-five, he has studied in Manhattan and in California. He thinks, "Winsor McCay is the greatest comic-book artist of all time," and is an enthusiastic fan of Frank Frazetta and classic magazine artists Norman Rockwell and N.C. Wyeth. The draftsmanship and composition of his illustrations here certainly reflect those masterful influences.

Greg Petan is 21, a graduate of the American Academy of Art in Chicago. He's at the very beginning of his professional career. Working as a successful freelance portraitist, he has also done architectural renderings and been a sought-after bass guitarist in several Chicago-area rock bands. His four illustrations here are the first he's ever done.

Charles Rosenthal studied four years at New York's National Academy of Design in the 1960's. He is primarily interested in fine art, as is plainly shown by the classic style of his drawing for "The Trout." His only previous illustration experience was for an article in *Chemical Week* magazine. We very much hope to see more of his work in years to come.

Art Thibert's first published illustrations appear with four stories in this book. Twenty-four, he's a comic-book fan and hopes to be a comics illustrator, having worked on his skills since childhood. We found him exhibiting his drawings at a West Coast SF convention, and are pleased with the results.

Greg A. West's illustration for "Dream In A Bottle" was done for his friends Jerry Meredith and Dennis A. Smirl, who authored that story. They're all associated with *Space Grits*, the amateur publication of their Charlotte, North Carolina SF group. West, 35, is employed in the art department of a yearbook-printing company, and is almost entirely self-taught.

Gary Meyer, our cover artist, is well known for his technical and aviation advertising art, and equally so for his film posters and music album covers.

He is a winner of awards in many art specialties, and notably versatile. He did the continuity art for *Star Wars,* designed the look of the train for the "Supertrain" TV series, and created the *Chicago 13* album cover.

His posters for *Das Boot* and other major productions have also been used as book covers.

His work for us here represents one of the few occasions on which he's had time to do a book cover directly.

CONTEST RULES

1. All entries must be original works of science fiction or fantasy. Plagiarism will result in automatic disqualification. Submitted works may not have been previously published.

2. Entries must be either short-story length (under 10,000 words) or novelette length (under 17,000 words).

3. Contest is open only to those who have not had professionally published a novel or novella or more than three short stories or one novelette.

4. Entries must be typewritten and double-spaced. Each entry shall have a cover page with the title of the work, the author's name, address and telephone number, and state the length of the work. The manuscript itself should be titled, but the author's name should be deleted from it in order to facilitate anonymous judging.

5. Entries must be accompanied by a stamped, self-addressed envelope suitable for return of manuscript. Every manuscript will be returned.

6. There shall be three cash prizes for each quarterly contest: 1st prize of $1,000.00, 2nd prize of $750.00 and 3rd prize of $500.00. In addition a cash prize of $4,000.00 shall be awarded to the 1986 Grand Prize winner.

7. There will be four quarterly contests commencing from October 1, 1985 and ending September 30, 1986.

a. October 1 - December 31, 1985
b. January 1 - March 31, 1986
c. April 1 - June 30, 1986
d. July 1 - September 30, 1986

To be eligible for a quarterly contest, an entry must be postmarked no later than midnight of the last day of the quarter.

8. Each entrant may only submit one entry per quarter.

9. Winners of a quarterly contest are ineligible for further participation in the contest.

10. The winners of the quarterly contests will be awarded trophies or certificates.

11. A 1986 Grand Prize winner will be selected from among the quarterly winners from the period October 1, 1985 through September 30, 1986.

12. Should the sponsor of this contest decide to publish an anthology of science fiction and fantasy works, winners will be contacted regarding their interest in having their manuscripts included.

13. Entries will be judged by a panel of professional authors. Each contest may have a different panel. Entries will not be judged by L. Ron Hubbard or his agents. The decisions of the judges are final.

14. Winners of each contest will be individually notified of results by mail, together with names of those sitting on the panel of judges.

This contest is void where prohibited by law.

A milestone in the science fiction genre, Mission Earth reads with the distinctive pace and artistry that inimitably hallmarks L. Ron Hubbard as an unequaled Master Storyteller.

From light years away, the Voltarian Confederacy sends a mission to stop earth from self-annihilation. However, a villainous faction, the Voltarian Secret Police launch their own plan to sabotage the mission.

Hilariously told from the alien villain's point of view, this high-speed adventure brilliantly and imaginatively fuses action science fiction with rich comedy-satire and biting social commentary in the great tradition of Swift, Wells and Orwell.

Volume 1 — THE INVADERS PLAN

"Remember how you felt the first time you saw Star Wars? This book will do it to you again."

ORSON SCOTT CARD

Volume 2 — BLACK GENESIS — Fortress of Evil

"Marvelous satire by a Master of Adventure."

Anne McCaffrey

"Assassins, dope addicts, wrestlers, mobsters, anarchists, New York cabbies and other characters provide even more targets for Hubbard's satiric barbs, and the action is as effectively drawn as ever."

XIGNALS

WATCH FOR VOLUMES 3-10 COMING IN 1986/1987.

Vol. 3 — The Enemy Within
Vol. 4 — An Alien Affair
Vol. 5 — Fortune of Fear
Vol. 6 — Death Quest
Vol. 7 — Voyage Of Vengence
Vol. 8 — Disaster
Vol. 9 — Villainy Victorious
Vol. 10 — The Doomed Planet

MISSION EARTH IS ACTION, ADVENTURE AND HILARIOUS SCIENCE FICTION SATIRE AT IT'S BEST!

GET YOUR COPIES TODAY!

Volume 1, THE INVADERS PLAN and Volume 2, BLACK GENESIS available now wherever fine books are sold. (See tear out order form for special offers.)